CARDINAL VON GALEN

CARDINAL
VON GALEN

by

HIS CHAPLAIN

THE REV.
HEINRICH PORTMANN
Dr. Jur. Can.

Translated, adapted and with an Introduction by
R. L. SEDGWICK

JARROLDS · LONDON

JARROLDS PUBLISHERS (LONDON) LTD.
178–202 Great Portland Street, London, W.1

AN IMPRINT OF THE   HUTCHINSON GROUP

London Melbourne Sydney
Auckland Bombay Toronto
Johannesburg New York

The original German edition was published in
1953 by *Aschendorffsche Verlagsbuchhandlung, Munster
(Westf.)* under the title of *Kardinal von Galen, Ein
Gottesmann seiner Zeit*, and bears the Imprimatur of
the present Bishop of Münster, dated August 3rd,
1948.

First published in Great Britain 1957

*Set in eleven point Baskerville, one point
leaded, and printed in Great Britain
by The Anchor Press, Ltd.,
Tiptree, Essex*

CONTENTS

5

PREFACE

The first twelve chapters of this biography appear in this
edition in a much abbreviated form. The reason for this can be
given very briefly. The biographer writes for a public of
German Catholics, ecclesiastics and laymen, many of whom
had known the Cardinal personally or had heard him preach
or read his Pastorals; for such a public he has given a very
detailed account of the Cardinal's family, of his early life at
home, at school, at the university and the seminary. He also
writes very fully of long and arduous years devoted to parochial
work, both in Münster and Berlin, and of his close and intimate
relations with those under his pastoral care, with his clergy and
seminarists.

The translator and editor cannot but be aware that if this
work is to interest readers of English, whether they be Catholics
or members of other Churches, it will be because the Cardinal
fought a great fight against Hitler and Nazism. His aim has
therefore been by a selection of the most striking passages of the
early chapters to give a picture, designed for these readers, of
the world in which the Cardinal who fought this fight was
born, a member of an ancient Catholic noble family, simple
and patriarchal even in the closing years of the nineteenth
century, for which ancient traditions, particularly those concerned with religious matters and family authority, were all in
all. Not less relevant are the selected passages dealing with his
education.

The translator and editor, however, ventures to hope that
his selections do full justice to the author's admiration of and
devotion to the Cardinal. This applies also to certain portions
of the early chapters, chiefly concerned with the Cardinal's
pastoral work, his relations with his clergy and his own
domestic life, which are represented not by selections but by
summaries. N.B. Such summarized passages are marked at
beginning and end by five stars, thus *****. The Cardinal's
three famous anti-Nazi sermons do not appear in the German

9

edition as they are sufficiently well known to German readers. Extracts are given in this edition in an appendix.

I am indebted to the late Mr. H. E. Fulford, of Lincoln's Inn, and Mr. J. Slingsby Roberts, of Brighton, for their valuable help and advice.

R. L. S.

INTRODUCTION

After my reception into the Catholic Church in 1922 at Worcester I went to Bonn to study, and there became friendly with the young Baron von Hülsen, a member of a famous Prussian Protestant family, who had joined the Church in the same year. He later became a Benedictine priest, and was 'lost in Russia' serving as a chaplain. It was from him that I first heard something about the future Cardinal, then a simple priest working in Berlin. Von Hülsen described his impressive appearance, his pastoral zeal, his saintliness and asceticism, and made the prognostication that he would one day achieve the Purple.

It was not until 1939 that I first saw the Lion of Münster, as Clemens August, Cardinal von Galen, came to be called by his countrymen. I had gone to the Vatican to do my service as a Privy Chamberlain of the Sword and Cape to His Holiness, and his name was down on the list of bishops making their *Ad Limina* visit, when they give the Pope an account of their dioceses.

There was no need to point him out in the thronged *Anticamera Segreta*. I remembered the Baron's description. He towered above all others, and when I knelt to kiss his ring, and spoke a few conventional words in German, I was conscious only of stern but friendly eyes and a majestic presence. When I saw him again in 1945 in shattered Münster I was wearing the uniform of another Sovereign, and the Cardinal, whose memory was prodigious, remembered me and laughingly commented on it by way of greeting.

In July, 1941, I was seconded from the German department of Military Intelligence to the Political Warfare Executive (P.W.E.), a secret organization responsible for psychological warfare and propaganda of every kind.

Shortly after the heavy R.A.F. bombing attacks on Münster during that month the text of Count von Galen's sermons reached us. A translation of these remarkable and courageous addresses appears in the Appendix of this book, where it will be observed that the Bishop used the occasion of these raids by the 'external' enemy, as he called them, to give added emphasis to his castigation of the 'internal' enemies of Germany, by which he meant the Gestapo and its affiliated organizations.

The Bishop of Münster had presented the British propagandists with most powerful material. At that time things were going far from well for the Allies. Our propaganda was based on truth (of course at times selective), and a straight presentation of the facts; but it was by no means easy to try to manipulate German opinion in our favour by psychological means when in the military field we were losing all along the line. Then, like manna from heaven, as some thought, there fell this rich fare upon our empty plate, and every department of P.W.E. pounced avidly upon it.

Among the numerous transmissions sent out by the B.B.C. there was one specifically addressed to German-speaking Catholics who numbered well over thirty million. Catholics could never, *qua* Catholics, be reconciled with the persecutors of their Church, nor by 1941 could they any longer doubt Hitler's hatred of Catholicism. This fact we had been driving home day after day, contrasting Hitler's policy with the British attitude towards Catholicism, both in England and in the missions in Africa, India, etc. The von Galen sermons (and there were later others by Cardinal Faulhaber, Archbishop of Munich; Bishop Bornewasser of Trier, and Bishop Count von Preysing, of Berlin, who was created a cardinal at the same consistory as von Galen in 1946) indicated declared spiritual opposition to the Nazis.

We worked also on the historical basis that German Catholics had always disliked the Prussian hegemony in Germany. Memories of 1866 (the defeat and exclusion of Catholic Austria) and of the *Kulturkampf* were still alive, and were fostered by our propaganda in this programme.

We had to bear in mind (and many of our propagandists could not or would not) that Germans do not believe in political democracy, *as we understand it*, and in my opinion this is still true today. Later, in 1945, Bishop von Galen never tired of assuring me of this. The democratic middle-class parties and the Social

Democrats were intellectually bankrupt and discredited in the eyes of most Germans long before 1933. But our line of approach was that German Catholics did believe in God-given human rights, which formed the basis of our democracy. Aided by these sermons our transmissions sought to show that National Socialism constituted a grave menace to the family, and it was essential to stress in our propaganda that the defence of the family *must have a religious basis*. Political arguments would not impress German Catholics, who were suspicious of social reforms based on the vagaries of 'progressive' politicians.

At the same time it must be pointed out that more harm than good was done by the exploitation of Cardinal von Galen's and other German bishops' sermons and pastorals in programmes which were palpably inspired by other than Christian ideals. Unfortunately they were not confined, as they should have been, to the Catholic programme. Their use in others laid us open to the charge of cynicism, which the Cardinal was not slow to tell me when we met in Germany after the cessation of hostilities.

It must also be made clear that as England is not a Catholic country we saw to it that our Catholic programmes did not stand alone; they were supplemented by transmissions for German Protestants. Co-operation between the Churches was happily increasing during the war in this country in the social and political fields; confessional animosities were decreasing both here and in Germany. We were thus able to present Britain to the Germans, whether Catholic or Protestant, as a Christian country. Whether this can be said today is another matter.

As soon as the Occupation began I was appointed Controller-General of Religious Affairs for the British Zone. One of the first major problems facing us was how to control the hordes of foreign workers press-ganged for labour in Germany, and who had now been freed after three or four years of the strictest discipline and police surveillance. While the war was on our propaganda had, by means of a 'Trojan Horse Campaign', created in the German mind a pronounced Anticipation-Neurosis regarding the treatment likely to be meted out to them by these erstwhile labour-slaves. This was accentuated in many Germans by a feeling of guilt; the old German saying,

'*Was Du nicht willst, das man Dir tu, da fueg auch keinem andern zu*', was symptomatic in this direction. Hordes of these released workers roamed the countryside by day and night, looting and raping.

On July 1st, 1945, Bishop von Galen preached a sermon at Telgte, a place of pilgrimage near Münster, protesting against the lack of control by the occupational authorities of these Poles and Russians. I was sent to see him and ask him to tone down some of his speech. Among other things, the Occupying Powers took strong exception to his use of the word *fordern* (demand).

The future Cardinal was then living in the *Collegium Borromäum*, the only one of Münster's several theological colleges and seminaries to escape total destruction; his own palace had been razed to the ground, as indeed was eighty per cent of the city, and the *Borromäum* was the only building left standing and conveniently placed to the cathedral which was felt suitable to house him. As I approached the College I noticed that it was badly damaged, and climbing the stone stairs which led up to the episcopal rooms the whole place seemed to shake on its hollow foundations. The rain was pouring in at many places. The room the Bishop used as a study, with a small bedroom leading out of it, was sparsely and simply furnished: an old sofa—even in happier days he had no aesthetic taste, and furniture 'was for use only'; two or three chairs, a few books, and one rug; on the wall, a large crucifix, and that was all. From behind a much battered desk, strewn with papers, the Bishop rose from his typewriter to greet me. During our conversation which took place alone, no interpreter being necessary, I studied him closely, and will try to describe him. In this book Dr. Portmann does not do so beyond referring to his height. To German readers so familiar with his looks and appearance it was unnecessary.

Above me towered a colossus of a man whom I judged to be about six foot seven with appropriate girth and build. He looked like a Prince of the Church, every inch of him, though then without the trappings of such a Prince. He presented himself, for a bishop, in a Spartan simplicity of vesture: no purple *zucchetto*; a faded black cassock edged with purple, and buttons of the same colour, many of which were sadly frayed; a simple pectoral cross hung about his neck, not suspended on the customary chain, but on a much tarnished gold cord. The only other sign of his rank was the biggest ring I have ever seen. It had to be, for his hands, though finely shaped, were huge. His snow-white hair was closely cut after the German fashion—almost *en brosse*. The physiognomy was noble and aristocratic: close-shut mouth, sternly set with thin lips, prominent jaws and nose, a capacious brow; the head long of form. The eyes, which inspired confidence, were of a soft grey above which lay long, bushy white eyebrows, carefully brushed, which beetled when he grew indignant. The whole head suggested a powerful mind well under control. Except when he smiled or laughed, and I was soon to learn that he had a fine sense of humour, his appearance could not be called happy. On the contrary his features bore the evidence of much sorrow and worry, of much strenuous labour wrought in this world and an anticipation of more to come. No one could fail to mark the austerity and self-discipline in his expression. When he spoke, there was in his voice, which was only occasionally loud, a mingling of controlled quietness and animation which made him master of those around him. His laughter had the ring of a jovial mockery about it that was quite unforgettable.

For me the meeting, after so much had happened since I last saw him, was a moving experience. Here visible in the flesh was the legendary being: the defier of Hitler and all his works; the man whose sermons we had exploited by fair means and by foul—the Lion of Münster himself, who was just as ready to roar at us as he had been to the Nazi leaders. When I saw him after his return from Rome wearing the long scarlet *Cappa magna* of a cardinal, and with all the accoutrements and panoply of his exalted rank, as he moved slowly in procession to the ruins of his cathedral, I could not remember ever having seen a more distinguished and Olympian figure among his colleagues of the Sacred College. *Ecce sacerdos magnus* in every sense of the word!

Of his character it is more difficult to write. Others who knew him intimately over a long period of years are best qualified to speak. There are many who saw him as a saint, and confidently expect that one day the Church will raise him to her altars. I was never close enough to him to know of this

except to say that in any contact with him one was conscious
of some inherent saintliness as soon as he began speaking.

Apart from this, and not wishing to anticipate the decisions
of Holy Church,[1] let us for a moment look at him as the man as
we in the Army of Occupation found him. His names were as
numerous as his qualities: Jesus, Maria, Joseph, Ludgerus,
Clemens, Augustinus; added to these he was an Eminent
Cardinal of Holy Roman Church, and a count in his own right.
You were certainly aware of his aristocratic background: on
occasion he could be imperious and dismiss one with a gesture;
but he was also a man of unfeigned simplicity and humility,
and he admired you if you stood up to him, even if he could
not agree. There was nothing of the Prussian Junker about his
make-up.

Of himself and his family he said, 'We von Galens are
neither particularly clever nor good-looking, but Catholicism
is in our bones.' During the war many stories about him
reached us in England, some of them apocryphal; but though
he denied most of them when I taxed him with them he let
some pass in a modified form. Two or three are worth relating.
Once, during a sermon in his cathedral, he was denouncing
Nazi contamination of family life and extolling the sanctity of
the marriage bond. A young Nazi thug, who was posted at the
back of the nave, called out, 'You as a celibate have no right to
talk about marriage and children!' Clemens August (as he was
affectionately known throughout his diocese) brought his huge
fist thumping down on the edge of the pulpit, and retorted, 'I
will not tolerate in my cathedral any reflection upon the
Führer!'

At midnight Mass one Christmas before the war the Bishop
prefaced his sermon with this story: 'Notices have appeared on
the authority of the Gestapo that all persons of non-Aryan stock
must leave the church before the sermon begins. If this be so,
then we must expect to hear a Child's voice say from the crib,
"Come along, Mummy, we are not wanted here."' The
Cardinal told me that he had not said this from the pulpit but

[1] Translator's note: Since this was written, it has been reported in the
Catholic Press, October 19th, 1956, that Mgr. Keller, the present Bishop
of Münster, has ordered the diocesan process—the necessary preliminary to
a beatification—to open in regard to the late Cardinal.

that he had frequently related the story publicly and in the presence of Nazi officials.

Once he is said to have threatened to carry the monstrance containing the Host alone through the streets of Münster if the Nazis banned the traditional Corpus Christi procession as they had threatened to do.

Cardinal von Galen was a great patriot: he loved his country, but was fully alive to the faults of his countrymen whom he had no wish to denigrate. He based all his actions on the words St. Peter used at the Council of Jerusalem, 'We ought to obey God rather than men.' On several occasions I was asked by my chiefs to try and extract from him some statement of collective guilt. Such requests drove him to a frenzy of anger, and were soon abandoned. He respected the British up to a point, but he never really liked them except individually. He was severely critical of what he called our 'spirit of compromise and vacillation'.

'You promised in your propaganda,' he once said to me, 'that you would come as liberators, and the first thing you do is to throw innocent people into concentration camps without preferment of charge and without trial. My own cousin, Count Max von Galen, is now in one at Corvey near Hoexter. He was never a member of the Party, and when he protested at his imprisonment, he was told "you have been in the Army and that's enough for us".' (I was able to effect his immediate release shortly after this conversation.)

'At one moment,' the Cardinal continued, 'you order non-fraternization, at the next you cancel it and complain if we are cold and hostile. You make us tear down or dismantle our factories, and ere the dust has settled you order us to build them up again. You take away our weapons even down to an air-gun' (he said this in 1946), 'and I prophesy that before much time is out you will ask us to arm again, so that we may be a bulwark between you and Russia.

'You are inconsistent, tough in the wrong way, and this softness mixed with your sensitiveness at what I and others say in criticism of your actions increases our humiliation at the thought that you have twice conquered us.'

B

Now the Cardinal's faults, and of course he had them, were national rather than individual. The German inferiority complex had not wholly escaped him. Although he hated and had denounced Nazi crimes he found it difficult to believe that German soldiers had committed atrocities. If he did, his memory was short. The rape of other countries was to him a necessary part of war. To him two wrongs did not make a right, and that was the end of it. Here I think some appraisal of the German mentality is necessary.

To begin with there is the paradox of German achievement and political barbarism. On the one hand there is an immense contribution to · knowledge: historical and philosophical, literary and scientific; the leadership of the world in music; great business enterprise; heavy industries; shipping; banking. Against this we must set a strange political ineptitude—an incapacity for self-government; an admiration for war as such; emotional coarseness and instability. Some of the reasons for this state of mind are historical.

Germany was never subdued by Rome: there is an unbroken pedigree back to barbarism, and Germany was never part of the Mediterranean culture of Europe. She wasted her vast energy trying to hold Italy instead of consolidating a national state. Then came the great independent Duchies, the predatory and brutal tradition of German 'Chivalry'. The huge-scale Thirty Years' War emphasized the tradition of militarism. The failure to create a unitary state when England, France, Spain and the Dutch had achieved one caused them to have their Elizabethan Age in the twentieth century. Following on this was their inability to attain overseas colonies, due partly to geography and a preoccupation with Baltic trade. When belated unity came it was from the most reactionary state of Germany—from Prussia, not Austria.

To this historical aspect we must add the psychological if we are to understand something of the complicated mentality of these highly gifted but essentially neurotic people.

As the Germans were not within the pale of the European tradition they developed a strong inferiority complex coupled with a persecution mania, which was quite unjustified since they have achieved great things, and have had a far better deal geographically and economically than the · Slavonic and

Balkan peoples. But over and above everything there has persisted a sense of frustration; they have always considered themselves the unappreciated missionaries of 'culture'.

Let us look briefly at their collective psychology. Both Goethe and Heine recognized the ambivalence in the national character, 'Alas, two souls within one breast. . . .' Submissiveness and brutality; the admiration for militarism; the prestige of the officer class and the inferior position of women; sentimentality and the *Totenwunsch* (death-wish); student romanticism and melancholy; the pre-war intellectual tyranny of the examination system and the statistics of student suicides. It is interesting to note that German mythology is the most defeatist in Europe. Their humour is elementary, their artistic taste normally execrable. But behind all this is a tremendous force and herd courage, toughness and hero-worship. The word *Kameradschaft* is proverbial.

The inferiority sense is balanced or compensated by ruthless and feverish efficiency and hard work. For years under Hitler they had no knowledge of the outside world like the Russians, and vast numbers of them genuinely believed in Rosenberg's Nazi mythology, Jewish conspiracy, encirclement, that America was dominated by gangsters, and that the British Empire was a blood-stained tyranny.

These characteristics, developed in the light of the historical background, go some way to explain the German mentality, and there are some who would add the language with its clumsiness, violence and undoubted power—the antithesis of French, Italian and Latin lucidity. Did the language make them or they the language?

Such national traits, a result of the past, have been greatly intensified by Nazism, which was not only a consequence of World War I, but also the *expression of deep-seated aspects of the national character*. Nazism was a lower middle-class movement mistakenly backed by big business; it was caused by revenge for 1918, by unemployment, by the political failure of the Social Democrats and upper middle-class leadership generally.

For centuries every German has feared Russia—a legacy of fighting the Slavs for so long. This fear of Bolshevism was another contribution to the rise of Nazism. When the proletarianizing of the German middle classes came there was a deliberate breaking of old standards (great emphasis is laid on this fact by the Cardinal in the book), and the establishment of rule by a calculated appeal to motives of fear and jealousy. When the old framework broke the 'little man' ran for shelter to the dominant organization. Symbols and gestures were developed which led to a reversion to a sort of tribal totemism. The satisfaction was psychological rather than economic; new institutions of primitive glamour took the place of the old dull ones, and there was a deliberate disruption of routine. Ordinary ambition and self-respect gave place to emotionalism and sadism. Hitler himself spoke of his 'mutton-headed people'.

The tragedy of the whole thing came from the paradox of German culture and barbarism—Bach and Belsen.

It must not be thought that Cardinal von Galen was always criticizing us. Far from it: where praise was due he gave it generously, as the following incident will show.

In Jan., 1945, General Templer[1] expressed a desire to meet all the Catholic archbishops and bishops resident in the British Zone, and asked me to arrange a conference at Lübbecke at the end of the month when he proposed giving them an overall picture of conditions and problems in the territory.

The meeting went off well, the bishops being greatly impressed by the General's manner and his brilliant report; he spoke through an interpreter for two hours without notes, ranging over a vast canvas, and showing a complete mastery of every subject involved. Between the two sessions I entertained the bishops to luncheon, and was the only officer present. Conversation started with a general appreciation of the manner in which they had been received; the provision of coffee, cakes and cigarettes had surprised and pleased them. All expressed their astonishment at the freedom of speech allowed to them both as regards the questions they were free to put and the fact that their comments were listened to politely and patiently. This was stressed by von Galen himself. He had been greatly impressed by General Templer. Turning to his fellow bishops, he said, 'The General handled us very

[1] Now Field Marshal Sir Gerald Templer, C.I.G.S.

adroitly . . . (*Er hat uns sehr geschickt behandelt*). Not only was he charming but clearly knows his job.' The notorious German curiosity, an integral part of their psychological make-up, was well illustrated by the many questions about the General which I was then asked. Was he a regular soldier? How old was he? Had he been wounded? Did he admire the fighting qualities of the German soldier? Did he get on with the Russians, the Americans, etc.? The Bishop of Osnabrück said, 'You Englishmen can do what we have never learned to do, laugh at yourselves as the General did this morning.' The same sentiment was expressed later to me by Dr. Kampe, the Bishop of Münster's private secretary and interpreter. Speaking of the conference generally, he said, 'You do this sort of thing so much better than we do.'

The Bishop of Münster then paid this tribute, and it was noticeable that when he spoke all the others were respectfully silent, including the Archbishop of Cologne (in spite of the latter's seniority as Metropolitan), so great an influence did von Galen wield. The Archbishop of Paderborn told me aside that the entire German hierarchy regarded him as *the* Church leader in Germany.

Bishop von Galen: 'It is clear from this morning's conference that the English have a strong tradition of religious behaviour, and that our Catholic principles are receiving sympathy and understanding which we could not expect from the Russians. I for one shall tell the Holy Father that we are dealing with Christian gentlemen. . . .' The Archbishop of Cologne agreed and spoke to the company for a few minutes on the Wehrmacht and civilian camps set up by the British. The fact that an admission had been made during the conference that in some instances conditions in the camps were unsatisfactory, and that if mistakes had arisen regarding unjust arrests, these would be rectified, drew warm tribute from him. 'This makes us understand the English word "fair-play"—a word we have heard so often.'

The Archbishop of Paderborn then took the chair for a moment. 'So many of us see things solely from a parochial point of view. We are all of us prone to regard our diocesan difficulties as unique. This is partly due to lack of communications, transport difficulties, and our inability to move about the zone. It is also due, in some measure, to the isolation we have suffered during the past years, and the propaganda to which we have been subjected. This morning, for the first time since our defeat, we have been able to see the picture as a whole. We have had the whole canvas clearly sketched. I, for my part, now realize, more distinctly than I ever did before, the immense difficulties which face us—both the conquerors and the conquered, and in my opinion, this has been the most valuable part of today's convention. It is our duty as bishops to impress upon our flocks the necessity for loyal co-operation of our people with the British military and civil authorities.'

The bishops concurred with these remarks, and Bishop von Galen, turning to me, admitted that the overall picture was new to him, and that we had done a better job than he had thought. 'But there's still room for much improvement,' he added with a roar and a laugh, 'and I'm an impatient fellow!' He then asked the Archbishop of Cologne if he might speak on the Eastern problem. Turning to me he said he felt it his duty to speak very frankly about our Russian Ally, and that if the subject was distressing to me as a British officer, I could of course leave the room. I said I would remain if he had no objection.

Bishop von Galen: 'Excellencies! You will recall that this morning I raised the question of the Eastern territories with the *Herr General*. He was not prepared under any circumstances, he told us, to discuss problems involving quadripartite agreements. Although I appreciate the General's position, I cannot myself, and neither can you as German bishops, be silent on this subject which cries to Heaven for justice! (*Welche einen Himmelschrei um die Gerechtigkeit ausstoesst*). We must protest to the world against the evacuation of Germans from the Eastern territories, especially Polish-occupied territories, e.g. Pomerania, Breslau, Upper Silesia. For centuries they have been German. The manner in which these wretched folk are forced to abandon their homes and all their possessions—often with less than an hour's notice—makes one shudder. They are forced to make a written declaration to the effect that they are leaving voluntarily. Old and sick are taken to mass camps, relatives are put to forced labour; hundreds suffer rape, violence and robbery while crossing the border.'

Bishop von Galen then stood up and spoke with great vehemence. 'How can we bring this to the notice of the world? It is our bounden duty to do so. Short memory is a German failing, but it is by no means peculiar to us alone. I know similar crimes have been committed by Germans all over Europe, but I was not silent then. Two wrongs do not make a right. I know that the Cardinal-Designate of Berlin, Bishop von Preysing, who has the most up-to-date knowledge of all on this subject, will speak to the Holy Father about it when he is in Rome.'

The bishops then debated the Eastern question at some length and eventually the Archbishop of Cologne and Bishop von Galen decided that all the bishops should sign a joint declaration of protest which von Galen should hand to the Pope. This document would also be given to the American, South American and Spanish cardinals when they were in Rome.

Dr. Portmann devotes a whole chapter of his book to the Rome journey and the difficulties connected with it. It might well be called 'A Chapter of Accidents', but none of them was of my making. The Army did all it could to assist the cardinals-designate, but the Foreign Office was far from helpful. Despite the author's good-humoured account he could not know what had been going on behind the scenes, and naturally I was not disposed to enlighten him of the muddle and intransigence on the part of the F.O. I can only say that there would have been serious international repercussions if the two German prelates had not arrived in time for the consistory. The Russians had made things quite easy for the Bishop of Berlin, and so had the Americans in the case of Cardinal Faulhaber of Munich. Here is my own account, to supplement the author's, of what Cardinal von Galen called 'A Second Pauline Voyage to Rome, and Nearly as Bad!'

Immediately after Vatican Radio had announced the names of the new cardinals, and without waiting for any formal request from the Germans, which came later, I began putting the machinery in motion for their transport to Rome.

Although I urged expediency there occurred a series of exasperating delays from London. The cardinals wanted to fly, if possible, but I was told no plane was available. I pressed the matter further and was at long last given an air route from Bueckeburg via Frankfurt and Vienna. The R.A.F. would provide the plane. The cardinals were informed of this, but the route was then changed to a direct flight from M.-Gladbach over the Alps. This was inexplicably cancelled by the F.O. at the last moment, and I began to be seriously worried. We in the Army had to carry out the policy laid down by the F.O. without questioning, and that was that. To make matters worse there was a curt refusal from the same source to afford any money exchange facilities to their Eminences either for the journey (which was ultimately made by train) or for the purchase of their robes in Rome where their German currency was useless. In the end I was informed that they would fly from Münster in General Sir Brian Robertson's own plane which he had put at their disposal, no other being forthcoming.

On Feb. 6th, 1946, I went to Münster and conducted the two cardinals-designate to the city's airfield at Handorf. On the way they expressed some surprise at the number of cancellations, and the refusal to change their money, but apparently now all was well as far as the journey went. As soon as they saw the General's plane on the field there was a general cry of dismay, and von Galen said: 'That bird isn't big enough even to carry me. We want an eagle, not a swallow.' This proved to be so after weighing: it was far too small for the two prelates and their *suite*, and long before this I had sent Transport all such necessary details. Owing to storms the telegraph lines were down, and I could not get through to H.Q. There was nothing left but to take them back to Münster while I returned to H.Q. at Buende for further instructions.

Now the Army had done all it could to facilitate the trip, and by now the General of my Division for Internal Affairs was exasperated. 'I don't care how you do it, Sedgwick,' he said, 'even if you take 'em in a wheelbarrow; but get them there. That's an order.' I spent the whole night sending signals, and at last succeeded in getting permission to take them by car to Karlsruhe, where places would be reserved for them on the leave train from Calais to Villach in Austria; there an American plane would be laid on to fly them direct to Rome. The only transport I could get was a station waggon for the *suite*, and an ancient Daimler, which had once belonged to the late Queen Mary, for the two prelates.

There is no need for me to describe here the nightmare journey to Karlsruhe. Dr. Portmann has already done so in detail. The unprecedented weather, the endless breakdowns of the 'Koenigin Maria', as Cardinal von Galen rather irreverently christened the Daimler (though he had a great respect for the Grand Lady, as he called her). When I jokingly pointed out, after the third enforced halt, that the car was really of German make, he said with a twinkle in his eye, and a jab in my ribs, 'That's what comes of the company going English!'

At Karlsruhe I was informed that the leave train had been cancelled owing to a storm in the Channel. This was the last straw. But when I told the cardinals that our hopes had been again dashed I realized what I was up against. The two men were by now firmly convinced that these delays and accidents were all part of a plan of the F.O. to prevent them from reaching Rome in time. Nothing I could say would convince them to the contrary.

It had rained incessantly for a week, which had made the going exceedingly trying for two men not in good health at the time; there had been four breakdowns, one of which had involved spending a miserable night in the car without food or drink; there had been four or five changes of route; they had been refused any money accommodation, and were, to all intents and purposes, penniless. And now they were stranded, knowing that I had no further plans, which was true. Cardinal von Galen, by now near to tears, got out of the car stiffly, put his hand on my shoulder, and said: '*Herr General*, you have done all a man could do to help us. You have telephoned and telegraphed day and night. It is not your fault. You must now take us back to Frankfurt, and if by tomorrow morning something concrete is not forthcoming we must return home, and I shall make a formal protest to the Commander-in-Chief. This is the revenge of your Foreign Office for my having stood up for what I believed was just and right.'

I again assured the Cardinal that he imagined this, and we drove back through the night in ever-increasing tempest and

storm, arriving at Frankfurt at midnight. I left my woebegone
flock in the care of the nuns at the Marienhospital. My driver
was worn out and asleep at the wheel. After getting him
accommodation, I sat in the back of the Daimler to think. It
was useless to try and communicate with H.Q. Suddenly I
remembered that I had an American opposite number in
Frankfurt, the colonel in charge of Religious Affairs for the
American Zone. After a long search I found his billet; he was
away in Munich, but a young captain had been left in charge.
He turned out to be a Catholic, and a man of great resource
and charm. While he plied me with refreshment, I told him
my story. Together we telephoned till the early hours, but
could get nowhere. After a prayer for help to Our Lady of
Telgte, Cardinal von Galen's Protectress, I snatched an hour
or two's sleep, and awoke with a plan. I would try the French.
I knew there was a small liaison mission in Frankfurt, but the
captain was not very sanguine about their ability to help, still
it was worth a try.

We arrived at their office at 6 a.m., and found an elderly
major still on night duty. I told him of my plight. He heard me
out with great courtesy and then spoke. '*Mon Général*, I am
appalled at what you have to tell me. One does not treat
Princes of the Church in this cavalier way. As members of the
Sacred College they are supranational, and France will accord
them every facility for their reaching the Eternal City. If the
captain here will reserve them a compartment on the officers'
leave-train for Paris tonight I will guarantee the rest. In the
meantime I will telephone to the Quai d'Orsay, and expect
you back here within the hour.'

I could scarcely believe my ears: it was all so quick. But
my prayer had been answered. We had already been four days
on the road, and the consistory was drawing ever nearer. I
went back to the captain's house for breakfast, after which we
both heard Mass at a neighbouring convent chapel.

. Back at the French mission the *Commandant* greeted us
with a smile, a handshake and a glass of magnificent Armagnac!
'All is arranged,' he said. 'I am instructed by the Quai d'Orsay
to ask you to convey to their Eminences the expression of their
profound respect, and an assurance that they may now consider themselves the honoured guests of France. My Foreign

Office will reserve seats on the Paris–Rome Express in which other French cardinals will be travelling two nights from now. The Quai d'Orsay will provide accommodation at a Paris hotel for tomorrow night for the cardinals and their entire *suite*, and will be happy to defray all expenses *including the tickets to Rome*.'

Having conveyed my own gratitude for this remarkable offer we took our leave in an atmosphere of great cordiality. The captain went off to reserve two compartments in the train leaving for Paris that night.

At the Marienhospital I informed the cardinals of the new plan, but found them in a difficult frame of mind, to say the least of it. They had little faith in the French assurance of help, and were for going home then and there. It was not until I had brought them the tickets to Paris and shown them the French and American visas that they consented to make this last attempt.

Before we left that night the good captain gave me a roll of French money to hand to the cardinals: it was not sufficient for their Roman tailors, but it was something, and a gesture they greatly appreciated.

After a comfortable night during which I had been able, for the first time since we started out, to entertain the whole company to a decent dinner in the restaurant car, we arrived punctually at our station at 10 a.m. Drawn level with the platform were three cars from the Quai d'Orsay, sleek, black and impressive. Three French officials knelt to kiss the episcopal rings, and after a few words of welcome we were soon speeding to our hotel. Before the two prelates went to rest Cardinal von Galen came to my room. He embraced me and said, with a catch in his voice: 'You have performed a miracle, *Herr General!* How did you do it?' 'You must ask Our Lady of Telgte,' I replied, and he beamed with delight. A few minutes later I took him a bottle of champagne. '*Ach!*' he cried. 'I can't remember how long it is since I last tasted the stuff, but I know I always liked it!'

Later, the Nuncio gave them a splendid luncheon, and von Galen entertained the distinguished assembly of French cardinals, archbishops and bishops with the story of our adventures, which he told with much good-humoured banter.

The French were not amused, but the Germans, now in good *Stimmung*, made light of our misfortunes, and the Lion of Münster, raising his glass, uttered the only words of English I had ever heard him use. ' "All's Well that Ends Well", as your Shakespeare says; but we are not at the end yet. . . . !'

That night I conducted them to the Rome Express. When I told them that I was not coming with them, they were astonished and dismayed. I had known this all along, but did not like to tell them before. When the journey was first proposed General Templer was willing and indeed anxious that I should accompany them all the way; but for some unknown reason the Foreign Office would not allow me to go. Heaven knows why. Thus I missed the most impressive consistory ever to take place. I would have given anything to have been present.

     .   .   .   .   .

When the Cardinal died, it fell to my lot to inform the Holy Father. None of my chiefs was available at the time, and I had to draft the telegram myself. It ran as follows:

> Regret inform Your Holiness of sudden death of the great Anti-Nazi Cardinal von Galen following operation for peritonitis.

The next day I was hauled over the coals for using the words 'Anti-Nazi'. The Foreign Office objected to these words. But I think the Commander-in-Chief was pacified by the Pope's reply, which I will quote:

> For I.A. and C. Div. (Religious Affairs). For Brigadier Sedgwick.
> Acknowledging deep gratitude thoughtful message condolence occasion death beloved heroic Cardinal von Galen. His Holiness bids me convey Commander-in-Chief, yourself, and members British Control Commission expression his profound appreciation.

     .   .   .   .   .

Thus I end my brief glimpse of a great Prelate, Patriot and Man. Two photographs of him hang on my study walls. In one the Cardinal is seated at his desk; above his signature he had written for me: 'To Brigadier Sedgwick with gratitude. Peace and Justice.' The other was taken a few hours after his death. He had crossed the bar and seen his Pilot face to face. Both serve to remind me of the greatest German I have ever met.

R. L. Sedgwick

CHAPTER I

THE ANCESTRAL PORTRAIT GALLERY

'ALTHOUGH I am fully convinced,' wrote Clemens August Count von Galen in June, 1925, at that time Parish Priest of St. Matthias' in Berlin, 'that the grace of God has called me and raised me through the priesthood to a position, the dignity and duties of which are incomparably higher than those of the nobility of this earth, I cannot and will not forget what I owe to the noble family through which God has given me life, the privilege of being brought up for His service and other innumerable benefits in body and soul. . . . I hope therefore that the family chronicle which I have planned will serve to pay some part of my debt and will contribute to the maintenance in my family, as a continual inspiration to them, of those noble traditions and ways of thought which are the best legacy bequeathed to us by our forefathers. . . . I would wish that my testimony to old traditions of which almost all possible witnesses have passed away should be as accurate as possible, and I will therefore begin with my grandfather, Hereditary Chamberlain Matthias von Galen. I have not known anyone who could of his own knowledge speak of what happened before his time.'

On the summer evenings of 1925 the thoughts of this Parish Priest serving in a great city turned more than was usual with him to his western home. For nearly two decades he had had a cure of souls in Berlin, that sea of hard-pressed human beings who too were seeking a home. But how few found what they sought! He himself had never found a home there but had remained a stranger in a great metropolis, suffering for the sake of God and immortal souls.

The castle of Dinklage was for centuries the seat of the von Galen family. There the Freiherr Heinrich von Galen, a man of foresight and energy, had settled and begun that close connection of the von Galen family with Oldenberg which has lasted for three hundred years. It was of his ancestors whose faded portraits hang on the walls of the corridors and rooms of

the old castle that Clemens August thought when as a bishop
he bade defiance to those who dared to insult his forefathers, 'I
do not know whether those, who today presume to decide
what is the essence of the German spirit and what German
blood requires, could, as I can, prove that the German spirit
has been for centuries the jealously guarded inheritance of their
families, that no drop of foreign blood runs in their veins and
that this can be demonstrated by the records of seven hundred
years.'

The Bishop's grandfather, Count Matthias von Galen, born
on the 12th September, 1800, was the eldest son of the Hereditary
Chamberlain Count Clemens August von Galen and his wife
a Freiin von Ascheberg. In 1803 father and son were created
hereditary Counts of Prussia. In 1825 Count Matthias married
Anna Freiin von Ketteler, a sister of Bishop William Emmanuel.
Although Matthias' youth was passed in the age of rationalism,
he acquired in his father's house that firm faith, unaffected
piety and those strict principles which he retained throughout
his life and which made him an example to many, particularly
his own sons.

In his own household and family he ruled with absolute
authority, rectitude and affection. He was a kind master to
servants and household officers. But over his thirteen children
his authority was absolute. Adult, even grey-haired, sons
never ventured upon a comment on their father, still less a
criticism. He indeed took part in the general family life and its
festivities but had no wish for recreation and pleasure for
himself. He walked with his young children but never rode
with his sons, never hunted or shot either with them or alone.
Personally very simple and unpretending he brought up his
children to self-denial and frugality, but without suppressing
the cheerfulness and vigour that are properly characteristic of
youth. Thus he did not prohibit riding, hunting and fishing for
his sons. Only they must absolutely obey the rules of the house
and conduct themselves in an orderly manner. Effeminacy he
hated. We shall find a man of the same character in his grand-
son the Cardinal.

The family life in Dinklage and Assen might have lacked
warmth and sunlight under the grave and unswerving leadership of Grandfather Matthias but for the presence of his wife

1. The Cardinal's grandfather with his eight sons in 1862:

Paul

Friedrich   Clemens   Bernhard   Max Gereon   Wilderich

Hubert   Count Matthias   Ferdinand

2. The Cardinal in childhood (1885) with two
sisters and a brother holding a hobby-horse.
Left to right: Franz, Agnes, Clemens-August
and Paula

Anna von Ketteler. She must have been an incomparably affectionate mother and mistress who united a superior mind and the nicest tact with personal humility and an inexhaustible spirit of self-sacrifice. Her greatest joy was quietly to help the poor and sick.

The eldest child of Count Matthias was a daughter, Maria. She married Count August von Spee. Three of her sons became priests. Friedrich, the eldest son of Count Matthias, renounced his hereditary rights and became a priest. He died in 1864, when Parish Priest of Lembeck.

Passing into the family portrait gallery, we meet with three striking figures, men in uniform, younger sons of Count Matthias. The eldest of these is Wilderich, who served in the campaigns of 1864 and 1870. He was naturally excitable, even vehement, but in later life acquired great self-command and even spoke humorously of his occasional outbreaks. As an old man he heard Mass daily.

Count Paul was full of enthusiasm for a restored German Empire, which he hoped for as did the majority of German Catholics. Devoted as he was to the old imperial family of Hapsburg, he entered the Austrian Army and became an Imperial Chamberlain. The war of 1866 was tragic for the von Galen family, Wilderich and Paul being on opposite sides in the struggle. Count Paul settled in Tirol in the castle of his wife's parents and thus founded the Austrian branch of the von Galen family. Like Wilderich he was outwardly of a vehement temperament but the inner man was pious and jovial with tender feelings for the old castle of Dinklage. The Cardinal, when studying theology in Innsbruck, learned to value and love his uncle.

Count Clement, the third soldier son, differed greatly from his elder brothers and was of a mild disposition. He died in 1908.

We now pass to other portraits of the thirteen children of Grandfather Matthias. One of these is of the youngest, Hubert von Galen. Next to him is the youngest daughter, Clementine, who died unmarried. Another portrait is that of the Countess Helena, the wife of the Hereditary Bailiff Droste zu Vischering Clemens, the greatly honoured leader of the German Catholics. Following his example, the Countess Helena for a half a century took an active interest in public life, in the struggles, sufferings and victories of the Church.

We are near to the door of the ancestral portrait gallery. Two of the pictures are portraits of priests, Bernhard and Max Gereon von Galen. Then we leave the gallery, bidding farewell to the faces that seem to be gazing on us. All, both men and women, have passed away. God greatly blessed the patriarchal Matthias: his descendants include two bishops, eight priests, two theologians and sixteen nuns. In writing his family chronicle the great Cardinal himself became our guide to the castle of his ancestors: he himself opened the door to us and pulled up the curtains. We have thankfully followed his leadership. We recognized the features of the great Cardinal in the faces which we beheld, in their way of life, their resolution and vital energy, in their piety and depth of soul and in the zeal which inspired them.

CHAPTER 2

THE ANCESTRAL CASTLE

THE 5th May, 1941, marked the beginning of a series of Confirmations in the deanery of Damme in Oldenburg. We[1] left the railway at Badbergen, the station nearest to Dinklage, and reached the castle, where we were to stay for most of the confirmations, by car. I shall never forget the first few hours after our arrival at the castle. The Bishop was unusually vivacious and communicative. The heavy burdens of his office seemed to fall from him in a world which had been his childhood's paradise. As we approached the castle, he pointed to a window. 'That was the bedroom of my dear parents; there I was born on the 16th March, 1878.'

We passed over the suspension bridge. 'Do you see the two lime trees on the right and left of the bridge? How long have they been there? I can tell you. On April 27th, 1890, my brother and I made our First Communion in the parish church of Dinklage. The next morning my father took us aside and said: "Here are two small lime trees, you must plant them yourselves. Whenever you see them you should remember the day of your First Communion." The Bishop's voice trembled with emotion as he uttered the last sentence. Then he went on in silence. I remembered that on the 27th April, 1940, Count Franz, who had come to the Bishop's private chapel together with other close relations, served the Bishop's Mass: thus was the golden jubilee of Communion Sunday celebrated. We approached the chapel which is outside the moat. 'How often did we, as children, morning and evening, pass this way. Every evening after supper our father led the way, with him our mother, then we children and the servants. Father said the whole rosary in the chapel and a long evening prayer. It was often a real trial when I was so tired. But how happy am I today, when I have the rosary in my hand and these recollections of my childhood come again into my mind. I never forget

[1] The biographer was the Bishop's domestic chaplain and attended him at Confirmations. (Note by Translator.)

35

that in my childhood the old Dinklage Christmas carol with its charming old traditional verses was sung; one verse tells us how the dear Holy Child enters the cottages of the poor but not the manor-houses of the rich. Well, we children always thought to our own consolation that our home was not a manor-house (*Schloss*) but a castle (*Burg*).'

We stood before the chapel and looked at the escutcheon of the founder and his wife, cut in sandstone, wolf-traps and a pot-hook. 'Yes, my dear grandfather Matthias and my grandmother built this house of God.' The path led us into the wood: in the midst of it we passed by a statue of Our Lady: here years and years ago the children attended the Month of May devotions, here they sung '*Maria zu lieben*', and learned the tender prayers which they remembered all their life, 'O Mother of the Divine Child who sweetens all suffering.'

On the following morning before dawn, the children and their elders assembled in the parish church before school hours; the authorities forbade the interruption of school routine. Then the Bishop confirmed the children of his own home. During the ceremony the organ suddenly played the melody of a song known only to the people of Dinklage, which they sang on special occasions. The Bishop was deeply moved: for some time he could not continue the service, so affected was he by recollections of a pious childhood.

Both his parents, Count Ferdinand Heribert von Galen and his wife Elisabeth, by birth a Countess von Spee, grew up in the same traditions: the holy Catholic faith was the foundation and the never-questioned guide of the thought and life of all the inmates of Dinklage Castle. Count Ferdinand, who inherited the estate from his father Matthias, was a Catholic of absolute thoroughness. After serious reflection and with a great sense of responsibility, he entered into matrimony, after long interior struggles and self-examination upon the question whether he was not called to the priesthood as were three of his brothers. God blessed his marriage, as his father's was blessed, with thirteen children. Fully conscious of what his task was, he was as a father both the head who ruled the family circle in Dinklage and the unquestioned centre of all its interests.

The mother, naturally lively, cheerful, with many interests, agreeing with the father in matters of moment and her out-

on life, enjoyed his full confidence. In the happiest way
vas the complement of the serious and silent father.
affectionate influence on his whole nature earned
ie' father's inexpressibly tender and chivalrous love.
for my mother's good always took the first place with

children were strictly educated. Obedience, order,
lity and industry without fail were required: the life
: of Spartan endurance and frugality. This was in
with the character of the old castle, which lacked
water and bathrooms and in which most of the rooms
t be heated. By such a life were the young children
Clemens August among them: plain and simple he
all his life, straightforward and hard, strong and
positive and angular, unyielding and inflexible, he
l of the world of his childhood and youth. Punish-
: rare: a severe reproof from their father was more
the cane is in many families. The thought that they
'e their parents was for the most part sufficient to
to act rightly and to overcome temptation. The
nything a child wanted or asked for ended the
e was no begging by the children or weak yielding
ts.

op learned in his parents' house not merely his
t the particular character of that piety. A religious
rrounded all the inmates from morning to even-
r they breathed. A faith which the scepticism of
r infected, and on which nothing made any
nded down to him as a priceless inheritance. For
of heaven, both then and in later life, were as
s as the things of ordinary life. God the Father,
leemer, the Mother of God, and the saints of
mere distant entities dwelling on high but
he knew himself to be surrounded. He lived
and hourly as if they were present in body:
ed in the earliest years of his childhood. All the
hey left home, were taught their catechism
and were prepared by her for their First

g the day's work began with Mass. Anyone

late at Mass got no butter on his bread at breakfast. Absence
from Mass meant no breakfast at all.

At the age of ten or eleven their father put his boys on
horseback and taught them to ride as in former times he had
taught his recruits. From the feast of St. George, 1889 onwards,
when their father was in Dinklage, a daily ride was part of the
day's programme. At that time Clemens August usually rode a
Hungarian black, great at bucking, who often threw his
young rider on the sand. Sporting-guns came some years later
a gun was not to be treated as a toy. Their father seldom shot
himself, but he understood his sons' passion for sport: some of
them were very keen, others less so. When he saw them start to
go shooting, he wished them good sport and often added the
warning, 'Take your guardian angel and St. Hubert with
you!'

There was no shooting or riding on Sundays and feast
days and their father was very reluctant to use the carriage on
those days.

It is a matter of importance in noble houses to preserve the
growing children from the dangers of an exclusive education
with its excessive narrowness and seclusion. Even in their early
years they must acquire wider views, get their minds awakened
to the fact that a world of another kind surrounds them and
learn how their fellow men live. In Dinklage the children were
not brought up to keep a distance between themselves and
community generally. They played with others of their age in
the neighbourhood, went with them to religious instruction
and themselves saw or heard how their father and mother
helped the needy in a spirit of Christian charity. In early years
their father personally visited the poor in their homes,
finding that this was, owing to his station, very embarrassing
them, he gave up doing so and smaller gifts were distributed
by their mother. Almost daily petitioners visited her: all were
listened to, most of them helped. She and her daughters prepared and distributed innumerable garments for the poor.
Christmas families recommended by the clergy always received
gifts of clothing. The children treasured in their hearts the
example thus set them by their parents for their guidance in
later life.

The ancestral castle was a greatly loved home. It

placed in a world full of warmth and blessed security, watched over by a noble father, guided by a gracious mother, sheltering brothers and sisters all in complete accord. There was the root of the strength which the priest and bishop so markedly displayed in later life. His childhood's kingdom remained with him and bore him up. To the last hour of his life till he was called to his eternal home he was loyal to his home and all it stood for.

CHAPTER 3

EDUCATION

SOME·years after his two eldest sisters had left Dinklage for
ever to enter as novices the Convent of the Sacred Heart in
Riedenburg near Bregenz, Clemens August ran his finger over
the map of the mountains and valleys of the Alps. At last he
found what he was looking for: Feldkirch in the Vorarlberg.
Proudly but also sadly he showed it to his brother Franz.
'That's where we are going, to the Jesuit Latin School.' They
looked at one another anxiously. On April 27th, 1890, they had
made their First Communion in the parish church of Dinklage.
They felt that this was the end of their childish paradise, at
least to some extent. Life was becoming more serious. But their
elder brothers Friedrich and Augustinus had already gone to
Feldkirch, that was a comfort.

Weeks and months passed by. The two lads from Oldenburg had entered into the spirit of the school: they soon felt
that they were members of a community. They had indeed
learned in Dinklage to have regard for others: here they had to
give practical effect to what they had learned. And this is the
real object of education in a community, to rub down the
corners of one's character. They made their first attempts at
Latin grammar. The Bishop in after years modestly admitted
that his brother was better at languages than himself.

When he came to Feldkirch as a twelve-year-old boy
Clemens August was already big and strong but strikingly thick-
set and clumsy, so that he found sport and games rather distasteful. But he soon shot up and became the tallest of all the
pupils, reaching the height of six foot six. Then he acquired a
passion for games and sport; mountain climbing and toboggan-
ing opened his lungs and steeled his muscles. He took a keen
interest in musical studies and became a very fair baritone and
player on the French horn. It was not surprising that the
appetite of the young giant, sound as a bell, living in clear
mountain air, left nothing to be desired. No one ventured to
make fun of him, it would have been ill advised. But it was only

in the stage plays, in which he always got the part of the sturdy and athletic footman, that he used his fists; never on other occasions. He was equally beloved by all, both teachers and pupils.

The Stella Matutina, as the school was called, was, under the protection of the Mother of God, full of the spirit of the great Jesuit Order. Here Clemens August sat for four years at the feet of St. Ignatius' sons: there he stayed for Christmas and Easter: holidays were limited to two months in summer and were spent at Dinklage. The mere mention of these facts is sufficient to indicate the profound impression this education made upon the young lads, building up their character in the years in which they were growing up. We can understand what these four years in a Jesuit school meant to them.

In the summer of 1894 the two brothers left the Stella Matutina and the beloved mountains for ever. The Jesuit school was not recognized by the Prussian Government and the last two years of their school life had to be passed in the Catholic public school of Oldenburg at Vechta. They soon made friends with their companions who in some cases remained their friends for life. This experience of a community was certainly of great importance to Clemens August, who hitherto had for the most part been brought up in a world of class distinctions. The young men's horizon broadened, their judgment acquired a wider reach, their understanding of the everyday life of their fellow men grew deeper. These experiences were indispensable in the case of a future priest. The way of life in the small town of Vechta, in some respects primitive, was also of educational value.

At Vechta both brothers felt themselves in their native air. Sundays were passed at the Castle of Dinklage only ten miles away. Thus they enjoyed at home and at school a beneficial combination of hard work and pleasant relaxation. The pleasures of home life in all its aspects were theirs. Clau brought down his first fallow buck in the Dinklage preserve; in other preserves he shot roebuck, hares and partridges. He was an enthusiastic and successful shot. At that time the bicycle was a novelty and the two brothers were bold riders of this dangerous machine.

The leaving examination took place in the summer of 1896.

The great joy of the brothers was mingled with sorrow: Pia, their youngest sister, had died a short time before at the age of ten.

After leaving school the two brothers stopped at home until Easter in 1897. A splendid time they had, resting on their laurels when still young. But some hours of the day had to be devoted to study, particularly of books on religion and philosophy. Their father knew the value of philosophy and history, and he therefore decided to send both sons in the spring of 1897 to the Catholic University of Freiburg in Switzerland for two terms. There they were to 'learn to think' as an introduction to the profession of their choice.

Amidst glorious mountains the young students enjoyed fresh air, physically and mentally. Scientific study, uninfected by the feeble disillusioned liberalism of many German universities, was pursued in a crystal-clear atmosphere and with a Catholic breadth of view.

In the spring of 1898 at the end of the winter term the brothers crossed the Alps and entered the country all Germans long for—Italy. For the first time Clemens August saw the Eternal City. He passed three months in Rome, every week of which had its influence on his future. Guided by their elder brother Friedrich, the Freiburg students wandered through the venerable streets and squares, through the churches and catacombs of Eternal Rome. For the first time Clemens August knelt at the tomb of the Prince of the Apostles under the mighty dome of St. Peter's. It might be said that every hour he laid a stone of the bridge which many years later brought him again under the same dome as a Cardinal sharing in the glory of the papal throne set upon the Confessio Sancti Petri. The students enjoyed the memorable experience of hearing the papal Mass said by Leo XIII at the age of eighty-eight. On their return journey they passed through Assisi, that little town by which every German Catholic is so deeply moved, and Florence.

Clemens August had had a vision of the extent of the universal Church. His love of the Church, of the Pope, of the bishops and priests, had grown: everything that was taken for granted at home, reverence for the Holy See, the bishops, the clergy of all degrees, was confirmed by his first vision of the

Holy City seen as in a beam of splendid colours. We read in the family chronicle; 'In my home no criticism of any act of the ecclesiastical authorities was ever heard. Priests must always be spoken of with reverence.'

The two brothers made a retreat at the Benedictine Abbey of Maria-Laach. On their way home from the Abbey Clemens August told his brother of his decision to become a priest; it was no surprise but from now onwards the two inseparables went different ways. At the beginning of the summer term Franz went to the University of Freiburg in Breisgau, Clemens August in the autumn following went to the Canisianum, the Jesuit Theological College in Innsbruck.

The new student, head and shoulders taller than all his fellow students, excited a good deal of attention. Keen-sighted but infinitely good-humoured, he never let them get a sight of the aristocratic side of his character; he had an antipathy for any kind of pretentiousness; he was blunt and frank in his speech. He was now able to get all the further practice in the mountain climbing which he had started at Feldkirch and during his term in Switzerland that he wanted.

Clemens August was not merely sound in body: his intellect and his soul had the same quality. His self-possession combined as it was with real modesty marked him out as a leader and led to his appointment by the Rector as *bidellus* or link between the college teachers and the student body, two hundred and fifty strong. His clear judgment and natural ability made his studies easy to him. He had not indeed any ambition to become a teacher; theory was not in his line; his temperament led him to fact, to close contact with the lives of men to whose help he wanted to dedicate all his strength. His principal interests were therefore in the various spheres of practical life, in questions of ecclesiastical politics, the relations between Church and State, between the State and science, the State and education, the State and the family. Social questions were also studied and also problems of moral theology and sociology. On these questions he followed his father's line of thought. Nothing but a society resting on God can produce tolerable social conditions: there can be no Paradise on earth. This truth he had already learned at home: under his Jesuit teachers his convictions on these matters became still deeper.

At Feldkirch and Innsbruck certain particular features of his character and piety developed. His conviction of the corruption of human nature through original sin was continually reinforced. The yearly retreats which in later life he regularly made under Jesuit direction and his daily meditations on supernatural truths were particularly concerned with the subject matter of the first part of the exercises of St. Ignatius, sin and eternity. The natural consequence was a pessimistic view of human life and of human nature.

In 1903 Clemens August was admitted to the ecclesiastical seminary of Münster. With other men of his year, who enjoyed his comradeship and friendship, he received the seven minor orders. Guided by a Rector of deep piety and a most conscientious Sub-rector, he was consecrated priest in the great cathedral church on the 28th May, 1904, Bishop Hermann Dingelstad being the consecrator. A few days later he left his beloved seminary after bidding farewell to all the students of the year junior to his own. This was not an established usage: all the more does it explain the profound reverence which a priest of that year had for the Cardinal's memory after his death.

CHAPTER 4

THE YOUNG PRIEST

On a glorious Sunday morning in June, Clemens August, just appointed an assistant priest at Münster Cathedral, crossed the Cathedral square newly invested with his unique dignity. What must his feelings have been in this sacred place where so many of his forefathers had knelt and to which he had belonged from his birth? His family and Münster Cathedral had grown together: on this day his eyes often rested on the epitaphs and monuments of cathedral dignitaries of noble families. Beyond the high altar in the von Galen chapel was the grave of the great Christopher Bernard von Galen, and that of Dean Friedrich Christian von Galen who died in 1748.

He preached his first sermon at Whitsuntide in the little church of Angelmodde near Münster where he had been sent to give his assistance for the feast. The Bishop later recounted that it was so hot that his sermon suffered from the heat, but apparently was not very stirring because some peasants actually went to sleep. He was so frank and humble about his own efforts.

The duty assigned to the new assistant priest was that of attending on his uncle, the suffragan bishop: it must have been a special disposition of divine providence which placed him in the early years after ordination by the side of the saintly bishop. As a strong churchman the Bishop was a *persona minus grata* to German Governments. His proposed appointment by Bishop Johann Bernard to an office in Vechta was frustrated by the Oldenburg authorities, those of Hesse took a similar course when he was chosen to be Bishop of Mainz, as did the Prussian authorities when he was proposed for the see of Fulda and subsequently of Osnabrück. He bequeathed the crozier given him by his brother Paul to the Church of Our Lady of the Seven Dolours in Telgte,[1] subject to the condition that, if any

[1] Telgte. Township, pop. 4,456, in former Prussian prov. of Westphalia, N.W. Germany; after 1945 in North Rhine, Westphalia, on Ems and 7 m. E.N.E. of Münster. Possesses fine church, 1654, with miraculous picture of Our Lady (approx. same date) and privileged chapel and altar. Also memorial to warlike Bishop von Galen (1661), the Fuerstbischof who subdued the Anabaptists.

one of the von Galen family attained episcopal rank, he should, so long as he lived, have the use of it. He died on the 5th November, 1908.

In 1906, when the health of his uncle was failing and he could no longer undertake fatiguing official duties, Clemens August bade farewell to Münster and its cathedral. At his uncle's side he had got to know, through visits his uncle made to administer confirmation, an important part of the diocese: it was a varied diocese, partly urban, partly agricultural and partly industrial. This too was providential as he was destined to be Bishop of Münster. He now left the diocese in which his home was situated to take up parish work in Berlin at the parish church of St. Matthias, which according to an old tradition was always served by clergy from the diocese of Münster.

Clemens August soon perceived the difficulty of pastoral work in a metropolis: he set to work with all the idealism of a priest. His then Rector, now dean and honorary Canon of Emmerich, reports that he excelled in pastoral work. Day by day he set out upon his visits both to cellar dwellings and attics and to elegant residences on the Kürfurstendamm, but he preferred the poor quarters. He dried many tears: many petitioners came to his door; his liberality was known; in this way he became the father of the poor. But amongst all the need and poverty, how much sin and crime! St. Ignatius was profoundly right when, in the first part of his Exercises, speaking with such bitter and uncompromising earnestness, he brought the souls of his sons and of all priests face to face with sin and the last judgment.

In his later years he was fond of telling how as President of the Catholic Young Men's Association in Berlin, it fell to him to take part in creating the Association's building: how he sought for a suitable site and found it near the Anhalter Station in the heart of the city and how he constantly reminded the ecclesiastical authorities in Breslau of the absolute necessity of such a building. He remained President even after Cardinal Kopp had appointed him *Curatus* with a separate cure of souls of the Clemens-Hofbauer Church which was connected with the Association's house and was also built by him.

He loved the family atmosphere of the Young Men's Association; it reminded him of how he and his family got together at home. His addresses to the young men always dwelt on four great objects which they were to strive for; they were to be good Christians, good citizens, first-rate men at their work and, above all, ideal fathers of families. Many a young man in his years of apprenticeship, despondent among the dangers of a great city, was helped and strengthened by him. He considered it an important part of his duty to watch over the company they kept and the books and newspapers they read.

The Clemens-Hofbauer Church which he served lay among modern brick buildings; it was daily visited by many worshippers, especially by deputies from the Imperial and Prussian parliaments. As *Curatus* he lived in a flat over the rooms of the hostel of the Young Men's Association: he and three clerical colleagues formed one household which was looked after by the Grey Nuns. Important visitors seldom shared their plain fare: there was no time for that. He himself had only two rooms, furnished with monastic simplicity. In a corner there was a row of long pipes which had resisted the incursion of the smarter cigarette. Even here he wanted to be loyal to family traditions.

Clemens August was an assistant priest and *Curatus* in Berlin from 1906 to 1919. His father died at the beginning of this period, his mother at the end of it.

On January 5th, 1906, God called to Himself in a peaceful and holy death the Hereditary Chamberlain Count Ferdinand Heribert von Galen. Like his father Matthias he died in the Christmas season. Clemens August's mother bore her husband's death with the courage of a Christian, even with rejoicing in the supernatural sense, and after he had passed away recited the Magnificat with complete self-command. But still, after his death, a quiet sadness overshadowed her natural cheerfulness. She could not make up her mind to leave Dinklage Castle, the scene of such lasting family happiness, and to take up her residence in the dower-house in Münster. Her daughter Paula Ursula remained with her and together they lived a quiet life in Dinklage for fourteen years, wholly devoted, one may truly say, to the service of God.

On the 24th March, 1920, on returning from her usual afternoon visit to the chapel, she had a stroke when going up the house steps. She was able to receive the last sacraments while still fully conscious. On the 26th March, the Feast of the Seven Dolours, she quietly passed to the eternal life. Twenty-six years later, again in the last days of March, she called her great son home to join her.

3. 'Clau' and Young Mischief in 1888

4. Going out to shoot: summer holiday in Dinklage in 1899

CHAPTER 5

PARISH PRIEST IN BERLIN

IN THE year 1919 the *Curatus* of St. Clement's was called upon to leave his beloved little church and the great family founded by Adolf Kolping[1] which had grown so dear to his heart. With the consent of the bishop of his native diocese, he had been appointed Parish Priest of St. Matthias'. He returned to the great community, which he had left nine years before as an assistant priest, with very few household goods. It was the same thing with his eating and drinking: here too we find he chose that life of abstinence which his deep religious convictions pointed out to him. Franciscan nuns had charge of the kitchen. At his very moderate midday meal, eaten in the company of his assistant priests—throughout his life he invariably aimed at a community life—he would not allow a word of criticism of the food. In this he followed the traditions of his home and his own instinctively monastic ideals. 'Fasting,' Pfarrer Holstein tells us, 'was a serious matter for a man who was so big and large of limb. In Berlin in the middle of the day we got back from our teaching rather late so that we usually had our meal at 1.45 p.m. Up to that time he took nothing beyond a small bit of dry bread and a cup of black coffee. Of course this impaired his vigour. I told him that his severe fasting injured his nerves and that this was bad for others as well as himself. The only result was that he did not cut down his fasting but redoubled his efforts to control his nerves.'

We shall find that Clemens August, when later he became a bishop, was still the same man. In one thing only did he not quite conquer the old Adam; even during times of fasting he did not quite give up his long pipe; to do so would have affected his capacity for work too much.

One of his assistant priests has written of the spiritual life

[1] Adolf Kolping, *b.* 1813, *d.* 1865, a Catholic priest, was the founder of the German Catholic Young Men's Association. (Note by Translator.)

of the Parish Priest of St. Matthias' in a touching manner:
'Every Saturday evening he went into the room of his senior
assistant priests and knelt down and made his confession.
When he was entering upon his annual retreat, he always
came to me previously and asked me to tell him what it
was he ought to be specially on his guard against and what
were the faults he ought to correct. The humility and the
spirit of pious endeavour with which he received admoni-
tions, which it was so difficult for me to give, as well as his
subsequent efforts to correct his faults, were touching and
deeply moving.'

Such basic elements of his character, which show his
tenderness and greatness of soul, cannot, in a biography, be
passed over in silence: in the picture of his life they supply the
colourings of greatest beauty. On the silver jubilee of his
ordination, he gave to every assistant priest who had served
under him a portrait of himself as a bishop. Underneath the
portrait he wrote: '*In domo Dei ambulavimus cum consensu*—We
have walked in unity in the house of the Lord.'

By his wish the nuns who had charge of the house placed
their chapel over his own room; he wished to be quite near to
his Lord; only a flight of stairs divided him from the sacra-
mental presence of Our Saviour. One of the nuns tells us: 'One
evening I came into the chapel to make a visit and saw that the
Parish Priest von Galen was in a seat near the altar. After a
short pause he rose, went to the altar, knelt there, stretched
out his arms so as to embrace our small altar and brought
his face very near to the tabernacle. He knelt for a long time in
prayer.'

Almost every afternoon he went to the cemetery, for which
he had built a new Church of the Holy Souls, to read his
breviary among the graves and, at times of fasting, to make
every day the Stations of the Cross. He constantly visited the
sick. Except as a pastor of souls he made no visits. He refused
invitations to lunch or dinner in lay society; he did not even
keep in touch with the nobility. When any of his women
relations stayed in his house, it was his custom not to join them
at table because he wanted to have the company of his assistant
priests at the midday meal. In very truth he was a man of a
monastic way of life and of a monastic rigour. He made his

own the great prayer of St. Francis Xavier, '*Da mihi animas, cetera tolle*—Give me souls, take from me all other things.' The Holy Sacrifice celebrated with awful veneration was the beginning of every day; every morning included a half hour of meditation. These were the sources of his strength in the wilderness of a metropolis. Whether he was restoring penitents in the confessional or climbing to the garrets of the forsaken, the image of the Good Shepherd was ever before him: he sought to be like unto Him. It was not his work to preach eloquent sermons in the pulpit of the imperial capital; his language was plain and his voice was not to any great extent modulated. Yet his sermons had their effect upon folk of simple faith. More than once his plain, deeply pious way of preaching brought back hearers to the confessional. Every word came straight from a personality humble in faith, working for Christ, speaking with the warm, beseeching, imploring accent of a shepherd or guardian of a flock seeking to guide his sheep.

A few months after his induction he had a mission preached in his parish. During the mission the news came that his mother had had a stroke, but his colleagues had to press him to go to his home as he thought that he should not leave his people at a time that counted for so much. But when he saw his mother she had passed away.

He once found that the three-year-old son of a woman who was asking for an alms had not been baptized; he immediately took them both into the sacristy and with the consent of the mother baptized the child. At another time he was visiting a sick man whose invalid wife was struggling to draw fresh water for him; he went straight into the kitchen and got the water for him. His compassionate heart urged him to deeds like these. A pastor and benefactor of the poor and sick!

A lad was present at a school breaking-up who had taken to bad ways. The teachers did not welcome him when he came in and took no notice of him at all. The poor boy in his wretched clothes was put to shame. When the Parish Priest saw what was happening, he got up, took the boy by the hand, and made him sit near him, talked to him during the breaking-up festivities and mentioned him in his closing address. This story was told by a Berlin priest, who as an elementary schoolboy had taken

part in the breaking-up, when the Parish Priest of the story was
being raised to the Sacred College in Rome.

The greatest of his pastoral joys were the great feasts of the
Church. He never slept on Christmas Eve. At midnight he said
Mass in the nuns' chapel over his room; afterwards he prayed
in his room until five o'clock when Masses began in the Parish
Church. Then he preached of the love of the Holy Child
for us and gave Communion; then he returned to his confessional until the time for High Mass, after which he went
home. In spite of his fast he showed no weariness; in utter
joy he said, smiling to his assistant priests, 'It was a beautiful
feast.'

The Holy Week celebrations of the Passion of Christ were
likewise felt to be profoundly sacred. And it was a great joy to
him when in the years after 1918 the Corpus Christi procession
could pass from the church into the city.

There was no side of pastoral work on which he had not
thought deeply and formed his own judgment. He continually
meditated on the questions of the day; problems such as the
development of religious feeling in a great city such as Berlin
was occupied him continually. There was not a meeting or
conference of the parochial clergy of Berlin at which he had
not a decided view on the questions to be discussed. And
indeed he really had something to say on them which was
valuable and useful. Judgments formed so independently might
indeed in some respects seem one-sided, but his birth and
upbringing had endowed him with an intuition of what was in
the fullest sense Catholic, his healthy instinct was his guide.
Hence came the uncompromising manner with which he
challenged with unswerving logic the unchristian tendencies of
the time. In his opinion the revolutionary ideas of 1918 had
had a pernicious effect even within the Catholic world. He
saw with anxiety that the youth of the day was growing up
without regard for authority and without reverence, that the
modern man was becoming more independent and presuming,
seeking ever to criticize, how the old restraints founded on
piety were being ruthlessly broken through even in ecclesiastical matters and where priests, bishops and the Pope were
concerned. All this pained him deeply. From his youth Clemens
August had felt that his relation to the Holy Father had a

special meaning for him, founded in loyalty, which no one was allowed to touch. A single hostile word, even if in some respects justified, aroused his passionate anger. He wished to be a loyal son of the Church with no reservations, and a good son cannot endure that the faults of his own father should be brought to light.

In the years after the First World War the decline of authority was accompanied to a great extent by a decline in morals. Clemens August had grown up morally pure and had passed through the severe school of the Jesuits. From the bottom of his heart he detested anything that was indecorous. He insisted that the Decree of the bishops upon the continually increasing licence in women's dress should be read and immediately acted upon. Two young girls of good Catholic families were refused Holy Communion: this led to a sharp conflict between the Parish Priest and the girls' fathers. Clemens August saw that he could not continue to act with such rigour. But it pained him deeply to be compelled to be a passive observer of the decay of sound morality and of modesty: he perceived intuitively that in the western world a terrible avalanche would fall upon the institution of marriage and upon family life. Here too he was right.

Berlin, where Clemens August's work lay, was on the mainstream of political life. Social questions prevented him from ever resting. Like Emmanuel von Ketteler he saw the multitude of the poor, without root, without means and without religion, drift into a way of thinking that broke with all tradition. And he had pity on the people. The pre-war monarchy was gone, popular rule was the order of the day. It was a turning point in history. The Parish Priest of St. Matthias' kept out of the political arena: he often found it hard to do so but that was his own choice. He saw that century-old values were sinking into the dust and with them belief in God and the Church. Years later, on the 8th July, 1945, speaking as bishop amidst the ruins of the Münster Domplatz, he declared that it was in the time following upon the revolution of 1918 that the ground was prepared for a godless state: the godless state opened the way for the rise of the Hitler régime. If man believes that all power proceeds from the people and not from the Eternal God, the State rests on purely human foundations and these are fragile. This godlessness in the foundations of the State, he thought, was to be found in the Weimar Republic, and he could not adhere to it. It is true that in later years he staked his life in the cause of the inalienable rights of human personality, but even so he remained firmly convinced that the ballot-box alone cannot give the people a truly Christian life. And so at the beginning of the new democracy of 1945, he represented to the authorities of the Allied Powers that if the German people were made a present of freedom from outside, there could be no guarantee that in the course of party conflicts a particular party might not again win over an overwhelming majority of the people and set up again a dictatorship and all in the name of democracy.

Clemens August stood for a conservative patriarchal tradition. Men of religious convictions and of unblemished character must be the leaders of the people, in village, town and State, men who had given proof of their capacity for leadership and really and relentlessly sought the good of the community—and not their own good. He had grown up in a patriarchal world and in that world he wished to pass his life.

The metropolis, therefore, in spite of all that it had to give, was part of a world that spiritually was an alien world. In Berlin he was still the child of and one with the broad Westphalian land and its silent woods. He perceived that the poison of dechristianization and godlessness was spreading from the great cities over the countryside. Even the Catholic West, therefore, caused him anxiety when he thought about it. In January, 1928, his nephew Bernhard attained his majority and thus became an Hereditary Chamberlain and head of the von Galen family. In a long letter addressed to him on that occasion his uncle implores him, with all the force of a father imploring but also warning a son, to uphold the old traditions in Dinklage, to live among the people there as a real Catholic nobleman closely united to them and to set them an unfailing example as did his forefathers.

But Clemens August's Berlin years were nearly at an end. In 1929 Bishop Johannes Poggenburg called the son of the Red Earth[1] back to his home after twenty-three years of unremitting labour in the capital. He had given to that

[1] So called because of its red colour due to rich mineral deposits.

capital the best years of his life. He took a sad leave of his congregation and his clerical brethren. Before he gave his hand to his assistant priests, he knelt before each of them, begged for his priestly blessing and also for his forgiveness for any wrong done to him.

CHAPTER 6

ST. LAMBERT AND ST. LUDGER

ON THE 24th April, 1929, von Galen, whom the Bishop had appointed to be Parish Priest of St. Lambert's, the municipal and market church of Münster, the capital of Westphalia, ascended for the first time the steps of the pulpit to read, according to the prescribed ritual consecrated by the usage of many centuries, the gospel of the Good Shepherd. For the first time he saw at his feet the great flock entrusted to him. He was conducted to the font, to the tabernacle and to the confessional, respectively symbols of the full powers of the *pastor animarum*.

The Burgomaster of Münster, wearing his golden chain, together with the town councillors, occupied a place in the choir and after the ceremony visited the residence of the Parish Priest to bid him welcome. The sincerity of his address was a clear proof of the immutable Catholic foundations of public life in Münster.

The Parish Priest, however, had seen in Berlin as the years passed how Christianity was more and more excluded from public affairs. Materialism and the exclusion of any world beyond that of our present experience had seized on men and led them bewildered far from the right road. After nearly twenty-five years he had returned to the cathedral town of his homeland. What changes had taken place as a result of the first great war and the perplexing post-war years! The public life of the city had maintained the traditional observances but was not much of this merely formal?

In the year 1932 the Parish Priest of St. Lambert completed for publication a work[1] which caused a sensation. It dealt with the secularization of human society, the rejection of God and His laws. Since the end of the Middle Ages, during which religion and life were in the closest connection, a gradual but lamentable evolution had been in progress leading men away from the supernatural to the world of nature and its values. This secularization, the author says, had in our time penetrated

[1] *Die Pest des Laizismus und ihre Erscheinungsformen.*

56·

into the Catholic ranks like a plague. He lays great emphasis on original sin, of which too little account is commonly taken, he cites the First Epistle of St. John (chap. ii, verse 16): 'What does the world offer? Only gratification of corrupt nature, gratification of the eye, the empty pomp of living: these things take their being from the world, not from the Father.' (Translation of Monsignor R. Knox.) He who has not a due respect for these truths is an opponent of the Christian creed and Christian ethics. Are Catholics vigilant and armed, proof against the slowly penetrating infection which, if we yield to it, threatens to destroy in us the foundations of our Christian faith?

A year later and the proof of this forecast began. The delusion of National Socialism got a foothold and poisoned the mass of the people. There were certainly many who, firm in a faith which guided their lives, instinctively detected that the wind which was blowing over all spheres of life and bringing with it the promise of a new world was a wind that blew from hell. But how many were they who failed to perceive the essential nature of the current events because they had already given themselves over too much to the things of this present world? The Parish Priest of St. Lambert was indeed right when he raised his voice in warning as he did in the work he published in 1932 and called Catholics to an examination of conscience. The public had never before had experience of his relentless pursuit of objects which were Catholic because they were primitively Catholic, nor of his constant effort to inspire the nobility of his day with the spirit of his own father and himself so as to be, while renouncing all thought of self, the leaders of Catholic and public social life.

In the year 1933 the Parish Priest of St. Lambert's made this entry in the Parochial Chronicle: 'On Monday, March 6th, notwithstanding the unanimous protest of the town council, the flag of the Hitler party, a red flag with a swastika, was flown from the council house. After the conciliatory declarations of Chancellor Hitler at the opening of the new Reichstag, the bishops on the 28th or 29th March withdrew their warnings about participation in the National Socialist movement. It was consequently possible to permit that at the High Mass on April 3rd preceding the entry upon office of the new town

councillors the National Socialists should be present in uniform
with their party flag. The Parish Priest made a grave appeal to
the congregation.'

On the following 1st July there were further and longer
entries as to the protest of the Parish Priest against the disso-
lution of the Young Men's Association.

The mask of the innovators was falling from them. The
struggle had begun. After the death of Bishop Poggenburg in
January, 1933, there was, as usually happens when an episcopal
see is vacant, much discussion. The public asked questions, the
Press gave advice and suggestions, the clergy spoke of various
possible new bishops. It soon got abroad that Dr. Francken, a
member of the Cathedral Chapter, had suddenly left for Rome
by air. The discussions went on.

One summer morning, the postman delivered a letter from
the Papal Nuncio at the clergy house of St. Lambert's. A few
days later the Parish Priest told his senior assistant priest that
he had to make a journey but did not tell him why. In Berlin
the Nuncio Monsignor Orsenigo disclosed to him that the Holy
Father intended to appoint him to be Bishop of Münster. But
he added that there must be absolute secrecy both in Münster
and in Berlin. The Parish Priest took the night train back to
Münster. He went straight to the church from the station to say
Mass. No one had taken any notice of his journey, but the
sacristan noticed that his boots had not been cleaned. On the
following days there was a lot of gossip mixed with grins
among the assistant priests about the dusty uncleaned boots. At
last all ended in loud rejoicing when on Sunday, the 2nd
September, 1933, the High Cathedral Chapter caused it to be
solemnly announced from the pulpits of the diocese that the
Holy Father had appointed the Parish Priest of St. Lambert's,
Clemens August Count von Galen, to be the successor of St.
Ludger.

The hearts of the faithful were full of pride and joy. They
trusted the bishop-elect absolutely. They knew his piety and
the Catholic strength of the race of von Galen.

Under the provisions of the then recently concluded
Concordat, Clemens August, as the first bishop appointed
under the Third Reich, had to take the oath of allegiance
before the Prussian President of the Council of Ministers,

Göring. The Bishop took a New Testament with him and, as a precaution, his pectoral cross also. And in fact there was no crucifix available at the Ministry: excuses were offered and also an assurance that next time, that was to say when another bishop was appointed, proper provision would be made. Göring, in view of the fact that this was the first swearing-in under the Concordat, read a discourse to which Clemens August replied with due deliberation and according to a text that had been previously settled. After the discourses Göring gave a lunch at which he emphasized the necessity of getting the clergy on the side of National Socialism. The Bishop replied that according to the Concordat the clergy were not to take part in any party politics, to which Göring rejoined that to be a good National Socialist it was not necessary to be actually a member of the party. When in later years Göring's popularity and moderation for the time being were praised by those more intimately connected with the Bishop, he would have nothing to do with any favourable forecast; he asserted that in his view Göring was not a whit better than the rest of them.

Clemens August had to pay a series of visits to the chief personages of the Reich. Adolf Hitler acknowledged his card by sending his own by post. So that he could see the grey-headed President personally, the Bishop prolonged his stay in Berlin by a day. Hindenburg inquired with interest about the Bishop's homeland; he had a clear recollection of Oldenburg from manœuvres in the eighties of the last century; he spoke also of his being wounded at the battle of Königgrätz. When the Bishop on taking leave promised that he and his flock would pray for him, Hindenburg thanked him and asked that they should do so.

Ordinary folk, as was already noticeable, had limitless confidence in the new Bishop; a sound instinct led them in the confusion of the time to look for safety and rescue from the aggressive Catholicism of one of the race of von Galen. Still there were certain groups who had their own views; some were cheerful and hopeful, others depressed and fearful. The first group consisted of those in high places in the National Socialist Party: they placed their hopes in the 'man from the right' who would drive the refractory sheep of West Germany into the brown fold. But God's will was that that anticipated union of

Church leaders with men of the right and the military element, which had been the subject matter of so much publicity, should develop into a very considerable and forcible combination with the aid of which the Bishop in the subsequent years was able to deal the Nazis some very hard blows. The second group raised a dubious forefinger for this reason—they doubted whether in view of the depressed social position of the German people it was really prudent to place a mitre upon the head of a nobleman. But in fact this aristocrat had a heart open to the poorest and to the incurable; to them he dedicated his life. A third group thought that his oratorical powers left a great deal to be desired. In a few weeks the men of this group were not merely convinced of their error but very glad that they had been wrong. Prophecy is difficult. This was verified in the summer of 1933: men had their varying views but guidance came from God.

.   .   .   .   .

* * * * * The consecration of Clemens August von Galen took place in Münster Cathedral. The consecrator was Cardinal Schulte, Archbishop of Cologne, assisted by the Bishops of Osnabrück and Trier. The congregation included both a large number of ecclesiastics, some Knights of Malta and representatives of the province and the municipality, but also columns of the S.A. and S.S. carrying their red flags on which the swastika was displayed. After the consecration the new Bishop addressed the congregation from the cathedral pulpit. It was, he said, his marriage day, inasmuch as the consecrated ring on his finger was symbolic of the marriage between a bishop and his see. He then took his seat upon his throne to receive from the clergy their oath of obedience.

In the evening there was a torchlight procession which passed in front of the episcopal palace. On the following day, the feast of Christ the King, he celebrated his first Pontifical High Mass in the church of St. Servatius. * * * * *

.   .   .   .   .

Many brown uniforms had been seen at the Bishop's consecration. Before the ceremony the episcopal palace presented an unusual picture. The banners bearing the swastika pushed their way, independent and unconcerned, among the deputations from the various Catholic unions with their flags; the S.A. lined the road on both sides. After the ceremony the Party office-holders, beginning with the Gauleiter and coming down to the smallest S.A. Führer, marched past the Bishop, gave the Nazi salute, expressed their congratulations and finished with a second Nazi salute. The Bishop's practice was to spare himself the Nazi salute inasmuch as he gave a very abridged version of it. The highest-ranking S.A. Führer in Münster, who originally had not been invited to light refreshments in the Borromäum, asked for an invitation as being due to his rank, but when he presented himself he was not admitted. The Catholic president of the N.S.-Gnaden thought it expedient to make a cold and colourless speech at the luncheon table—very significant of the situation of the time. The Bishop said subsequently that a Protestant would have done better.

In the first months after the Bishop's enthronement it seemed as if the relations between the National Socialist authorities and himself would be strictly correct. He left his card upon those holding office in the Party or the Government who had been present at or had congratulated him upon his consecration. He also at a later date called upon the Gauleiter Meyer at his house.

CHAPTER 7

THE GREAT BISHOP

DURING the decade before National Socialism became dominant, Clemens August had read the signs of the time and found them gloomy. Now that the Dictator had come, was he dazzled as were so many in the Christian camp? Did he really believe and have confidence in Hitler's declaration in the Reichstag about the loyal co-operation of the new Germany and the Christian Churches? There certainly had been brief moments when Clemens August had still quietly hoped that the poisonous teeth of the wildest of the adherents of National Socialism would be drawn by men, possibly from the conservative camp, who combined strength and Christian faith. So the Bishop of Münster, like all the German religious leaders, had to wait and feel his way. He could not publicly pronounce an anathema until the hostility of the new movement to Christianity had become clear. Then, when he could doubt no longer, he fought the fight through as no other bishop did. But who in March, 1933, at the time of the Reichstag declaration and the Concordat to which it led, was competent to unmask the hellish gang? And had a blow been struck, who could have relied on support from the German people of sufficient weight? All were dominated by the hypnotic watchword that the new men must not be deprived of the chance of standing a test of their worth. Hence the tragic period of waiting, looking on and groping during which National Socialism was able to get such a firm hold, quite unopposed as it was, that no physical or spiritual force originating in Germany herself was able to dislodge it.

If we are to form a correct judgment of the events of these years, we must keep steadily in view the several stages to which reference has been made and their respective contributions to the final result.

The end of the year 1933 and the early part of the year 1934 were marked by some controversies of a lesser order, which however served to define the respective positions of the parties concerned. The Bishop paid close attention to the

literature of National Socialism. In his first Lenten Pastoral of
the 29th January, 1934, he opposed the fundamental doctrine
of the new thought, the worship of race. Christ, he said, knows
of a higher type of unity founded upon blood in that redemption shared by all which unites in Christ men of all peoples and .
of all'times who have been ransomed for God by the blood of
Jesus Christ. But this Pastoral, although it touched upon an
essential question with which later controversies were concerned, does not formulate any provocative propositions; such
were yet to come. A few weeks later the Bishop sat down to
write his Easter Pastoral. He was now quite certain where
National Socialism was going; he was absolutely convinced
that it was his duty to meet the danger of a gloomy and brutal
foe robbing his diocese and his country of their faith with every
means of defence that his episcopal office put in his hand and
with the help also of God's grace. Absolutely clear speech was
now necessary to open the eyes of right-minded people, to
warn the thoughtless, the superficial and the frivolous and
protect them from being misled. The Pastoral was read in the
cathedral in the most solemn manner in the presence of the
Bishop wearing his mitre and carrying his crozier so that all
present should know that a new epoch in the ecclesiastical
history of the diocese had begun. It was heard by the thousands
of the congregation in breathless silence.

We have to remember the state of public opinion at the
time. The National Socialist propaganda had confused many
minds: the objective of National Socialism appeared to be the
good of Germany; it had given the German Catholics the
Concordat. It was true that men could not close their eyes to
the spread of a new heathenism, but many thought that movements of that kind were not wanted by those now the leaders of
the Party and the State who stood for 'positive Christianity'.
The Bishop's words fell like a clap of thunder on to the mentality which passing from groping to waiting and then to
hesitating finished by thinking collaboration still possible. The
rulers of the State as such were not indeed directly impeached,
the warning was directed to what might lead both State and
people into an abyss. In two churches the reading of the
Pastoral led to interruptions which were in fact protests. Two
of these protestors, S.S. men, came to the Bishop's palace at

midday and politely asked for the text of the Pastoral, which they and others found offensive. The Bishop gave them a copy and advised them to read it carefully. The Party had got nervous and there was a lot of telephoning. The Burgomaster called up the Vicar-General to ask whether the Church was taking a new line when so far everything had gone on harmoniously. The Pastoral caused a widespread sensation even outside the diocese. Clemens August had publicly challenged his opponents and he began to be the man the public trusted.

* * * * * After Easter 1934 the Bishop's defence of the Catholic position against National Socialist ideology continued. In an address to an audience of between twenty and thirty thousand men and youths at Billerbeck he spoke of the Christianity of our forefathers. He vindicated Widerkind, Grand Duke of Saxony, who, in National Socialist writings, was exalted as a typically German hero whose Christianity was but a mask. Rosenberg and his errors were refuted.

In June, 1934, he spoke at Xanten where the jubilee of St. Norbert was being celebrated. After preaching in the cathedral he addressed an audience of young men and women on the Domplatz.

He was the chief mover in instituting an episcopal conference for North-West Germany, meeting periodically or specially to discuss urgent matters of ecclesiastical politics. Cardinal Schulte immediately seconded his efforts, calling the first meeting at Bensburg. The views of the bishops as to the way in which the fight against National Socialism was to be conducted naturally varied. Clemens August held that each bishop must follow his own conscience: it was not for another bishop to judge him. In important matters he tried to get the bishops to take the same line, and on many occasions he frequently gave a lead to the see of Cologne. But he held that the ultimate responsibility rested with the bishops individually; each one was the pastor of his own flock.

On the 5th July, 1934, he summed up before a chosen body, the Knights of Malta, his thoughts upon the great themes of conscience and responsibility and the part they should play in the fight between the two ideologies. Divine providence, he declared, which without merit on his part had made him a priest and a bishop, had conferred on him the signal benefit of belonging to one of those families whose most eminent members for seventy-five years had belonged to the brotherhood of the Knights of Malta of the Rhineland and Westphalia. In these families and in the dear home of his forefathers, the Catholic faith and the life guided by Catholic principles had for centuries had their home.

Divinely revealed truth had been the foundation of all their thinking and the touchstone by which all human theories and opinions were tried and judged. Gratitude to divine providence should be all the greater when they saw that many of their fellow men in Germany did not share in these gifts; they had fallen into error though they may have meant well. They mistook partial truths for the truth itself. Recent experiences had taught us how a ruthlessly one-sided propaganda of novel ideas and dazzling slogans could lead whole masses into error by its dominating influence. If the enemies of faith and of Christ had at their disposal such powerful means of spreading their influence, everyone must be watchful that neither he nor the souls entrusted to his care bowed down to idols, and that in spite of the constant accusations and calumnies against the Church and her ministers, our child-like confidence in her, our mother, in her doctrine and guidance was not impaired by indifference or estrangement.

The danger to the Catholic faith in Germany could not be neglected. No greater evil could happen to their dear country than an injury to or possibly even the extirpation of the Christian faith and Christian life. At his consecration he had solemnly sworn that he would stake all to protect her from this evil. The Holy Father himself in the Bishop's hearing had publicly declared that the Catholic faith in Germany was attacked and in danger and that German Catholics must meet the danger with vigilance and courage. * * * * *

The Bishop concluded his address to the Knights of Malta in these words: 'Where do we stand in this struggle? Where do you stand? I hope it may be said that the Knights of Malta of

E

the Rhineland and Westphalia are taking their stand with fearless, chivalrous loyalty as the living shield of the Immaculate Bride of Christ, often heavily laden and despised, our venerable mother the Holy Catholic Church. I hope that public avowal on your part and the devotion of your lives to duty will confirm what I will now say. Armed for the fight, regardless of ourselves, ready for sacrifice, we defend the priceless inheritance of the Catholic nobility, the possession of the Catholic faith, the moral teachings of Christ, the means of grace and the Blessed Sacrament in which the blood of Our Saviour purifies and strengthens us. Be steadfast and fearless in this holy fight. God so wills. Preserve for your children this unspeakably priceless possession. Preserve for your descendants, in your Catholic noble families that unrelenting uncompromising Catholic bearing, that unconstrained life in the Church which becomes a second nature and which in spite of many afflictions is our warranty of true joy in this life and of a holy death in the arms of God.'

The Bishop's address bore witness to his profound anxiety as to the future of Christianity in Germany. He saw the fearful danger and never paused in his efforts to meet it.

The day of the Party rally of 1935 for the Münster region arrived. The Bishop had early news of the plans of the day, particularly of the expected attendance of Rosenberg, and he had written to the Provincial President to express his deep concern as regards Rosenberg. On the other side there was a corresponding atmosphere. Rosenberg spoke from a platform erected in the Neuplatz where of course he got a large audience. The Party had gone to a lot of trouble to bring in bodies of S.A. men from the specially 'brown' areas of Westphalia. The applause as heard through the loud-speakers was to some extent noticeable when Rosenberg uttered his abuse of the Bishop, but residents on the Neuplatz asserted that it was markedly restrained. Personal attacks such as these, conceived in the tub-thumping style, left the Bishop quite cold. He was more concerned about the attitude of the President and the danger of the mass of the people being egged on by irresponsible demagogic speakers. During the Party rally, when so many were present who had come in from outside the city, the position was extremely tense.

The reply of Catholic Münster came the next day, on Monday's Great Procession. The swastika decorations of the Party rally had disappeared and caused no trouble. The throng was overwhelming. Rosenberg and company had brought about an increase in those taking part from the seven thousand of the previous year to about nineteen thousand. After the Procession, when the Bishop was escorted back to his residence, he got a tremendous ovation such as had not been heard for ages past. There was an uncanny tension and sultriness in the air. The Bishop appeared at an upper window and the wave of rejoicing and enthusiasm surged up to him. He stood up there like a fighter and spoke. Never before had he put matters so dramatically as at this moment. He pointed out that in the Bishop's Palace in which he stood, Caspar Max Droste zu Vischering, who dared to raise his voice against Napoleon in Paris, had dwelt; that the Confessor Bishop Johann Bernard had been taken to prison from there; such times had now returned; he assured all present that he would never yield to the enemies of Christianity and the persecutors of the Church. All stood there entranced. Solemn anger and invincible determination inspired his words. One of the audience said to a companion as they went away, 'How blind the brown men are to rouse the Lion of Münster.'

The Bishop's friends and foes remembered very clearly when the day of the Great Procession of 1936 arrived what had happened in the previous year. The police roped off a great part of the Domplatz so as to prevent any large numbers of people assembling and the Procession on its return to the cathedral passed between the ropes. 'I am going into the pulpit,' said the Bishop, addressing the Provost. There, while the congregation looked on in amazement, the Bishop thundered forth his solemn indignation: 'What does this use of force mean? Can the shepherd be severed from his flock? Can the police divide Catholics from their own bishop by ropes and chains?' (There were loud cries of 'No! Clemens August! *Heil, Heil, Heil!*') 'They cannot be divided; they are ever one and today in inseverable unity they have followed their Saviour through rain and storm. Sorrowful times, my dear people of Münster, are at hand but I know that steadfastness will prevail.'

When the Bishop left the cathedral the police could not

keep back the throng. Children and youths, as ever heedless, were the first to leap over the ropes; others followed and finally the police were so hemmed in that they were carried like a wave towards the Bishop's Palace. Loud acclamations were heard under the open window of the Bishop's study. He came to the window and a hurricane of applause met him.

In 1937 the police again met with a check. The close of the Procession was to be filmed in an impressive manner for purposes of foreign propaganda directed to refuting alleged persecution of the Church in Germany. But just at the spot where the photographers and Gestapo had arranged to set up the cameras, there was no bishop to be seen.

Rosenberg in Münster, the Great Procession, police cordons on the Domplatz: all enter into the picture of Catholic resistance in Western Germany. Similar spontaneous demonstrations continued as the years passed. It was one of the few ways left of showing loyalty to the chief pastor of the diocese.

These striking demonstrations of Christian loyalty went to the Bishop's heart but they could not conjure away the dark clouds on the horizon, ever more threatening and sinister. We know today that in that dreadful decade the gates of hell did not prevail against the Church in Germany, but the Blessed Anne Catharina Emmerich was truly right when over a hundred years ago she said that hell would be let loose. A gigantic tower of Satan was being raised, nothing else than a hellish abortion. Of a lustre that dazzled, of glorious colouring, of gigantic dimensions and an ardour that bade defiance to any violence, possessing pluck and dash, vaunting uniform and rhythm, such was the structure of what was called 'the Movement' which was able to spread delirium and stupefaction over a nation. Reason and judgment were banished or overclouded. Millions knew not where they stood in the midst of an artful combination of truth and error, of idealism and violence, of substance and show, of salutary authority and brutal abuse of power. This conglomeration of good and evil was what the devil contributed to National Socialism. 'Hell itself is let loose with its deceit which may mislead even good men,' wrote the Bishop in his Easter Pastoral for 1934. We recollect how men were fascinated and carried away by the buoyancy with which National Socialism seized on problems and seemed to solve them. Unemployment disappeared, economic life was cranked up, money circulated. Even the old became young. As to the younger generation, how could they not be filled with enthusiasm? Everything went well with Adolf Hitler: there was even Hitler weather. Men of judgment saw the course of events with pain and anger; others were dubious but concluded that it could not all be traceable to the devil. The hesitators who were searching for arguments to justify collaboration by themselves and others were not a small body. Who will cast a stone at them today? What was being thought and done in other countries? There men were amazed and those at the head of affairs negotiated with Hitler, exchanged addresses of congratulation with him, recognized him as the head of the German State, and yet—they let the building of the Tower of Babel go on.

We must keep all this ever present to our minds so as to be able to see how infinitely difficult it was for the German bishops to combat the paganism and godlessness which the National Socialist leaders without any intermission were using as the foundation-stone and pillars of this monstrous Tower, to open the eyes of the Germans to the kind of work that was going on and to instruct them as to the impending fatal consequences for the future of Germany. We know today only too well that the whole of the National Socialist literary production was made to serve as open or hidden propaganda of the new paganism; that Christianity and the Church were attacked in a subtle manner and the ideas of the new paganism were instilled into the young at meetings and in the labour service. Catholic publications which should have been able to resist these ideas were crushed underfoot; finally only the pulpit remained.

The Bishop considered it to be his most sacred duty to uphold the truth of the gospel against the wild teachings of the godless movement and to state that truth in a way that was clear as crystal. His Lenten Pastoral of 1935 was against that pantheism which denied a personal God and asserted that the true God was embodied in the race of men of German blood. In a sermon preached on the 22nd March, 1936, he refuted the charge that Christian faith and the belief in an eternal life are a hindrance in this world and in the work of German restoration.

A few months later, on the 6th September, 1936, he preached a powerful sermon against the totalitarian State: 'An obedience which subjugates men's souls, which intrudes upon the sphere of conscience, that innermost shrine of human freedom, is the crudest form of slavery.' He stigmatized not merely the theories of the National Socialists but their crimes as well. He spoke of the imprisonment of ecclesiastics, the delay in bringing them before an impartial court, the graves of those whom the Catholic population regarded as martyrs for the faith, but the manner of whose death was a carefully guarded secret. This reference to the events of the 30th June, 1934, and the murder of the Berlin Catholic leader Klausener was understood in official circles and the Bishop received a letter expressing surprise that he had touched on the subject.

The propaganda of the foes of the Church stooped to the meanest methods. All remembered the trials for alleged currency and moral offences. Thanks to God, the true character of these trumped-up charges was revealed by the clumsy way in which they were brought forward, so that they wholly failed to convince men of sense. But it was the National Socialist literature that the Bishop considered really dangerous. Day by day and week by week poison trickled into the minds of the people. In 1936 he himself read in the cathedral a Pastoral dealing with this, adding on the spur of the moment comment expressing his indignation. After quoting a leading article from a National Socialist journal, he could hardly go on speaking, so deeply moved was he at the calumnies hurled at the Church. He cried out in the cathedral, 'A man is a rascal who does not stand up and resist when his mother, brother and father are wrongfully attacked and slandered.' National Socialism soon recognized it was difficult to convert the old; it therefore used all the subtlety of its propaganda and its worst terrors against the younger generation. All Catholic youth organizations were abolished as the years went by. Thanks to God, it was no easy task: our young men and women on certain occasions resisted even unto blood. As no banners could be openly displayed, secrecy and disguise were brought in and their loyalty to their unions and societies thus maintained. The Bishop's paternal love and care for the young of the Church was boundless and his heart bled when he had to stand by and see that his public protests and sermons had no effect on the rulers—outwardly at any rate.

The tyrants also forced their way into the schools and, imitating the iconoclasts of other ages, profaned the crucifix of Our Lord and Saviour. So long as Church history is written it will contain a page in honour of the heroic and victorious struggle of the Catholics of Oldenburg. The crucifix remained in the children's schools and the hands which were raised against the image of Our Saviour have withered.

The building of the Tower of Babel went on, a sinister growth. Misled Germans, intoxicated by a wild romanticism, added stone to stone, endlessly. In the spring of 1937 Pope Pius XI pronounced his curse against the godless State. The Encyclical *Mit brennender Sorge* tore the mask off the tyrants before the eyes of the world. The German bishops received unambiguous guidance from the father of Christianity. Then 1939 arrived: with it the war. The Tower which was a monument of satanic pride, of the superman who wars against God, shone out with all its sinister brilliance; then it showed rent after rent; it tottered and split; the years went by and it fell and in its fall buried whole nations. For centuries the prayer has gone up to God, 'Except the Lord build the house . . .'

CHAPTER 8

APOSTOLIC JOURNEYS

[N.B. This entire chapter is a summary of the original
passages.—Translator.]

* * * * * THE earlier chapters give us a picture of the wholly
Catholic world in which Bishop von Galen was born and
educated for an ecclesiastical career and in which he worked
for many years as a priest, and to these the chapters describing
his work as a bishop are a natural sequel. Their detailed descrip-
tions of, first, the frequent journeys made by him to visit all
parts of his very large diocese and, secondly, of his ordinary life
when at·home in Münster are, like the earlier chapters, a
description of a wholly Catholic world. The significance of the
whole for readers of an English edition lies in this—that we get
not merely a picture of a Catholic world in·many respects
different from that of Catholics of Great Britain and the
United States, who for the most part live and work among
those who are not of their Faith, but a description of the field
on which the Bishop fought his last great fight, a fight in which
he could neither give nor ask for quarter.

The Bishop's journeys were far more than journeys under-
taken with a view to administering the Sacrament of Confirmation, they were events for the several towns and villages
visited. There is some analogy between them and the progress
of a prelate of the Middle Ages. Some particulars from the very
detailed German text may be noted: the Bishop is starting out,
not in the old-fashioned carriage of his predecessors with its
baroque ornaments, but in a car with his driver, chaplain and
personal servant. When they had passed the city gates, the
Bishop takes his breviary and reads the travellers' prayers, those
old appeals to Almighty God to protect and guide wayfarers
even as He protected and guided Abraham, the people of
Israel and the Wise Men from the East. May He send the
Archangel Raphael to escort them on their way!

Houses and streets are soon left behind. Münsterland in
spring with its wayside crucifixes and statues of Our Lady, its

high church towers and quiet graveyards, receives them. Münsterland was close to the Bishop's heart. How he loved the people, homely and taciturn, loyal and strict in their conduct. He is depicted as approaching Emmerich and telling the driver to go slower. 'If we get there before our time it will be serious. Dean Sprunken was my Rector in Berlin and I should not like it if he seemed annoyed with his old assistant priest.' At the city boundary he is met by processions of cyclists and horse riders with an open carriage decked with green branches of fir and flowers. The riders and cyclists are delighted when the Bishop, who thanks God he can leave the car, inspects the horses and gives an expert's opinion on them. Then he gets in with a final blessing for all the faithful of the neighbourhood who had erected a splendid triumphal arch.

In the early years of Nazi rule the Burgomasters welcomed the Bishop at the town boundaries. This was soon changed: riders and decorations were given up as was the old traditional procession of clergy and laity, and the Bishop was received at the church door. On his arrival the informal demonstrations of the people were almost indescribable. Children, carried or on their own feet, young men and women, parents—all thronged round the Bishop. Year by year there was this proof of the depth and sincerity of the people's love for their great bishop.

Then the Bishop enters the church and preaches to a packed congregation. He speaks clearly and unambiguously of the spirit of evil of the hour. The spies of the Gestapo are in a dark corner under the organ: he knows it but cares nothing. The spies, breathing rage, saw the result of the anti-Christian propaganda, of the attack on Christian teaching as un-German, of the charges of alleged immorality, of the suppression of Catholic literature. The crowd in the church, in front of it and in the streets, was the answer. And these thousands were there of their own free will and ran the risk of being denounced and possibly injured.

Of course there was a prudent minority who wished to remain in the Church but thought that the Bishop's Pastorals were too strong. He might give the 'noble Führer' a trial and then all would be well!

The Confirmation took place the next day. The Bishop's address was for young and old alike, plain and pious with the piety of childhood. When catechizing, as the custom was, he always managed to include a bit of downright humour. When he left the church hordes of children and young persons thronged round him, cheering and shouting. Time and again he had to come to the window of the clergy house and speak a few last words to the young folk and tell them to go home.

The Bishop was always very desirous of including visits to schools in his programme. He would greet the teachers and give an instruction to the children so as to bring to public notice in the fullest sense the connexion of the Church, the teachers and the pupils. It was still possible to do this in the early years of the Nazi rule. But it sometimes happened that he was met by the headmaster in S.A. uniform and by a resounding 'Heil Hitler' from the well-drilled pupils. The teachers were in some cases hesitating between the Church and Nazism, others had gone completely Nazi. Finally in 1938 the fist of the new heathenism crushed the denominational schools. It then depended on the individual teachers whether they would give religious instruction or curry favour with the Nazis by giving it up. These were anxious days when some of the children had their minds poisoned even by teachers who were once Catholic. There were other teachers who held out and relied on the Bishop.

There were also visits to the hospitals and institutions conducted by Sisterhoods. He fought for the defenceless Sisters in 1941 when they were banished from their homes.

Other journeys were made to consecrate new churches. It was his great ambition to consecrate many and he was deeply grieved when the outbreak of war put an end to church building.

His last journey, in the human sense a terribly tragic journey, was made in 1945. It took him to places where war had destroyed whole towns with all their churches. He exhorted people and priests to submit to the will of God. * * * * *

CHAPTER 9

A DAY IN THE BISHOP'S PALACE

[N.B. This entire chapter is a summary of the original
passages.—Translator.]

* * * * * THE author describes in great detail an ordinary
working day in the Bishop's Palace. A summary of a typical
day's work will be a complement of the account of the Bishop's
journeys.

The Bishop left his bedroom at 6 a.m. and entered the
palace chapel where he spent half an hour in prayer and
meditation. A few minutes before 6.30 a.m. a seminarist
arrived to serve his Mass which was attended only by residents
in the palace. At 7 a.m. a second Mass was said by his
chaplain while the Bishop made his thanksgiving. The Bishop
then took the seminarist to the breakfast-room. This was his
way of getting to know the views, thoughts and wishes of the
younger generation of ecclesiastics who were at the threshold
of their ordination. The Bishop's conversation, sometimes
serious and sometimes humorous, put an end to his guest's
shyness. On fasting days the Bishop ate only two pieces of dry
bread dipped in coffee but he urged the seminarist to a bolder
attack on the fare before him; students, he said, have to work
hard and should eat accordingly.

After breakfast the Bishop sat down at his writing-table
immediately. First he read one or more chapters of the Bible
and in this way usually went through Old and New Testa-
ments in the course of a year. Then came the time for his long
pipe, whose fragrance his biographer believes to have contributed greatly to the efficiency of his work. Before visitors
arrived he worked not with his pen but with his typewriter:
there he was always a beginner, using only one finger of his
right hand. When he came to matters of weight and moment
the noise of the keys was interrupted by a loud and long
coughing. He called it the von Galen cough. Then everyone
in the house knew that another storm against the 'browns' was
brewing. But the long pipe was always by him; a loyal friend.

75

Then came the visitors: on some days the stream between 10 a.m. and 1 p.m. was continuous. First came Monsignor Leufkens, a skilled draughtsman of ecclesiastical decrees which not infrequently got through the network of National Socialist legislation. He had been a fellow student of the Bishop and remained a friend who always cheered him up. Then came priests who had to fight in the front line against the evil spirit of the time for the rights of the Church in education and social work. Then laymen so pressed by persecution that they were at their wits' end and came to the Bishop as a last resource. At a time when the power of evil was making greater and greater inroads on Christianity, the burden resting on the Bishop became heavier and more painful and impaired his vital energy.

The Bishop's correspondence consisted mainly of appeals addressed to him and was another heavy burden. Some part of his anxieties was shared by a council of his clergy meeting in the afternoon from time to time to which he stated what the urgent problems were on which he sought their advice. On these occasions he always appeared wholly calm and sure of himself so that in those trying years many felt they could rely on him. He knew he was the rock and must show no weakness.

At 1 p.m. the Bishop, when not detained by visitors, went to the dining-room, where a plain and homely meal awaited him. At table he closely kept to certain customs acquired in his ancestral castle which were perhaps not entirely modern, but he was indifferent to that.

After his meal he had a rest and a short sleep. At 2.30 p.m. he took coffee. Then he went into the garden, played in summer with the two tortoises, jested with the good old gardener, a mine of information about the Deans and Canons of the last sixty years. Then, now alone, he crossed the bridge over the Aa into the shaded park. Here and here only amidst the fierce controversies of the day, whether in Münster or outside, was he unnoticed and unobserved. He would light his cigar and utter some ejaculatory prayer. He had the authority of a Jesuit father when he himself was but a youth for holding that smoking at prayers is not right but that pious thoughts when smoking are right.

After half an hour's walk the Bishop usually went to the

chapel to say his office. Meanwhile the first afternoon visitors
arrived, usually groups of young men from various parts of the
diocese, recruits who had taken part in manœuvres in Münster,
men from a distance who were passing through : some came out
of curiosity but others were moved by enthusiasm and gratitude, especially after the sermons of 1941. But the Bishop was
also capable of dealing with swindlers who had escaped the
eagle eye of his servant and chaplain (who dealt also with the
hysterical callers) and the biographer saw and heard him
thrust a young man out with, 'Off with you, you low swindler !'
More serious were cases of persons who got in in disguise
hoping to kill the worst enemy of National Socialism. There
were found amongst the Bishop's papers three mysterious notes
fastened together. The first two contained only words that
made no sense: the third was typewritten by the Bishop himself. The notes without meaning had been separately posted by
the Bishop of Berlin; the Bishop had combined them and was
warned of a possible attempt on his life.

The Bishop passed the evening alone in his study, where he
read the paper or turned the wireless on for a short time. Afterwards he read either a work on religion or philosophy or a
historical book on the theological controversies of the Reformation. Such works had great interest for him and he often
pondered on the analogy between the Reformation and his
own time, which witnessed that tragedy, which was so bitter for
Germany, of renewed controversies on religion.

Thoughts on death and eternity ended the day. At 11 p.m.
the Bishop, now tired out, went to the chapel where the
sanctuary lamp guided him to the altar. He knelt and placed
his hands upon the altar: he was alone with God. * * * *. *

CHAPTER 10

HOLY WEEK AND EASTER

[N.B. This entire chapter is a summary of the original passages.—Translator.]

* * * * * THE mind and soul of the young son of a noble family had been moulded and formed in a profoundly conservative religious world according to the laws and customs of a Catholic tradition many centuries old. The sacred gift of faith had been handed down in his family from generation to generation, from the Middle Ages to our time, his forefathers had been the living bridge which handed on that gift. In the Bishop's spiritual life his firm grip on tradition cannot but be noticed. How often did he say with deep emotion that in the early years of his childhood his mother had been his only religious teacher! The Catholic life led by his parents in the Catholic Church was ever present to his mind as an inviolable and irrefragable ideal, as the immutable guide of all his years of manhood. Modern tendencies and movements which seemed to him to be based on some passing fashion, either in liturgical or in other matters, certain aspects of which involved a change of emphasis or a one-sided insistence on certain theological propositions accompanied by a neglect of other truths, made absolutely no impression on him.

His own faith was founded on a systematic theology which resolved all difficulties just because it was supported by a piety of childish simplicity, by profound humility, and by that joy derived from meditation which beginning with the fear of God and the four last things led him on to fervent love of Christ in the Blessed Sacrament (of which he had given testimony in establishing Perpetual Adoration at St. Servatius) and to devotion to the rosary, to relics and pilgrimages. The history of our redemption by Jesus Christ in all its detail was repeated for him in the course of each ecclesiastical year. He lived through it, one may safely say, as only that man can for whom it is the most profound of all experiences. Every year he passed from the darkness of original sin over the road that led to the brilliant light of a redeemed world, from the desert abandoned by God to the grace and protection enjoyed by the children of God—the road that leads through the Passion to the joy of Easter. This stress on the two sides of a genuinely Christian life, release from sin by penance on the one hand and exaltation in the joyful feasts of Our Saviour on the other, gave to his spiritual life a marvellous harmony.

The Bishop's religious life was in all its detail founded on these convictions. Penance and atonement must be marked by real severity as it was in the time of our ancestors by the spirit of the *Dies Irae*. No place was allowed for concessions to human imperfections. Man must seek freedom from sin not only in the Sacrament of Penance but in a daily struggle against passion, base inclination and human weakness.

In Rome the Bishop had mounted the Scala Santa on his knees. Münster knew how often in the early hours of the morning he made the pilgrimage to Telgte. On the afternoon of every Friday he made the Stations of the Cross in the garden of the episcopal palace. In April, 1941, he renewed the consecration of his diocese to the Sacred Heart of Jesus, a devotion which he always loved and promoted.

At times of fasting he took a bit of white bread with a bit of black—no butter—dipped in black coffee. Nothing more before one o'clock. His health suffered in consequence in the years of struggle with National Socialism with their heavy and exhausting labours.

The Bishop's Holy Week and Easter is dwelt on by his biographer with much detail and pious comment. But in 1944 his cathedral was in ruins and the services of Holy Week were celebrated in St. Ludger's. Slowly and gradually these celebrations lost their splendid ceremonial. The long procession of seminarists in their surplices became shorter and shorter. Barracks and the steppes of Russia had taken most of them. Soon only the schoolboys remained to serve. The Bishop had now but a small flock which was driven out of the cathedral and finally out of the cathedral city. A sorrowful pilgrimage for the shepherd of the flock. The first Easter after the war he could no longer sing the alleluia on this earth: his earthly sufferings were over. * * * * *

CHAPTER II

THE SEMINARY

[N.B. This entire chapter is a summary of the original
passages.—Translator.]

* * * * * The Bishop attached the greatest importance to
his relations with the theological students of his diocese. The
Seminary, dedicated to St. Charles Borromeo, was in the
Domplatz opposite the episcopal palace. There more than two
hundred young men were studying. On the first Friday of
every month the Bishop said Mass in the chapel of the
Seminary. He wished to pray with and say Mass for those
whom he was to ordain. He continued to do so in the war
years though the number of the students was growing less and
less. In the course of years a spirit of trusting affection grew up
between the Bishop and the students.

He wished to get to know them and they were to get to
know him. The younger generation's prayers and thoughts
were in many respects different from those of the young men of
his youth. He laboured much to get to know the tendencies of
the more recent theology but he could not fully succeed; the
religious ideas of his own youth were too deeply rooted. He
could not enter into modern interpretations of old truths or
changes proposed by the liturgical movement. The basis of his
objection was the tendency of that movement to emphasize
certain truths and neglect others, to find spiritual value only in
actual celebration of the sacred rites and not in the prayerful
strivings of the faithful. The Bishop saw clearly the danger—
emphasis on the *opus operatum* and neglect of the *opus operantis*.

Clemens August also held that a dangerous tendency was
indicated by the subordination of moral to dogmatic theology.
Doctrine indeed holds the first place in the matters dealt with
by theological science. But the acceptance of the faith is in the
last resort—and this is what makes it hard—always an act: the
following of Christ is a doing. In the writings of later theology
the Bishop saw a certain danger to the firmness of faith, to its
immediacy and simplicity. Professor Wust, whose apostolic

80

5. Family gathering after his first Mass in the chapel of his home. *Left to right*: Frederick and his wife, Paula, Dom Augustinus, Franz, Clemens-August, Agnes and her husband, August and his wife. *Seated in front*: the Cardinal's parents with grand-daughter Maria

6. Among the priests of his family. *Left to right:*
Dom Augustinus, Canon Count von Spee,
Clemens-August, Dom Placidus von Spee.
Seated in front, Suffragan-Bishop Max Gereon

efforts he doubtless greatly valued, once came to him and gave him a copy of his book entitled *Uncertainty and Venture* (*Ungewissheit und Wagnis*). The Bishop told him that for him faith had no uncertainty, it was not a venture; he added, with a smile, that such books were only for his theologians. He found much in modern books and reviews that he could not understand, parts of them he thought hazy and extravagant. He was not one of those who held the less intelligible a statement was, the greater the profundity of the writer's thinking. He kept to clearly defined, penetrating definitions, antiquated and worn-out as the younger generation might think them. The National Socialist ideology had the same defect; it recognized nothing traditional and permanent but in every sphere of intellectual life replaced the old by the new. Modern man loves the unusual, the extraordinary, and what he finds stimulating and subtle. This even in the language of prayer. After reading some modern prayers the Bishop often said: 'I talk to Almighty God in a simpler way. It seems to me that men of today like to walk on stilts.'

But in spite of his old-fashioned views the Bishop respected the efforts and honourable endeavours of the younger theologians and tried to understand them, and all appreciated his paternal affection and care for them. The seminarist who served his Mass and afterwards breakfasted with him alone and could talk to him freely felt this especially, how he was interested in them as individuals and got to know their names. He was conscious of the great responsibility of admitting to Holy Orders only young men who were suitable and worthy. * * * * *

CHAPTER 12

THE CLERGY

* * * * * The Bishop held it to be a sacred duty to get to know all the priests of the diocese as well as he could. The clergy themselves recognized the close bond between their chief pastor and themselves: they confided to him all their anxieties, undeterred by difference in ecclesiastical rank or by the fact that the Bishop came of a noble family. Among the clergy themselves he wished to see and endeavoured to promote a genuinely deep spirit of brotherhood. His experience as a Parish Priest in Berlin had taught him the value of this, especially when it united a Parish Priest closely to his assistant priests. In their case his ideal was that they should live together in a clergy house. * * * * *

A book published at the beginning of the war put forward the proposition that an up-to-date and successful priest should be of a culture which reached the highest standard of the present age whether in literature or art or in other spheres, that he should embody the values of humanism. The Bishop shook his head. He held that an entirely humble pastor who bears his own cross is the man to save humanity alienated from God; as for academic elegancies, away with them!

The Bishop instinctively grasped the direction the great masses of men were taking, their decline into a state of disbelief and want of moral principles. Preach eternal truths and the four last things in modern style! That is as good as saying serve them up to the faithful watered down and sugared, as possessing only relative truth, as if one was afraid that to proclaim the entire inexorable truths might do man harm. Only the whole truth will make men free, give them a true conception of God in all their loneliness and misery and, thus, true comfort. This is the message which the priest must spread abroad.

The conversation of the spiritual father of a parish, the

82

Bishop held, should be of the things of religion rather than on literature or the theatre. A pastor of souls is not to be an ecclesiastical official more or less skilled in interesting the members of his community and of influencing them by purely human means. The typical pastor of human souls was to be pious, solid, thorough, patriarchal. He himself as a Parish Priest had been the embodiment of such a type and sincerity, zeal, attachment to human souls were qualities which were as alive in the Bishop as they had been in the Parish Priest.

In 1933 the Bishop became on his appointment the spiritual leader of all the priests in his diocese and found them engaged in a hard struggle to defend the Church against the new heathenism. In a few months those fighting in the front line appreciated the steel-like strength of their chief pastor, who would not retreat an inch from the position in which God had placed him and them. The murderous hand of National Socialism struck at that long line of priests who year by year did their duty as a loyal body of fighters, often heroically. One priest is called before the Gestapo, another taken into 'protective custody', another expelled from a school and prohibited from giving religious instruction, another is banished from the Rhineland and Westphalia. Imputations of all sorts were made. Where hatred or craft could 'eliminate a black' without arousing too much notice, they went to work without mercy. So far as he could, the priest attacked defended himself. The Bishop's strong hand was there for all whenever he could help. He never blamed anyone for imprudence in the conduct of the struggle and he was the last to reprove anyone for his temerity in committing the imaginary crime of listening to foreign broadcasts. Under the satanic tyranny of the system all priests who had been locked up or condemned suffered. To many of them the Gestapo suggested that they should give up their black coats: then they could get good places in Government offices. They had the courage to refuse. There were cases in which the Bishop could do nothing for the persecuted as his name was like a red rag and only did harm to the persecuted priests.

In these persecutions of the Church the Bishop held that the sufferings of the priests were works of expiation; but he yet at the risk of his life scourged the brutal deeds of the Gestapo.

We have in mind the two great sermons of June, 1941, in which he spoke of the cellars of the Gestapo and the concentration camps in which his priests were languishing. He was deeply affected on receiving the news of the deaths of his priests in Dachau. His words spoken at the grave of Dean von Hoetmer, whom he revered as a saint, applied to all the priests of his diocese who in the persecution had endured shame for Christ's sake, among whom were those in the summer of 1945 returning home from prisons or from exile.

The war broke out. Many of the clergy joined the forces either as chaplains or in medical units. The Bishop made great exertions to secure the release of any priest called up for combatant service: the Concordat had made provision for this. Greatly as the Bishop regretted the want of clergy at home, he was yet greatly consoled by the thought that his priests could be spiritual advisers and helpers of their comrades. Many a priest at that time was troubled in his conscience. They knew, or at any rate suspected, the wrongfulness of the war and that crimes were being committed at the command of men of German blood: they were convinced that the shame and infamy in which the German people were involved would, in the end, and in spite of what appeared to be a series of victories, lead them into an appalling abyss. Priests on leave would reveal the troubles of their conscience to their spiritual father who would give them comfort, encourage them loyally to do their duty for the sake of the souls of the soldiers and to assist them in the hospitals, on the battlefield and at the hour of death.

* * * * * The Bishop had during the war an enormous correspondence with his priests at the Front who wrote to him at length about their experiences, their success in their work as priests and also of their disillusions. All were replied to, the Bishop shared the priests' joys or gave them comfort. For the great feasts he sent a circular letter to tell them of the joys and sorrows of their homes.

The Bishop's collection of letters from the Front was lost when on the 10th October, 1943, the episcopal palace was destroyed. But the Bishop started a new collection and this was

found after his death, all the letters being arranged in chrono-
logical order. Nothing took too much time because the Bishop
felt he owed a special duty to those who were preaching the
Gospel amidst cold and heat, privations and dangers; they
were called too as disciples of Jesus Christ to set an example to
their comrades in the midst of moral dangers.

Many never came back: others returned ill or mutilated.
Some might think that they had sacrificed themselves for an
impious doctrine. No, it was not for the doctrine but for the
sake of God and immortal souls. They hated the war but
accepted and willed the sacrifice. This was also the Bishop's
way of thinking.

The chapter on the relations of the Bishop to his clergy
closes in a more familiar way. Social meetings of the clergy
principally with a recreational object were traditional among
German Catholics. The Bishop had given them great support
when he was a Parish Priest in Berlin: he continued to do so as
Bishop; he thought relaxation priceless. Even on his journeys to
administer Confirmation there were evening meetings of the
clergy: the Bishop was great as a teller of stories, witty and
quick at repartee. * * * * *

Fault-finders and malcontents were by God's grace so rare
among the Bishop's clergy that they hardly counted at all. A
Gestapo official in Münster was much annoyed because he
could find no one to act as a spy on the Bishop. No! The
Bishop had no trouble from fault-finders and traitors. On the
contrary, up and down the country, in towns and villages, the
outspoken sermons of 1941 were distributed by the priests and
read from the pulpit. This required courage. They wanted to
be like their Bishop, who feared neither prison nor death.

CHAPTER 13

NAZI STRATAGEMS

AMONG the weapons which National Socialism used against Christianity and the Church was an avowed campaign of calumny. It came into operation when, in the opinion of the governing leaders, their own situation rendered undisguised hostility impracticable. The Third Reich held firmly to these principles right down to its overthrow, although in practice they were only applied consistently during the first months, when the early leaders were laying the foundations. Thus it happened that many men of good faith, by accession to all manner of organizations, allowed themselves to become tied to the new world-outlook, at least in outward show, and some indeed in inward conviction. Christianity, they persuaded themselves, ran no danger; quite the contrary. People saw and heard how at the pilgrimage to Treves[1] in 1933, the S.A. performed the duty of regulating the traffic. On the films the Bishop of the town himself could be seen in company with the leading National Socialist officers of his diocese. On the evening before the Bishop of Münster's consecration, at the end of October, 1933, Dr. Donders, then Provost of the cathedral, walked through the spacious building with the party-leaders, in order to decide in detail where at the ceremony the formations of the S.A. and S.S. could most suitably take up their positions. The great deception worked by the Spirit of Evil, as the Bishop wrote in his pastoral letter at Easter 1934, was under way.

As soon as Nazism felt itself stronger, it began to wear the mask more loosely. Following a subtle system of tactics, it drove a hundred yards forward into the ecclesiastical front, and then, to deceive public opinion, drew twenty yards back. Responsibility for the aggression was thrown on the supposed excessive zeal of subordinates, and so, among the majority of people,

---

[1] Translator's note: The Diocese of Trier is a suffragan of Cologne and possesses many treasures including the Holy Coat of Christ, which, according to legend, was given to the Church of Trier by St. Helena.

always simple-minded, the waves of indignation were be-calmed. Then, at favourable times and opportunities, the advance was renewed and one could easily reckon how a frontal break-through to a depth of 80 yards deepened to 160 and then to 240. Propaganda and arbitrary exercise of authority were alike directed mainly to disparage the ideas and ideals of Christianity and so to render them distasteful and repulsive to the people. For that purpose, church institutions, such as religious associations, religious newspapers, confessional schools, were in great numbers simply suppressed. At the same time they took as their principal aim to undermine the influential position of the Catholic clergy and to whittle away the authority, respect and veneration which priests, bishops and members of Religious Orders had widely enjoyed in our country. They sought to pillory the spiritual shepherds as idlers and even as criminal offenders, so as to alienate their flocks from them and bring these over to their own side. The prosecutions for offences against morality in 1936 were the high-water mark in this stream of propaganda; the illustrations and articles in *Der Stürmer* and *Das Schwarze Korps* supplied it with weekly nourishment. In spite of all the inward resistance and indignation of the faithful, the harmful outcome for the Church could not fail to show itself. We remember that in public places, railway stations and waiting-rooms, people began to meet the Catholic clergy with a certain reserve, with looks, sometimes of hatred, sometimes of half-scornful compassion. The leadership of the National Socialists took good note of all this. Intoxicated with success, they strove, in courses of instruction and manuals for subordinate commanders, to spread it by ridicule still more widely, as a groundwork for more thorough and radical measures.

.   .   .   .   .

A period followed in which fanatical individuals had the impudence to hustle both regular and secular clergy openly in the street. Even in neighbourhoods with a preponderantly Catholic population, it could happen that half-grown louts howled after a priest the ribald couplet:

'Oho, master priest, your teaching's a mess,
For your hocus-pocus we couldn't care less.'

It was then a matter of temperament whether one at once administered a resounding moral box-on-the-ear to such rowdies, or, ignoring everything, went on one's way. At that time a priest was travelling by a late evening train from Hamm to Münster. The carriage was like a compartment of a tramway; one could view it from end to end and so late at night there were few passengers. Three young men got in; they were in their early twenties and slightly drunk. The sight of the priest provoked them. Their talk grew louder and ruder. They sang the ribald song against the Bishop of Münster. The priest sprang up, strode towards these shameless fellows and forbade them to treat him as fair game. They had not expected this. They stammered excuses to him, likewise to a railway official, who had been called in and wanted to take down their names and addresses on behalf of the railway police. On the platform at Münster they joined comrades from other carriages, among whom was a Nazi official in uniform. Without hesitation the priest approached this man, told him what had happened, and uttered, as strongly and loudly as before, his indignation at the disgraceful behaviour of fellows who were seemingly under his authority. Matters had reached that pitch. A hard, direct counterstroke was the only way to impress such a mob.

In November of 1938 the Synagogues in Germany were set on fire. The S.S. and S.A. purported to take over the duty of keeping order in the streets. They were thronged with astonished spectators, who fancied themselves back in the weeks of the Revolution, when the Reichstag building was burnt down. At that time in South Germany the residences of cardinals and bishops were broken into by brown-shirted bands. One need only recall the shameful events in Vienna and at Munich and Rottenburg. Shouting and yelling crowds did not hesitate to break into these venerable courtyards and halls, and even into the chapels. Bishops' croziers, their robes and vestments, were befouled, torn up and burnt. The mob had their hour. In these weeks the staff of the episcopal palace at Münster had to reckon with like possibilities. How easy it would be, under cover of darkness just outside the town, to unload from lorries roughs who were strangers to the place and then let them loose to raid the episcopal palace in the night. Quite seriously, the clergy then living there, Canon Vorwerk,

who had already been deported from Oldenburg, the Vicar-
General, Canon Ricking, who lived in one of the wings, and
the Bishop's chaplain, thought over the precautionary measures
which might eventually be taken. Appliances were installed
for alarm-signals, secret private telephone connections with
the presbytery of Überwasser, since, in case of a systematic
raid, one had to allow for the normally available communications being cut off. One had almost become accustomed to
the singing of the ribald song against the Bishop towards
midnight. To protest or complain was like pouring water
through a sieve. The bolt of the iron gate into the forecourt had
been several times wrenched away and replaced. At length its
replacement was given up.

On Saturday, December 10th, in the small hours of the
morning, about five o'clock, I was suddenly awakened. Heavy
stones crashed against the outside wall of my bedroom which
was in the left wing. Then came sharp blows against the
windows of the sleeping-rooms and living-rooms. The panes of
glass were shattered and even the slats of the blinds inside
them were cracked. Between dreaming and waking, I listened
for a few seconds: more stone-throwing, then complete silence.
I turned on the light, put on a dressing-gown and slippers and
went out through my own rooms, the floors of which were
sprayed with splinters of glass, on to the landing and staircase.
An hour later, I heard from the Bishop that the first stone-
throwing had shattered the window-panes in his study and on
the ground-floor. He added, laughing, that as long as we did
not get stones on our heads, we must be content and keep quiet.
About eight o'clock, I rang up the police headquarters and
told them the state of things, which the Chief of the Criminal
Service, as representing the headquarters, was apparently
shocked to hear. At the same time I drew his attention to the
uproar persistently repeated about midnight and the singing
of the disreputable song. I stressed that one could not help
getting the impression that all protest was futile and the police
attached no importance to stopping these occurrences. A few
minutes afterwards an officer of the Criminal Police appeared,
a very good Catholic, whose sons were still active members of

the North German Youth League. He counted the broken window-panes and the stones, then took down notes. Meanwhile I had informed the Bishop of this officer's personal standpoint and he thereupon expressed his deep indignation and used very sharp and sarcastic terms about the police, who were making themselves positively a laughing-stock. In the same connection he commented upon the feebleness and helplessness displayed in following up the robbery of the sacred picture at Telgte. The officer with a sad countenance nodded agreement with all that the Bishop said and promised to repeat it to his superiors. Shortly afterwards an officer of the Criminal Police telephoned on the instructions of the Police President, expressed his very deep regret, enquired details of the midnight scenes, promised a stronger patrol-service and asked that, in cases of a repetition, the emergency detachment should be rung up. The Provost of the Cathedral, Dr. Donders, went, together with two Parish Priests in the town, to the Police-President, who promised an immediate investigation of the incident and very severe punishment of the culprits. In consideration of this, the prospective denunciation from the pulpit on the following Sunday, which was much dreaded by the Party and by the police, did not take place.

The affair had quickly become the subject of general talk in the city. The first to appear in the forecourt were the customers at the market, then representatives of the older generation, who had attended the ten o'clock Mass in the Cathedral. They looked at the holes in the windows, the splinters of glass and the stones on the floors. On all faces alike one saw disquiet and indignation. Thus the incident acquired the notoriety of a public event. It had been suggested to the Bishop earlier that, as a gesture of protest, the broken window-panes might be ostentatiously replaced by wooden shutters or sheets of cardboard. He put that aside with a smile and the comment: 'We won't rub it in. They've got the worst of it anyhow.' So the glaziers were set to work with their long ladders.

A few days after this, the Bishop drove to Osterfeld in the rural deanery of Sterkrade to administer Confirmations there and in the neighbouring villages. Police officers guarded the presbyteries, especially at night, and escorted the Bishop's car on every drive from church to church and from school to school; the intention clearly was to nip any repetition of the scene at Münster in the bud. On outer walls of school play-grounds and on railway bridges one saw scrawled in large letters the slogan, 'Clemens August, you are not wanted here.' In places the tares sown by the enemy had been transformed into wheat, 'Clemens August, you are much wanted here.' This heartened and amused the faithful. At Osterfeld at St. Pancras there was a great demonstration by youth-societies. About this I find in my diary: 'The road back to the presbytery was filled by an excited crowd: we could hardly shield the Bishop from the enthusiastic and applauding throng of young men and girls who pressed after him. He had to show himself again and again in the doorway of the house: this doorway, the front garden and the windows were lighted up with electric bulbs and coloured candles, as though for a festival; again and again he was enthusiastically greeted by the young Catholics.'

This was one of the answers to the shameful conduct of the sinister elements at Münster. Provost Donders sent to Osterfeld a cutting from a newspaper which wrote of disorderly young men smashing panes of glass in telephone-boxes and at a clergy-house. I carefully made no mention of the episcopal residence. The purpose of this tendentious announcement was not doubtful: it was to divert attention from the scene at the palace, regarded as unedifying, and to render it harmless. This meant that on grounds of general policy there was a reluctance to carry matters at Münster too far. We could set that down as an asset. About a week after these events a higher official of the Criminal Branch of the Police appeared and in the name of Dr. Meyer, the Governor and chief administrator of the district, offered to enter a criminal charge against persons unknown. This was done. On this occasion the Bishop expressed his indignation very openly. The official declared that two of the suspected culprits had already been arrested that morning. In course of time one heard that the men involved belonged to the S.S. After the Local Public Prosecutor, then the Public Prosecutor of the Province, and then the State Public Prosecutor, had acquainted themselves with the case, it was finally referred to the Ministry of Justice. Not long afterwards war broke out and the culprits, whose names never became known to the public, came under the amnesty. The worthy Catholic official at the Police Office knew it all quite well beforehand when he said, 'They won't ever need to turn a hair.'

·After that Saturday the episcopal palace was never again pelted with stones. The nightly singing too notably fell off. The reason of the violent outbreak that night in January of 1939 was that, a few hours before, Rosenberg, who had just been named an honorary citizen of Münster, had spoken at a monster demonstration. As was afterwards found out privately, all branches of the Party were, after those excesses, strictly warned to work against such goings-on. The mask was put on again; the ground had not been made ready enough for all the ideals of National Socialism. War was imminent and there were other urgent matters to think about.

CHAPTER 14

CANONS IN EXILE

THE patronal feast of St. Joseph on May 4th, 1941, being the third Sunday after Easter, had been commemorated and the Bishop had taken part in the closing service of Perpetual Adoration in St. Joseph's Church. Soon after the devotion was over, a car stopped on the Square in front of the parish church of Überwasser and several men got out; one of them went up the steps of the Spiegelturm and pulled the door-bell at the office of Canon Vorwerk, a member of the cathedral chapter. The housekeeper opened the door. 'Good day; may I speak to the Canon?' 'Certainly; please take a seat here in the parlour.' Almost at once Canon Vorwerk joined them. Just then the bell rang again. They were no sooner in the hall than the door of the reception-room opened and the Canon came out. He saw the two men and said to the housekeeper: 'These are officers of the Gestapo. I am under arrest. Please pack my suitcase.' The housekeeper, an elderly and frail woman, trembled in every limb. The officers warned her that she would incur a very severe penalty if, before the middle of the next day, she let anyone else know of this incident. The telephone was at once cut off. Half an hour later the Canon disappeared in the car in the direction of the Gutenbergstrasse, where lay the notorious headquarters of the Gestapo. There he rested on a plank-bed until, shortly before midnight, two other officers appeared and ordered him to follow them. They boarded the night train to Hamburg. Even then Vorwerk did not in the least know what this forcible removal meant, whether merely deportation to another town, or internment in a concentration camp, or some other form of kidnapping. Only the next morning, after the journey from Hamburg to Schwerin, the local Gestapo there informed him that he was to be deported to the town of Brüel in Mecklenburg.

As soon as the Vicar-General's office got news of Canon Vorwerk's arrest, they rang up the local headquarters of the Gestapo for details and received the curt answer that he was being deported to Brüel without any statement of the grounds for this banishment. On that day the Bishop was driving into the rural deanery of Damme in Oldenburg to administer Confirmation. He drove round by way of Osnabrück, of which the widely scattered diocese comprises Brüel, in order to visit the Bishop of that town, or, failing him, the office of the Vicar-General there. He was informed that at Brüel there was neither a Catholic church nor any Catholics; it was an hour's train journey from Schwerin, the nearest place where any Catholic clergy could be reached.

Some weeks afterwards I received instructions from the Bishop to seek out Canon Vorwerk at Brüel and inform him about the episcopal steps taken on his behalf. On the morning of the Feast of Corpus Christi, I boarded the 10.28 a.m. express to Hamburg and had just stowed away my bag in a compartment when Canon Echelmeyer, lately appointed a member of the chapter, appeared in the doorway. Only an hour earlier we had assisted at the High Mass of the Feast in the cathedral. He seemed quite cheerful. The only thing that struck me was that he was dressed as a layman. I supposed that he was going to take part, as representative of the diocese, in a conference somewhere in a non-Catholic part of the country, and for that reason had chosen this unwonted attire. We were standing side by side in the corridor of the train, which was very full. When our talk turned onto questions of Church policy, he whispered into my ear in Latin, '*Favete linguis!* (Don't talk)—Gestapo!' So I held my tongue. At a favourable moment, I sought closer information about the suggested risk. It proceeded, he said, from two gentlemen; one of them was about forty-five, of average height, with a good middle-class, eminently respectable type of countenance, who was smoking a cigar that smelt like a good one; every now and then he talked in a lively way with us, particularly with Echelmeyer, as though he were an old acquaintance of his. The other was a man of spare build with a narrow face, younger and more reticent, a typical specimen of the North-German S.S. Echelmeyer, as diocesan president of Young Men's Clubs, happened, I supposed, to have come into some kind of contact with these gentlemen and I thought no harm. My only fear was that the card I had sent two days before to Brüel, announcing my arrival, might have fallen into the hands of the Gestapo; that card might have informed these officers of my plans and have prompted them to follow on my tracks. Before long, however, my elaborate series of inferences struck me as rather foolish. In the meanwhile the compartment had become less crowded and Echelmeyer and I were able to find seats beside each other; this gave him the chance to say to me, 'Those two are taking me away.' This struck me like a blow on the head. 'And can you be so unruffled in these conditions?' He smiled and went on with his story. Since Vorwerk's deportation he had reckoned with a like fate. In this respect he had received, moreover, a confidential hint from an official high up in the provincial administration. For that reason he had bespoken the lay suit well beforehand. 'At seven o'clock this morning,' he went on, 'I already saw the two fellows walking up and down in the Cathedral Square. When High Mass was over, they appeared in my house. After first showing their authority from the Gestapo, they declared that, much to their regret, they must take me into deportation. They had the railway tickets already; I need only pack my bag quickly. Then we could catch the ten o'clock train to Hamburg; otherwise we should have to wait till late that night for the next train, and that would be unpleasant for all parties. Soon afterwards we drove to the station in the waiting car; one of the men, quite inconspicuously, pressed a ticket into my hand and we passed the barrier like passengers on their lawful occasions.' I sat in silence. So matters had reached this pitch: not one person there on the train suspected how low-down a game was being played before the eyes of the public. The two Gestapo sentinels stood, as though accidentally, on the right and left of the carriage door; now and then they looked in quite ingenuously and kept their pistols in their pockets. The elder man was the notorious D.

At Rotenburg, a station between Bremen and Hamburg, the three got out. The tall figure of the Canon walked across the platform with these two Gestapo thugs on either side of him. He was going into banishment for four years in a township the name of which he had understood as 'Visho': he had only caught those two syllables in the intimation that the Gestapo officials gave him by word of mouth. On the map in the corridor of the train I found, after a rather long search, a place called Vissel-hövede, about 30 km. south-east of Bremen. Directly after my arrival at Hamburg I informed the Bishop by post of these experiences. On the Cathedral Square at Münster in the meanwhile, as I afterwards heard, the following incidents had taken place. From Echelmeyer's sisters, the Treasurer of the Cathedral, Father Finke, who lived close by, got news that the Gestapo were on the spot. He at once went to the Provost and then to the Bishop. They came straight away, further evidence that the Bishop in such circumstances did not hesitate to withstand the enemy to their faces. Unluckily it was too late. The car was just vanishing round the corner of the Michaelsplatz.

On my first journey into Mecklenburg, I reached Brüel at about eight o'clock in the evening. So this was the place to which the Nazis had sent Vorwerk, in a wholly non-Catholic neighbourhood. They meant him to live there as an outcast, shunned and treated with distrust by everyone; the inhabitants were all to keep an eye on him. His use of the railway was restricted to very short distances; even his walks were confined to a limited range. The police were to watch his comings and goings and report to the Gestapo. A room had been assigned him in the house where the local National Socialists had their headquarters. In that room every morning he used the sacred vessels and vestments he had brought with him to celebrate Mass alone; there were no Catholics in the place to attend. He was to take his meals at the Mecklenburger Hof, a small hotel close by.

Echelmeyer's situation at Visselhövede was so far more favourable that visitors from the West could reach him more easily, and a few Catholics, though you could count them on your fingers, gathered for Mass in a room adapted for the purpose. Vorwerk, however, took only a few days to get on friendly terms with the householders where he was lodged, an elderly, childless couple, who looked after him assiduously. Both were devout adherents of that section of the Lutheran community who had kept themselves independent of the

7. 'Uncle Bishop' with his little grand-niece
Elizabeth in Gevelinghausen

8. (*Top*) The children's friend
9. (*Bottom*) The last procession round the Cathedral : *from right to left* : Auxiliary Bishop Roleff, Provost Donders, Professor Diekamp and Canon Emmerich

National Socialist Government. Their pastor, who was extremely friendly, unfortunately died suddenly very soon after Canon Vorwerk came. Relations grew no less pleasant with the landlord and his family at the Mecklenburger Hof.

As was to be expected, the bulk of the population showed themselves at first rather aloof and distrustful. In those June days of 1941, when we were out for a walk, a peasant, seated on a reaping machine or at work in his garden, would often, in no mood of hostility or challenge, greet us with 'Heil Hitler'. We, who came from the West, were not used to that. In the following January (1942), when I visited Vorwerk for the second time, a marked improvement could already be observed: Regent Francken, the principal of the Theological College, and Councillor Ricking were able to note the same change on the occasion of their visits. As time went on, Canon Vorwerk was welcomed everywhere. He became an object of sympathy and even admiration. Scarce goods, such as writing-paper, were willingly put at his disposal in the shops. The friendliness of the people towards him rose, from month to month and from year to year, in much the same tempo as the curve of enthusiasm for National Socialism sank. In the autumn of 1943, he commented casually on this change: people were saying openly at the hotel that there were only two Nazis left at Brüel, the leader of the local Party branch and one other man, who was deranged.

Without investigation or judicial decision, the two capitulars had been spirited away behind a smoke-screen of secrecy. Because the Bishop, in strict accord with the wording of the Concordat, had appointed them to offices connected with the Cathedral, they were, as persons not agreeable to the authorities, driven into banishment. They underwent in fact the penalty which had been mooted for the Bishop, but which the Government dared not inflict on him. It was often conveyed to them, sometimes by insinuation, sometimes by threats, that, if they would renounce the offices he had bestowed on them, they would get their freedom. Faithfulness to the Bishop, however, carried more weight with them than a prospect of freedom at that price.

Typical of the Gestapo's methods was an episode in the year 1943. This is how Canon Vorwerk related it. 'During a conversation, the Secretary of the Gestapo at Schwerin blamed

G

me for having shown no signs, during the two years since I came, of drawing nearer to the general standpoint of National Socialism. If I would alter my attitude, I might thereby get many advantages. I answered that he could spare himself any trouble in that matter: I was a Catholic and should remain one. Thereupon he grew quite amiable and advised me to have confidence in the Gestapo all the same; the distrust I had expressed was quite unfounded. Two days afterwards I received a visit from a man who represented himself as a leading personage in the Gestapo and enquired about that talk with the Secretary. He declared that, immediately after it, that same Secretary had instructed him to procure the material for proceeding against me: he had taken on the job, but would report nothing to my detriment. He might thereby get himself into trouble, but he did not mind that, as he should like to be rid of his duties; he really could no longer take part in such disreputable intrigues.'

In the course of years repeated steps were taken from very various quarters to procure the return of the two Canons from exile. All efforts however proved unavailing. On the occasion of the heavy bombardments of Münster in 1943–44, by which the offices of Vorwerk and Echelmeyer were badly damaged, they obtained a few days of the furlough usual in such cases. No relief however followed from the measures taken in 1941; not even in 1944–45, when the leaders of the Third Reich had the flood-water up to their necks. Only the arrival of the enemy gave them freedom.

CHAPTER 15

HIS GREATEST HOUR

THE course of events was roughly as follows. One Saturday in July of 1941, a mild summer's evening brooded over the episcopal city. The sirens sang their ominous song. Out of the distance the iron roar of the gigantic birds of prey drew nearer. Folk looked up into the darkening night, wondering if those evil spirits of the air would once again spare the city and those who dwelt in it. There were bursts of flak; bombs fell on the harbour quarter and the post-office near the station. People were still standing out of doors and could not distinguish the bursting of bombs from the thunder of the anti-aircraft fire. Only on the following morning the people grew aware how widespread the devastation had been, when it was made known that the trains were not running to Telgte. Early the next morning long streams of people started on foot for that small township, whither for three hundred years the Feast of the Visitation had drawn the faithful of Münster. Before the war the Bishop had on foot led the procession of pilgrims, flaunting banners and mustered parish by parish. After war broke out these outward manifestations were forbidden. For this special intercession, he drove in the episcopal coach from Münster to the venerable mercy-seat of the Mother of God.

During Pontifical Mass in the thronged church of pilgrimage, he read out the general pastoral letter of the German bishops against the measures of euthanasia applied to the insane. To render the meaning clearer, he threw in at certain points explanations of some length. It was the prelude to his great sermon on the Fifth Commandment[1] four weeks later. In the afternoon the Bishop went on a visit to relatives in the Sauerland to share in the celebration of a golden wedding.

Night after night at Münster further attacks followed from

[1] Translator's note: In Catholic Bibles, 'Though shalt not kill.' The system of numeration based on the Hebrew text was made by St. Augustine. It is followed also by most German Lutherans.

the air. After the devastation of Lübeck, the provincial capital of Westphalia was apparently to be the target of the heaviest blows. The bombers drew near in low flight over the Aasee, which shone like a mirror in the light of the full moon. The first bombs struck the Cathedral and the Cathedral Square. Nearly the whole of the Sonnenstrasse was burnt down. The institute for women students was torn down by an aerial torpedo and a Sister of the Order was buried in the ruins. An unexampled panic gripped the population. Wild rumours ran round that leaflets[1] threatening attacks constantly to be renewed from the air had been dropped from enemy aeroplanes.

. In the evening almost the whole population forsook the town. At that time there was no question of protective cellerage, not to speak of underground bomb-shelters. People lay down out of doors in the moonlight outside the supposed limit of danger from splinters of flak shells. Towards midnight they heard the howl of the sirens, then the approach of the aircraft; then they saw the fires leap up against the calm night-sky. People hurried back into the town, round the bomb-craters and over heaps of rubble that blocked the streets, to reach their own dwellings, and, if need be, put out fires or retrieve possessions. An incendiary bomb fell during one of those nights through the roof of the Bishop's Palace onto a floor immediately below, but was extinguished in time. Many people, with luggage heaped on hand-barrows or tied to bicycles, went on foot into the neighbouring villages, or drove further afield in the crowded motor-coaches and stayed over a week outside the town. Proclamations, posted up on the walls by the authorities and the Party, summoned the men back to their work in factories and offices.

On Thursday, July 10th, the Bishop came back from the Sauerland. Two days before, he had enquired on the telephone about the details of the bomb damage and we had besought him to stay at least a few days and nights longer outside Münster. As soon as he returned, he sought out the places where the damage was worst and proffered to the sufferers heartfelt words of fatherly consolation. In the evening when the sirens again started howling, he could not be persuaded to seek

[1] Translator's note: Such leaflets were, in fact, dropped.

refuge in the cellar. He only did so after the experiences of October 10th, 1943. It was again observable in this instance that a purely theoretical estimate of probabilities has far less power to influence our outlook as human beings than practical experience. On that night of July, 1941, between Thursday and Friday no further attack happened, nor was there any in the following weeks. The panic, however, lasted for several days longer.

.   .   .   .   .

Now Satan himself took a hand in events. The Party and the Gestapo became his instruments in an undertaking which had dire consequences. Even the shrewd and capable District Leader, Meyer, thought that the favourable opportunity had come at last for a successful stroke against the Church in his district. The thoughts and plans which in those days of the air-raids prompted the leaders of the Party to active measures were stripped of all disguise four years later, when the correspondence of the district leaders was brought to light. The Lord had stricken them with that blindness which is a peculiarly satanic quality. They believed that they knew the Bishop; in truth they were very far from knowing him. With the bitter recognition of their own folly came the shock of the reaction: that was lasting.

On the afternoon of Saturday, July 12th, the Bishop received the startling news that the Jesuit Institutions in the Königstrasse and at Sentmaring had been confiscated. In spite of the intense heat, he betook himself at once, in company with the Regent Francken, to both buildings and caught the Gestapo in the very act of driving the inmates out from their Order's property: he called them and their instigators thieves and robbers. For the first time he defied the persecutors of the Church, literally to their faces. He did not do so out of any peculiar fondness for that kind of strife man to man. It shook him in his inmost soul that the Jesuit Fathers, at whose feet he had sat as a pupil and a student at Feldkirch and Innsbruck, should be flung into the street like helots. In this man, to whom conscience and responsibility, charity and faithfulness, were no empty words, something rose in revolt. The resolve broke from

him like a vow, 'Now I can be silent no longer.'[1] Those were his
words on the way home to his palace.

.   .   .   .   .

When he came back to supper in the dining-room, he had
already sat for an hour at his typewriter. Leaning forward with
his elbows on the table, he rested his head on both hands;
what he then said about the events of that afternoon was the
agonized cry of a man shaken to the depths of his soul. In the
course of years I never saw the Bishop so distressed; neither
before nor afterwards did he moan; only on that evening.
Silent and oppressive, the hours of night brooded over the
palace. Doors and windows were wide open. One heard only
the slow tapping of the typewriter; now and then the Bishop
coughed or cleared his throat. Only once he rose and came
upstairs to the floor under the roof, where a servant named
Rüsenberg and I, owing to a threatening thunderstorm, were
busy spreading a tarpaulin to stop the rain from pouring in
through holes made in the bombardment. Half-jokingly, he
warned us to take care not to get a bad fall and advised us to
pray to our guardian angel. With his long pipe in his hand, he
walked slowly back to his room. In that night he wrote the
words which in the eyes of the world have indissolubly bound
up his personality with the city of Münster. He was firmly
convinced that the enemies of the Church would soon put an
end to his life here on earth. Looking death in the face, he trod
the way of conscience and faithfulness fully ready to receive at
God's hands the grace of martyrdom. On the day of his
consecration as bishop, as a token that he was wedded to his
bishopric, the golden ring had been bestowed on him. The ring
should never be broken, so he had then vowed. The good
shepherd giveth His life for His sheep. Priests of his diocese were
suffering in the camps and dungeons of the Gestapo, or, driven
from their homes, were pining in loneliness. For them he wrote
in that night the words of righteousness, for the two Canons of
his Cathedral, Vorwerk and Echelmeyer, for the Catechist
Friedrichs and many others. Something of the strength and
ardour of the old feudal fealty rose up, one may say, hot in his

[1] '*Jetzt kann ich nicht mehr schweigen.*'

soul, when he wrote down the words, 'That I will remain bound to the Society of Jesus, my teachers, my educators, my friends, in love and thankfulness to my last breath' (Vol. I, page 126).[1]

Something of the noble spirit and valour in fight of mediaeval chivalry, whose hallowed ideal it was, with strong arm to give shelter to the weak, came to life in him, when he beheld the cowardly shamelessness with which defenceless members of a religious Order were robbed of their buildings and possessions. Great men of the Church and of German history were watching him from above. He beheld their path brightly lit up by the lightning-flashes of that summer night. It was his path also. .

That night was followed by a warm, summer morning. I celebrated the Holy Sacrifice at the Hospital for Nervous Cases, where few patients were now left. In the streets of the town there was no one to be seen. Somewhere a shoemaker was hammering in his workshop; a wireless was playing; a cat ran across the road. There was an uncanny stillness everywhere. About half-past ten the Bishop came hastily into my room and said it was time to start. A strange unrest had come over him. It was perceptible how he tried to shake this off or to hide it. On the way to St. Lambert's he talked at unwonted length with some young people who were passing, also in the sacristy with the servers. As soon as the priest had gone to the altar to begin the Mass, the Bishop followed him into the chancel. There he knelt a few minutes on the floor and then stepped slowly and heavily up into the pulpit. How often he had stood there as Rector of St. Lambert's! That day it became for him as the Mount of Olives. In his opening words still quivered all the distress and torment which had oppressed him in the foregoing night: the future that threatened him personally, imprisonment by the police, the cells of the Gestapo, the way to the

[1] Translator's note: This quotation is from a book the title of which may be rendered: *The Bishop of Münster: The Echo of a Fight for Divine and Human Rights* (Aschendorff, 1946). Another book was published by the same firm in 1948. These two books, when quoted in this one, are referred to as Vol. I and Vol. II.

scaffold. He may have prayed that God would suffer that cup of bitterness to pass from him; only His Will should be done.

After he had spoken about ten sentences, a wonderful strength and serenity came over him. That tall, pastoral figure stood forth full of solemn dignity; his voice had a sound of thunder as the words fell on the ranks of the spellbound hearers, some trembling, some gazing up at him with tears in their eyes. Protest, indignation, fiery enthusiasm followed each other in successive waves. As one reads the sentences of that sermon over to oneself, one can live through again the sense of solemn dedication imparted in that hour. The sermon was at an end. The lofty calm, the sureness of himself, the deliberation full of latent power, which on that morning at St. Lambert's were bestowed on the Bishop from the hand of God, accompanied every step and act of his in the next days and weeks. They never forsook him in the times that followed. In the sacristy a throng of clergy were waiting for him, who had witnessed that historic hour, among them his Auxiliary[1] and many of the chapter. All were deeply moved by admiration and joyful enthusiasm. Exhausted and smiling faintly, the Bishop drank a glass of water and left the sacristy. Among the clergy who accompanied him, Domvikar Holling asked me about the typescript; I did not however at that moment venture to part with it. After our return to the palace, the Bishop gave me his instructions that, if the Gestapo appeared, as seemed likely, I was quietly to hand over the typescript; he had stowed away in unlikely places two carbons of it, which would not reach the Gestapo's hands; but nothing must be said about that. The Gestapo did not turn up: they never crossed the threshold of the Bishop's residence.

In the evening the Bishop took part in the closing service of Perpetual Adoration at the parish church of Überwasser. A frightful thunderstorm with drenching rain was raging meanwhile over Münster. The priests at that church begged persistently for a copy of the sermon. To one of them, who

[1] Translator's note: Mgr. H. Roleff, Auxiliary bishop and Dean of the cathedral.

appeared soon afterwards at the palace, I handed the copy
that was meant for the Gestapo, in spite of the consequences
which, in case of a visit from them, were to be awaited. Three
hours afterwards the copy came back and was duplicated in
the following night by Domvikar Roth. On the next morning
it was taken over by Father Uppenkamp, whose office at once
got to work. From this stage onward, one can no longer trace
out the progeny[1] of that typescript from generation to generation. At any rate on the Monday evening the office of the
Caritas sent attaché-cases full of them to the railway-station;
thence they were scattered in smaller packets into the pillar-
boxes of several Westphalian towns. Copies were sent off
specially to all the leading clergy in Germany and also the
chief personages in the Army, among others to Field Marshal
von Kluge, who then commanded an Army Group on the
Eastern Front. All that had happened while the Party and
the Gestapo were rejoicing over their supposed successful
suppression of the document. When they awoke, it was too
late. No Gestapo could any longer hold back the flood which
was pouring through the broken dam. There had been no
planning beforehand; God Himself in His mysterious wisdom
had done all.

    On the Monday morning, directly after Mass, the Bishop
sat down at his typewriter. Then started the telegrams to the
Chancellery of the Reich, to Hermann Göring, to the Prussian
Prime Minister, to the Minister of Public Worship, to the
Minister of Justice and of Home Affairs, finally to the Supreme
Command of the Army. At short intervals they were taken to
the post-office. The Bishop smiled as he handed over the
telegram directed to Göring. The wording was somewhat as
follows: 'With the power at your disposal, it will be a small
matter for you to confer help and justice on those persecuted
by the Gestapo.' The Bishop believed that in this case the
influence of vanity might, as it sometimes does, work for good.
Göring however only answered in March of 1942. When the
palace and the offices of the Vicar-General were destroyed by

---

[1] *Generationenfolge über Enkel und Urenkel.*

bombs on Oct. 10th, 1943, copies of Göring's letter and of the Bishop's retort were in his brief-case. So these significant documents could be saved for posterity (Vol. I, page 319).

On that same day the Bishop had recourse personally to the President of the provincial administration, who declared however that he could not interfere with measures taken by the Gestapo, which was quite independent; he promised to bring the grievances and requests at once before the Chief President, Dr. Meyer. When the Bishop was informed that the Gestapo were occupied in sequestrating the Convent of Our Lady of Lourdes in the Frauenstrasse, he went there at once. The leader in this affair, the notorious Gestapo official D., asked the Bishop who he was. 'I am the Bishop of Münster, in case you don't know that.' 'We must carry out orders, my lord Bishop.' 'Nice orders and nice work,' was the retort. He talked with the Sisters. Repeatedly D. summoned him to leave the House. With great emphasis the Bishop replied, 'I have something to say here; I will not leave until I have finished.' The crowd shouted from the street, 'There are a lot of young fellows here; off to the Front with them.' The Gestapo knew at once that this was aimed at them and tried to excuse themselves: here too there was work to be done. The Countess Helene von Galen, a cousin of the Bishop, was arrested and shut up in a cell of the Convent; she was able, however, to escape. The convent at Wilkinghege, occupied by the same Order, was appropriated at the same time. The Auxiliary-Bishop took the long journey thither on foot, in order to protest in the Bishop's name against these violent measures and to supply the unfortunate Sisters with such succour as was humanly possible.

On Thursday, July 17th, the Bishop received from Dr. Lammers, the head of the Reichskanzlei, the short answer that he had forwarded the episcopal telegram to Himmler. In anger at this, the Bishop wrote a long letter to Dr. Lammers, which perhaps, from the historical standpoint, was the most significant document during the contest of the Church against National Socialism (Vol. I, page 156). On Friday, July 18th, about midday, a telegram came from the Supreme Head-quarters of the Army: 'Not within Army's province.' The Bishop received this disappointing answer just before leaving the palace to travel to Osnabrück. He wore the plain attire of a priest. The afternoon sun poured down on the city of Osna-brück when we crossed the Cathedral Square, as yet undamaged. We were received by the local bishop and the Abbot of Gerleve, who had been robbed of his monastery and was staying at Osnabrück. The Bishop at once sought out the Benedictine nuns, driven out from Vinnenberg, who had found a very inadequate refuge in an Osnabrück convent. While he spoke words of fatherly consolation to the Sisters, tears came into his eyes. On that same afternoon I received his instructions to drive from Osnabrück to Castle Dinklage in Oldenburg, a property of the von Galen family, in order to help with prepara-tions for housing the expelled Benedictine nuns over there. The migration became possible soon afterwards, and for a short time the Abbot of Gerleve lived there also.

A week after that first sermon, the Bishop stood again in the pulpit of the parish church of Überwasser. The Gestapo had persisted in confiscating religious houses. Hence the second mournful denunciation against the persecutors of the Church, whose pretensions to identity with the people the Bishop strongly repudiated. He tore the mask even more completely from the face of National Socialism and condemned both system and practices with extreme frankness and acerbity: he dared to quote the words, 'Whose God is their belly' of the National Socialist leaders. 'They are the hammer,' he said, 'we are the anvil, but the anvil is harder than the hammer.' This aphorism he gave to believers as a watchword for their worka-day lives. The words were prophetic. The hammer is shattered, the anvil abides. In that sermon he named with reverence his chivalrous father, 'who, with unremitting earnestness, guided, instructed and admonished my brothers and myself to defend with knightly protection all such as were unjustly threatened' (Vol. I, page 138). As he spoke these words of dedication to the Catholic heritage of his knightly forefathers, he was stirred to the inmost depths. On the way home from the suburb he said to Father Höping, who was accompanying him, that, both before and during the sermon, he had often recalled the sacred memory of his father, how many a Sunday morning during

High Mass he had knelt before that pulpit in that church and said his rosary.

The Gestapo persisted, according to plan, in forcing their way into Religious Houses, until on July 30th an order from the Führer put an end to these proceedings (Vol. I, page 166). The regional director, Meyer, feeling that his recent steps had placed him in a false position, began on August 1st to write his remarkable letters to one of the national leaders, Bormann. The Party and the Gestapo, up to the level of their supreme chiefs, had been thrown on the defensive. The echo of the words and deeds of the courageous Bishop had been tremendous. The good rejoiced and the bad ground their teeth. The post soon brought the first messages of gratitude and enthusiasm.

In the last days of July, at the time when Hitler stopped the storming of monasteries, the chaplain of the Asylum at Marienthal, Father Lackmann, paid a secret visit to the Bishop, in order to inform him that the removal within a given interval of the insane patients for euthanasia had been decided; like steps would be taken at the mental hospital at Warstein in the Sauerland. The Bishop sat down at his writing-table. A lawyer had drawn his attention to par. 139 of the Criminal Code and he gave information, as was indeed his duty, to the Public Prosecutors, the Police-President and the Captain-General of the province, of the impending crime which had come to his knowledge. Thus arose the sermon on the Fifth Commandment, a sermon which, in the judgment of the Ministry of Propaganda, constituted the sharpest attack against the State for scores of past years. On the morning of August 3rd he went up into the pulpit; never had St. Lambert's been so filled with people. Like a foreboding cry of lament, the words of the Bishop in that historic hour rang into every part of our unhappy fatherland, in bondage, as it was, to men stricken with blindness, 'The days will come when, of all this fabric you contemplate, not one stone will be left on another; it will all be thrown down.'[1] According to the newspapers in 1947, before the end of August, 1941, the measures for euthanasia had been suspended, but not till 50,000 to 60,000 persons had fallen victim to them.

On the morrow of the sermon on the Fifth Commandment,

[1] Translator's note: Knox version.

the Bishop appeared in the pulpit of the church of the Benedictine nuns at Hamicolt near Dülmen; it was on August 4th,
1941, the jubilee of the introduction of the Perpetual Adoration.
With right hand upraised, he called to the many faithful who
had streamed thither from the neighbouring townships, 'We
shall never rest until our religious orders are restored to their
cloisters; we do not acquiesce in the expulsion of your beloved
sisters from their convents.'

The three sermons had been delivered. In hundreds of
thousands of copies they spread rapidly through the land.
Later, in Feb. of 1946, Provost Dr. Otto Spülbeck of Leipzig,
among others, wrote as follows: 'Herr Thomassen reproduced
these sermons by the thousand, to spread them among the
people. For distributing them, several persons at Leipzig
were sent to concentration camps and some met their death
for it.' Rumours were spread about that the Bishop had been
arrested, also that the military authorities had interfered on
his behalf. The Party staged a campaign against him by way
of protest meetings up and down the country. The police-
presidency and the Gestapo tried by various devices to entice
him outside the country, in order to get him arrested at the
frontier and so render him harmless. The Bishop's name was
in everyone's mouth. Count Franz, the Bishop's brother, says
that during the following winter he felt great anxiety about
him. One day he said to him, 'What are we to do, if you are
locked up?'

'Nothing at all.'

'Then what is to become of your poor diocese?'

'My dear boy, St. Paul was locked up for years, but God
had no misgiving that the heathen would not be converted in
due time.'

Calmly the Bishop took the pastoral staff of St. Ludger in
his hands for a journey into the rural deanery of Dülmen to
administer Confirmations. Several people pointed out to him
how easily he might be attacked and murdered on the road.
He smiled at these well-meant warnings.

When he returned, among the many letters on his desk was

one from the Bishop of Innsbruck without a stamp. It had been handed in by a priest on the day before. This was the first letter he opened and read, that in August, the Holy Father had personally read the three sermons aloud to those most in his confidence at the Vatican, with expressions of the strongest approval (*see* Vol. I, page 46). The Bishop's eyes were moist. He seemed to behold the exalted figure of the Vicar of Christ, with the sermon in his hand: he seemed to hear the words, 'Yea, my son, thou hast done well.' For the Bishop this was the same voice of God which on that night, in his hours of agony, had spoken, 'Gird up thy loins, go forward, fear them not; I am with thee.' He had answered, 'O Lord, behold thy servant; I am here, I follow.' That was his greatest hour, the decisive hour of his heroic act of faith, which will some day, God willing, raise him to the altars.

In scholastic philosophy there is a maxim, *Agere sequitur esse* (Action springs from being). Out of the calm and depth of the Bishop's inner being grew the strength for his great action in those days. To quote Our Lord's parable, he was the good tree that bringeth forth good fruit.

While this book was in the Press, on January 27th, 1948, some original documents from the former Ministry of Propaganda were handed over to our new Bishop.[1] Part of them had already reached Münster in reproduction in August of 1945, and could be published in Vol. I, page 189–196, part of them were included a year later in Vol. II by means of mimeograph. Among these original documents, which bear the marginal notes and signatures of persons holding high positions in the Party, two pairs of documents are to be found which were unknown hitherto and are printed further on. The first pair betray the insincerity and inconsistency of the National Socialists. On the one hand, their propaganda taunted the Church with holding opinions like Bolshevism, and on the other Goebbels professed indignation when a German Bishop raised his voice against Bolshevism (*see* the Section 'Strange Methods', Vol. I, page 84 ff). The latter pair of documents reveal the powerlessness of the Party's leadership against the Bishop's sermons. Even Hitler, who deemed himself alone

---

[1] Translator's note: Monsignor Michael Keller, D.D., formerly of the diocese of Osnabrück.

equal to dealing with the happenings at Münster, kept silence. Would that we in the Christian camp, as many may now reflect, had already known at that time how powerless the dictator and his accomplices really were! How much misfortune could perhaps have been spared to the German people! Let us learn for the future. On those who, undismayed and uncompromising, fight against the enemies of Christianity, God bestows victory.

A SUBMISSION

Re Reference to Bishop von Galen in the *Journal de Paris*.

In an article in the *Journal de Paris*, Bishop von Galen is represented as a combatant against Bolshevism and described as one of the worthiest bishops.

Dr. Goebbels is indignant that such a blunder is possible. Party-Member Fritsche has received instructions to enquire carefully into the matter.

Signed T(iessler).

Berlin,
Nov. 19th, 1941.
    Ti/Hu.
(Documentary Ref. Z.d. A. La.)

A SUBMISSION

Re Reference to Bishop von Galen in the *Journal de Paris*.

In supplement to my submission of Nov. 19th I beg to inform you that Party-Member Fritsche has established the following:

The observations in the *Journal de Paris* reached it from the press-service of the German Embassy in Paris. Publication in the *Journal de Paris* followed through a Catholic writer.

Dr. Goebbels instructed Party-Member Hunke again to direct the particular attention of the Foreign Office to this article and to give Abetz (the German Ambassador) corresponding instructions about it.

Berlin,
Nov. 20, 1941.
(Documentary Ref. Z.d. A. La.)
Ti/La.

From Heinrich K.
Munich, Mühlbaurstrasse 27. (Marginal Note: Received Dec.
    4, 1941.)
To the Director of the National Organization for National
    Socialist Propaganda and Popular Enlightenment.
Party-Member Walter Tiessler.
Berlin, W.8.
Hotel Kaiserhof, Room 117.

Dear Party-Member Tiessler.
    After I had heard repeatedly during the course of several
weeks of the pastoral letter of Bishop Galen at Münster, I have
now had the opportunity of reading it. This so-called pastoral
letter is just a typical specimen of black propaganda. The
Catholic Church has, in respect of propaganda, already perpetrated unheard-of performances, but this pastoral letter is a
peculiarly clever example. I am convinced that not merely
thousands, but tens of thousands, of people have been taken in
by this letter, which has been reproduced over and over again
and disseminated everywhere. After long reflection, as I have
not heard what steps we have taken against it, I should like to
put forward the suggestion to you, that we should organize a
circulation of letters to answer it. If one or more rebutting
letters are duly composed and circulated, it should be possible
to take the ground from under the feet of this black propaganda.
I should be very interested to hear your views.
    With cordial greetings,
                          . Heil Hitler!
                              Yours faithfully,
                                  Heinrich K.

Directorate of National Propaganda.
National Organization for National Socialist Propaganda and
    Popular Enlightenment. Ti/La.
Berlin. Dec. 5th, 1941.
Hotel Kaiserhof. Room 115. Tel. 110014. Private line 2189.
(Marginal Ref.: Pastoral Letter of Bishop von Galen, Münster.)
To Herr Heinrich K.
Munich, Mühlbaurstrasse 27.

SECRET

Dear Party-Member K.
    I thank you for your friendly suggestion in the matter of
Bishop von Galen. In this connection I give you the confidential

information that the Führer is personally following up this matter and therefore himself decides all steps to be taken in it. The precise moment for needful action in it will be determined by the Führer, when he considers it most favourable for ourselves. Up till that time all measures, however attractive they may seem—and your proposal is very much so—must be deferred, so that they may be carried out with practical thoroughness.

Heil Hitler!

Yours faithfully,

T(iessler).

(Marginal Ref. Z.d. A. La.)

H

CHAPTER 16

A CHARACTER-SKETCH

WHEN, at this stage of the book, I venture to give some hints about the inner life of the great Bishop, I am fully aware of the difficulty of this daring attempt. It is not for me to draw the spiritual portrait of such a man in all its amplitude. I shall only make a slight effort, in order to complete and justify the chapter headed 'Passion-Sorrow and Easter-Joy' (cf. Holy Week and Easter),[1] by referring to single incidents, which I observed myself, to enable the reader to recognize the essential outline of the Bishop's character and temperament. This will put him in a position to range and estimate properly certain characteristic actions of his, which are not readily understood otherwise.

Only a few months after the Bishop's enthronement, contemporaries, even beyond the limits of his diocese, were already praising him as a fearless fighter against National Socialism. This marked an essential feature in his spiritual portrait. His words and deeds in the aftertime confirmed this early diagnosis by popular opinion. He had hardly, in the autumn of 1933, been appointed Bishop by the Holy Father, when he revealed his essential standpoint and outlook. It was expressed in the watchword and call-to-battle on the crest of his family, *Nec laudibus nec timore* (Neither men's praise nor fear of men shall move me). In the pride and strength of his youth it had been his joy to gallop on horseback through the country-side, and as a sportsman he was a good gun: in later years he was wont to declare that, had soldiering been his vocation, he would have become an airman, for in the air there was still knightly and personal combat: the individual man still counted. Indeed, when there was high purpose in the fight, he never shrank from putting his own life to the hazard. He never yielded an inch to an adversary, once he recognized him as such, and he left him in no doubt about it.

[1] *Passion und Osterjubel.*

114

After his nomination as Bishop, even before he was consecrated, he had enquired of Göring the time-limit for taking the
oath. When he did not get an answer at once, he asked again
by a telegram with reply paid; in Berlin they certainly looked
at it with surprise, but felt called on to answer. At the Ministry
he enquired whether there was a crucifix there; search was
made for one, in vain. Then, while the officials looked on in
astonishment, he pulled his pectoral cross out of his breast-
pocket, saying, 'I thought that would be so, and have brought
one with me.'

The new successor of St. Ludger, no one can deny, from his
first entry into office, adopted a line of conduct which was
thought out beforehand and of which the purpose was evident:
everyone could perceive, without possible mistake, his total
freedom from fear and his strict interpretation of the episcopal
duties and rights entrusted to him. This vivid and strongly
marked awareness of leadership bestowed on him, in the times
then to come, the unwonted sense of power that distinguished
his conduct and developed more and more into a conscious
mission against the errors of the day.

It may be that his aristocratic descent created a certain
natural background for his attitude. As the son of a Count[1] in
the ancient family of von Galen, he felt revive in himself the
strength of his forefathers, who through hundreds of years had
striven mightily for the Church, whether they had borne the

[1] Translator's note: Hereditary titles are more frequent in Germany
than in Great Britain because German titles pass from the father to all his
sons, who in turn transmit them to their sons; therefore it is only possible to
find British equivalents for the *heads* of German titled families. The British
counterparts of other titled members of such families bear either a courtesy
title or no title at all. The titles most commonly met with in Germany are
as follows: *Graf* (Count): corresponds approximately to an Earl. As with
other titles, it is usually followed by *von*, though in referring to a Count the
prefix is often omitted. *Freiherr* (Baron): equals approximately the lowest
degree of the British peerage. The title *Baron*, which is also found, is of non-
German origin. In conversation a *Freiherr* is generally referred to as *Baron*,
the prefix *von* being omitted. *Ritter* (Knight): corresponding in some cases
to Baronet and in others to Knight. A *Ritter* whose title is hereditary usually
owns a *Rittergut* or Knight's estate and takes his name from it. *Edler* (Noble):
approximately the same as Baronet. The titles *Ritter* and *Edler* are, as a rule,
of Bavarian or Austrian origin.

The prefix *von* corresponds most closely to the English suffix Esquire (in
the proper heraldic sense), denoting the right to bear arms.

There is not space to deal with the princely families, e.g. *Fürst*.

crozier, like Christoph Bernard von Galen, Wilhelm Emmanuel von Ketteler, or Max Gereon von Galen, or, in the parliaments of the Reichstag, had fought for ecclesiastical rights. All this bestowed on him beforehand, not only a strong self-confidence, but a positive feeling of superiority against his opponents. Years afterwards, in a sermon at Vreden (17th of November, 1937), he expressed this sentiment: 'It is no merit of mine, but the ordinance of God; far be it from me to pride myself on the fact that I spring from a family of the old Westphalian nobility. But it is a fact that documentary evidence shows that my forefathers, men of my name and my race, whose blood flows in my veins, have, for over 700 years here in Westphalia, in the land of Münster and on the banks of the Lippe, held hereditary estates. If anyone stands up and asserts that German blood speaks in him, I stand up here and assert the same of myself. . . . I don't yield to them. I protest strongly against anyone slandering my forbears, my father, my mother, and besmirching their Faith, their Christian life, as un-German and contrary to the genius of our race' (Vol. I, pages 243 and ff.).

Did aristocratic pride speak in such phrases? Yes, but not in the traditional sense. First and last, he wished to be a priest and a bishop. If anyone addressed him as Count, he either passed it by or emphasized that he was a shepherd of souls and a bishop. Above the dignity of a count, he held the dignity of a priest. For that reason he always behaved in the simplest and least artificial way, just as altogether he disliked anything elaborate or wilfully conspicuous. In Berlin he signed with his plain surname, 'Galen'. When, however, after 1918, the announcement was issued that the titles of nobility, *Graf*, *Freiherr*, *Von*, belonged to the surname and no longer denoted aristocratic standing, he signed himself, as a protest, 'Graf von Galen'. So, in certain respects, he did lay weight on his aristocratic descent. He regarded it as, first of all, an obligation. The medieval conception of the knight and nobleman, which sprang from the religious source of obligation to serve Church, State, and People, was the inmost kernel of his ideal of nobility. He was so thoroughly steeped in this ideal that he regarded nobility as meaningless where there was no will or effort to attain it. For that reason he positively hated the way of life of those members of his class who used their property and position to get money.

He felt a thorough contempt for the so-called *Erfolgsadel* in Westphalia, men who used their titles as stepping-stones to a commercial career. He stigmatized them as money-grubbers. He preferred a poor, but blameless, nobility to a rich one, which had forsaken healthy traditions and imitated the wealthy middle class by a life of pleasure. It was only natural that a scion of the old noble family of von Galen could not, in the years after 1918, reconcile himself with the quite different spirit of democracy and levelling down, which then pervaded Germany, that he could not feel happy when the traditional values, which in his eyes were the most sacred and had been so important for Christianity and the Church, were trodden by the Revolution underfoot. How, as priest and as bishop, he thought about these events in detail, has been set out in another context.

The ideas of the Third Reich could not modify his fundamental standpoint. There were times when, in righteous anger, he spoke with depreciation and contempt of 'that brown gang', as he called them. From day to day that choleric side of his temperament grew more and more prominent. We have written of his great sermons in the summer of 1941, of his outspoken and vehement rebukes to the Gestapo, whenever they desecrated a religious house, of his protesting telegrams to Ministries in Berlin. Even some years before those great events, there had been an occasion when, after the great procession, the police roped off the Cathedral Square. He at once went up into the pulpit and, as righteous indignation inspired him at the moment, condemned this arbitrary action in the strongest terms.

In a narrower circle also, in particular cases, which seldom reached the ears of the public, this trend of his disposition found vent. The following incident happened at an educational conference at a presbytery near Münster in the early years after 1933. The Chairman expressed the opinion that a wife and mother was of much more value in teaching than a spinster. The Bishop laid hold at once on the heathen and materialist theory, propagated by National Socialism, which underlay this remark. In anger, he struck the table with his fist and exclaimed, 'I won't listen to talk like that; Germany is not a stud-farm.'

So in the course of conversation sharp expressions fell from him, which displayed his aversions and dislikes. Sometimes, one must admit, he liked verbal fencing, to elucidate an intricate question and illuminate it from every standpoint; he was fond of taking highly controversial objections and so intentionally provoking an adversary to opposition. He did not fear contradiction, but took it in quite good part, provided it were honest and sincere. To many, especially to National Socialists, such a line may have seemed rough, even coarse and uncouth. Maybe that, even in his own camp, to some over-clever and over-prudent people, a more liberal infusion of moderation would have been welcome. Such people might have reflected that there is an anger which is righteous. Even the Redeemer Himself took hold of a scourge and drove out from the temple those who had turned His Father's house into a den of thieves.

What men are wont to call diplomatic dexterity and smoothness was almost wholly absent from the Bishop's vocabulary. In so far as such a mode of conducting life and affairs oversteps the prudence enjoined as a cardinal virtue and passes into the realm of deceptive ambiguity and calculated economy of truth, one can only say that diplomacy was his weakest side. On such slippery paths he had no ambition to excel. After the Capitulation in the spring of 1945, many people, some prompted by the best motives, regretted that the Bishop retained towards those now in power, the British and the Americans, the same outspokenness he had used to their forerunners; it would, they foretold, work out unfavourably in the future, whereas from a different attitude more advantage could be derived. On July 15th, 1945, such considerations, in a discreet shape, were put before him by a large body of clergy. Very earnestly, but with no sign of ill-will, he declared, 'I am grateful to you for your advice, but I shall go straight forward on my own way, as I have gone all these years: I look neither to the right nor to the left.' His watchword, to do one's duty, unmoved by praise or fear, was his guide through the changing times to the end.

The irascible and combative side of the Bishop's make-up is manifest in the great actions of his episcopal life. Was it the dominant side? The public never knew how suddenly his instinctive stiffness and rigidity, not to say obduracy, could change into a benevolent mildness and warmth, when reflection bade him subdue his natural disposition. A few examples follow.

The first was in 1910. He was an assistant priest at St. Matthias in Berlin. At the usual meeting of clergy on Monday evening, the conversation turned on questions of ecclesiastical art. Father G. opposed the Count. There was lively argument on either side, which became more and more acrimonious, until the sentence was rapped out, half in earnest, half in jest, 'Galen, your outlook in art is plebeian.'[1] Father von Galen, who was smoking his long pipe, sprang up in a violent fury. His eyes glowed like fire and he stood over against his fellow curate with clenched fists. All those present feared that in the next moment it might come to blows. In a second, however, a shudder passed over him, he recovered his self-command, and stretched out his hand to the amazed G., who grasped it with the words, 'Forgive me; I didn't mean to offend you.'

On an occasion early in his episcopate, a priest was to be entrusted with a difficult and unpleasant task. He had been a friend and fellow student of the Bishop and brought forward various pretexts for evading this duty. At first his tone was half-jocular, but finally he seriously and explicitly refused. The Bishop grew angry and exclaimed, 'If you take that line, I order you to do it.' A coldness and estrangement had intruded into their friendship. The Bishop seemed very soon to have grown aware that he had been too harsh. Before the day was out, he laid his hand on the shoulder of his brother-priest with a friendly gesture, as though asking forgiveness. After the Cardinal's death the priest told the story with deep emotion.

[1] Translator's note: 'Galen, Du bist ein Kunstbanause.' An opprobrious epithet, stronger than 'philistine'. In German an insulting term in spite of its respectable Greek origin.

In February of 1939, while visiting a school on the Lower Rhine, he had already begun to catechize a class, when the headmaster appeared, unexpectedly called him out of the classroom and informed him in the passage that the governing body had just sent an order on the telephone that the Bishop was not to be allowed to enter the school. That worked like a bombshell. Very angrily and loudly, the Bishop protested against such high-handed treatment. At the moment, the schoolmaster could not put in a word. When at length in the conference-room he was able to explain convincingly that he personally was quite guiltless in the matter and his viewpoint was that of a good Catholic, the Bishop's words displayed so much cordiality and kindness that the schoolmaster took his leave with tears of joy in his eyes.

In the same year, when the Corpus Christi procession was leaving the chancel of the Cathedral and the Bishop was bearing the Blessed Sacrament under the *baldachino*, the men who were holding it up hesitated in moving forward; the Bishop addressed a few words to them betraying irritation and annoyance. At dinner, he mentioned this incident and said he had lost his self-possession; while one was bearing the monstrance, one ought not to speak.

In the spring of 1944, the Bishop was walking from the Theological College to the Borromäum for an Ordination of Deacons. The way at that time led through the Bishop's garden and across the courtyard of the Ludgerianum. Suddenly he saw some workmen occupied in laying a new pathway across the courtyard of the palace. Angry that the municipal authorities had not asked his leave for this, or even given him notice, he betook himself to the place where they were at work and protested in the sharpest terms against such methods, 'those of Bolshevik Russia, where property was no longer respected'. For the rest of the way to the Borromäum he kept silence; one could feel that he regretted that, as a Bishop, he had attacked these simple workmen, who could only carry out their orders. In the chapel of the College he beckoned to a Capuchin Father to come to him, went with him to a confessional, knelt down there, and not till afterwards did he go to the altar and there vest for the Holy Sacrifice. None ever heard of this incident in his lifetime, but today I feel it a duty to communicate it to my fellow-men.

How strong the power was which continually in the Bishop's inner soul subdued his splenetic temperament with its components, impulsive roughness, downrightness and obduracy, and held it in bounds, is evident from the examples quoted. Of what nature was that power? It lay in the fundamental kindliness and gentleness of his disposition, in the thoughtfulness which was deeply rooted in his piety. That the Bishop possessed depth both of thought and of emotion in so high a degree constituted his peculiar greatness. Strength and hardness in him were united with tenderness. They served as complements to one another and created a remarkable unity. A professor at the University of Münster found the right expression: 'He was a giant with the heart of a child.' He always recognized the merit of the humble and retiring. In the Ludgerianum there was an old charwoman who through a score of years peeled the potatoes. The students gave her the Homeric name of Eurykleia. Many an afternoon the Bishop had seen this old charwoman go, with her back deeply bent, into the cathedral, to make the Stations of the Cross. He described this humble human being, who walked in the obscurest corners of the kitchens and cellars, as the most devout person in all Münster. For weeks, while the episcopal servant was ill, he acted as server to his chaplain at Mass, handed the cruets to him and bore the missal from one side to the other. He did just the same in 1945 in the Borromäum for the clergy of St. Aegidius, when there was no server on the spot.

One afternoon, while the Bishop, saying his rosary, was walking across the central graveyard, a man came along, whose daughter had died a few weeks before. The father was still full of deep sorrow for his heavy loss, and a doubting thought tormented him, whether he would see his daughter again in eternity as he had known her on earth, so young, joyous and unchanged. Priests, whom he had consulted before, had given the opinion that one could know nothing precise about recognition in the world to come. Now he saw the Bishop coming and he could ask him: he enquired with a beating heart. The Bishop, who felt with the father's grief, said in a most reassuring tone: 'You will see your daughter again as she was on earth. Now let us go to her grave and there say an "Our Father", that God in His Love may soon take her to Himself in Heaven.' He then took the man by the hand and they both stood in prayer by the child's grave. The father went home deeply consoled and will never, as long as he lives, forget those minutes in the churchyard.

In Berlin how much humility must have been required to confess his sins week by week to his senior curate! When in 1929 he left the capital, he knelt down before each of his curates and asked him for his priestly blessing. What did he say to a Protestant Colonel, who in the autumn of 1941 expressed his deep-felt appreciation of the three sermons? 'Ah, if you only knew, my one desire is that God may be satisfied with me.' His great self-knowledge enabled him to know quite well the limits of his powers. He often spoke with admiration of the faculties of others, adding, with humility, what a bungler he felt in the matter talked of. Without a doubt, dreams often reveal the life of the soul. Several times he told me how he had dreamt that he had come into a House which God filled with believers, had gone up into the pulpit and then not known how to preach about anything at all.

His susceptibility showed itself most plainly in situations which for him were strongly charged with devotional feeling. His eyes then always moistened and his voice for a moment began to tremble or to fail. If truth is to have its due, the Bishop's tears—his *donum lacrimarum*—cannot be passed over in silence. This strong man would cry like a child. He, who would not have faltered in ascending the scaffold, at certain moments could not hide his emotion. Is that a psychological riddle? No, this close association of steadfastness and sensibility is a distinctive mark of the Westphalians. It is wholesome that the people who, in the so-called iron age of Adolf Hitler, worshipped the Police-State as an ideal realm of manly strength, and also the decadent Rationalists of our day, should take note of this fact. The Bishop, who fought in the front rank against barbarity, had primitive Westphalian, primitive German, qualities, which he inherited from his forefathers.

This natural disposition was, in him, sublimated into the devotional sphere. In the realm of our Holy Faith lay that which moved him most deeply. On occasions that stirred religious emotion, tears almost always gathered into his eyes, often tears of joy. Examples here, too, will serve best to illustrate this side of the Bishop's spiritual life.

He had only just been appointed as successor to St. Ludger, when the senior curate of St. Lambert's came to speak to him about the ceremony of his farewell. He however declined to go through this ceremony at that time; he said it would be too severe an ordeal, and he would not be able to refrain from tears; he would, when opportunity offered, come after his consecration as Bishop; he would then find it less trying. At the farewell ceremony itself, he said, 'I beg all to forgive me, if I sometimes had to turn away applicants and petitioners, but I assure you that for each of them I at once recited a silent *Ave Maria.*' The newly chosen guardian of his people was however mistaken, if he thought he could conceal his susceptible temperament under his episcopal vestments. What affection he won among the faithful when, on his way to Confirmations, or to other affirmations of religious faith, he drove through the crowded streets! All thronged to greet him. His hand rose slowly again and again to give the blessing, his lips uttered the hallowed words in a soft and kindly voice; tears stood in his eyes, tears of thankful joy, at such fidelity to the Faith, at such steadfastness under persecution and manifold oppression.

One evening in the year 1942, he told how two Bavarian soldiers, men of an age to have families, had come to him and told him quite simply that, whenever they passed the Church of St. Servatius, they always went in to say a rosary for their wives and children at home. The piety of these men had so deeply impressed the Bishop that, when he spoke of it several hours later, the tears came into his eyes.

A mechanic from Münster, who was employed during the

war on the aerodrome at Handorf, had occasion to go to see
the Bishop; incidentally he told him that every day he had to
take the defensive against profane jokes about religion and
gibes against the Bishop himself. The Bishop took leave of this
courageous mechanic with tears and tapped him gratefully on
the shoulder. With what deep emotion he embraced his
ghostly brethren and members of his flock, when they returned
home from the concentration camps in 1945, they who had
undergone shame and hardship for the sake of Christ! Sometimes during the hostilities, priests, pursued by the Gestapo,
came to him, and asked whether it was allowable to avoid
arrest by that body, either by flight or by a voluntary offer of
military service. He did not forbid them either course, but he
stressed how precious, and indeed indispensable, was the ex-
piatory suffering of the priesthood. This shows that his kindliness did not extend to letting men shun their sterner duties.

His highest pitch of joy and satisfaction was when he heard
that a priest had sacrificed himself for the good of his fellow
men. After an air-raid he had gone to a church which had been
struck. He asked the whereabouts of the parish priest. The
answer was that he had, at the height of the bombardment and
anti-aircraft fire, ridden off on his bicycle to Haus Kannen,
to visit his sick people there. In the evening he told us this and
was so moved by it that he added, 'He is certainly a saint.' He
said the same things with sobs in his voice in the summer of
1945 at the grave of Father Wessing von Hoetmar; another
member of the cathedral chapter had brought home with him
from Dachau an urn containing his ashes.

When the recollection of his pious childhood, of his parents
of blessed memory, of the woodlands of his home, came vividly
before his mind, he was at times unmanned by melancholy,
that peculiar blend of feeling which springs from happiness
lived through, or sorrowful looking backwards on what was
beautiful, is gone and can never return. The same happened
when he simply recalled that the rosary, which he held in his
hands, had been many years ago strung by his mother at a time
when, on Sunday afternoons in winter, she was wont to
string hundreds of rosaries. During a Confirmation at Dinklage,
when the congregation sang an old chorale traditional in that
township, he was so overcome by emotion that he could

hardly utter the formulae of Confirmation. Such was the power exerted by the memory of his childhood's world, which, as he listened for the first time after many years to the melody of that hymn, rose up before him.

Awareness of his impressionable temperament brought the Bishop much anxiety and sorrow. In April of 1941, before the commemoration of the Sacred Heart of Jesus, he was greatly troubled; the fear tormented him that, at the moment when the act of consecration took deepest hold on him, his emotion might be visible. Bitter sorrow always overcame him when he had to behold the thankless indifference which requited the Love of Christ for mankind. At that commemoration, indeed, what he had feared happened to an excessive degree. On that same day, in what seemed a fit of depression, but with self-control and patience, he said that God had laid this cross upon him and he would have to bear it to his grave. He did indeed bear it to the last days of his life.

When he was invested with the Cardinal's Purple, symbolic of suffering, and walked through the applauding crowd in the Vatican, both there and in St. Peter's his eyes were full of tears, and he greeted the loving words of the Holy Father with trembling lips. Thus he stood in the camps of his fellow countrymen in Southern Italy, thus before tens of thousands of the faithful of his diocese in the Cathedral Square at Münster on the day of his return. What he regarded as a cross made truly his fame and his greatness. Those who loved him knew the breadth and depth of his heart. They knew that his soul was, above all, filled with love for God and man. This love grew in a life of prayer, of contemplation and of solitude with God.

How ardently he sought and loved the quiet, the stillness, of nature as God created it, how he traced the Spirit of God in all the beauty of His creation! When in May the nightingale sang, he would stand for nearly an hour of the night at the window and talk of it on the next morning. It was for him as a song from his happy childhood and the days of his youth, a song from the graves of his homeland. It gripped him, just as the hymn 'To Love Our Lady' (*Maria zu lieben*) always made him weep. Incidentally, he once, as has been mentioned before, came to speak, in connection with Pfandl's book, *Philip II*, about the Escorial, which, in that king's old age, became at the same time a royal palace and a monastery. How beautiful it would be, he considered, to spend one's last years on earth in such surroundings, a blend of the monarchic with the monastic. Indeed the Bishop was like a king, in his constant awareness that leadership was a duty laid on him; but he was also like a monk, dedicated wholly to God and scorning the world. The harmony of these two characters, elevation and dignity, sureness, calm, depth of sincere feeling and spirituality, could be clearly traced in his whole outward appearance, his tall, indeed gigantic build, his slow heavy walk, the steady carriage of his head, the kindly, affectionate look in his eyes.

The words Augustus Clemens, Latin form of his Christian name, expressed what lay deepest in his nature: one would fain write them under his likeness in death. In the small room of the St. Francis Hospital, where he died, his features were a few hours afterwards perpetuated by photograph. We all know this wonderfully impressive picture. The spirit of eternity breathed upon that countenance, when the soul forsook her earthly vesture. The likeness of one illuminate (may one say of one made perfect?) shines out from those noble features; kingly elevation is there in equal harmony with tenderness and infinite loving-kindness. It is the calm and harmony of a great soul, which filled his whole earthly life, and now, as a wonderful echo diffused from that likeness, abides with us for ever. Someone showed it to a four-year-old child and asked, 'What is he doing?' The questioner had expected the answer, 'He is sleeping.' But what did the child say? 'He is praying.' In the home of that child the likeness hangs beside a medieval Entombment of Christ.

CHAPTER 17

DOWNFALL OF THE CATHEDRAL

Sunday, Oct. 10th, 1943

ON A sunny afternoon in autumn, the bell of the Cathedral was ringing for Vespers. The Bishop was about to put on his rochet and betake himself to the Cathedral, when the sirens howled a full alarm. Meanwhile I was walking up and down my room, saying my Office. When the flak started, I changed my clothes, put my breviary in my coat-pocket and went down the staircase to the ground-floor, where the housekeeper, Anna Röggener, asked me whether it would be a bad business. I answered that, judging by former experience, that was not likely. Suddenly the anti-aircraft fire intensified, then the roar of aircraft grew threateningly near. We withdrew into the narrow passage between the dining-room and the kitchen; this passage, a year before, had been roofed over with reinforced concrete. We had hardly reached it, when we heard the uncanny screech of a stick of bombs. Spontaneously, we bent down, sank on our knees, uttered a hurried prayer and, in breathless tension, awaited the end. There was a frightful crash, walls tumbling down, beams and timbers splitting and striking against each other. Then thick clouds of dust spread a darkness like night. One clear thought emerged: 'We are saved, not buried; God does not yet will our death.' Next came the instinctive urge, 'Get outside.' We felt our way through the dust to the kitchen door, which was jammed, but could still be thrust open enough to go through, and thence down some steps into the kitchen. The Bishop's servant came running to us out of the boiler-cellar; he had heard our voices. The three of us felt our way through another cellar into the open. All the doors we passed had been burst open and jammed. As we found out a few hours later, we had in darkness taken the only way left which could lead us out of the ruins into the outer air. All other outways had been destroyed or blocked with rubble.

Outside, directly behind the dining-hall we stumbled on a
bomb-crater: that beautiful old hall, wainscoted with tiles of
blue Delft,[1] had been wholly demolished.

Like earth beside a freshly ploughed furrow, the rubble
lay in mounds beside the crater's edge, at the bottom, water,
seeping in from the soil, had already settled into a reflecting
pool. We could not see very far. The old, broad, ivy-clad wall
of the garden had been thrown down; the tool-shed was in
pieces; trees and shrubs were torn to shreds. We ran across the
bridge over the Aa into the park. Then the flak started again
like wildfire: a fresh wave of planes was drawing nearer. We
threw ourselves on the ground, hard against the trunk of a
thick beech tree, and pressed our heads into the ivy. Now again
came the moaning screech of showering bombs. The earth
heaved and shook us. Over us passed a rain of soft mould, rubble
and stones. It was a fountain of earth, the work of a bomb,
which had struck a few yards behind us. Among the upper
boughs of a huge tree to our right an incendiary had burst. We
saw little tongues of flame flicker everywhere in the branches;
here and there the burning twigs fell to the ground. The bare
trunk stood upright.

What was to be done now? We could not stay where we
were. We ran towards the tower of the Church of Überwasser.
A man lay dead on the square in front of it on the side towards
the Frauenstrasse. We saw houses on fire beside the Spiegelturm and thick smoke rising from the roof of the left-hand
tower of the Cathedral. From the first minute of the attack, one
thought had weighed like lead on our minds: where is the
Bishop? I ran back into the palace-garden. The flak increased.
Were further waves of aircraft drawing near? The air had
grown less murky; one could now see how badly the palace had
been hit. Between the dining-hall and the bridge across the
Aa, I met with the father-in-law of Keller, assistant in the
Vicar-General's office. He had just seen the Bishop standing
on an upper floor among the ruins. These tidings came like an
awakening from some frightful nightmare.

·   ·   ·   ·   ·

[1] Translator's note: Built by John of Leyden.

Running as fast as our legs would carry us, round bomb-craters and over ruins, we fetched the long ladder from the orchard. Then came a sight, which was both a shock and a relief: the Bishop, covered with dust and dirt, was standing upright in the doorway between his bedroom and his study on the second storey. When the back wall of the palace collapsed, the roof, the ceiling below the roof and the floor of the second storey had all slid down into the courtyard, so as to form a steep slope. One could climb up without a ladder by laying firm hold on the thick, angular, cast-iron clamps; after two hundred years they had at length failed to hold the heavy oaken beams together. Thick smoke was rising in the front room. The Bishop wished, first of all, to quench the fire which was breaking out. But there was neither a single pail nor a drop of water. The row of ready-filled pails had disappeared with the top floor, and the huge washing-tank in the yard below, which dated from the time of Bishop Johann Bernard and held 800 litres, was buried under a mound of ruins. The Bishop lay down and slid along the steeply sloping beams to the ground. I climbed down at the side and put a hand under his feet to check his slipping down too quickly. He made a joke of this, saying that his very loose shoes must on no account be allowed to fall through the gaps in the beams into the unattainable depths below. He would then have to run about barefoot; he already looked comic enough, after throwing off his cassock, in his leather waistcoat, short knee-breeches and long violet stockings. When he reached the ground, he sat down, quite exhausted, on the edge of a bomb-crater. It was a heart-rending sight. I could not get rid of the reflection that this man, who, at the hazard of his life, had striven against the brown-shirted barbarians, had been, on a sunny autumn afternoon, under the peacefully oversheltering towers of his own cathedral, pursued and endangered by the bombs of those very countries which, in their wireless propaganda against the Third Reich, had broadcast his sermons round the world.

The anti-aircraft fire subsided. The housekeeper, Catharina Bussmann, looked out through a back window in the upper storey of the old chancery; she was already fairly cheerful after her fright. So none of the Bishop's household had been harmed, although the man-servant alone had stayed in the cellar and

I

four or five direct hits had torn the building to pieces. The councillor at the Vicariate-General, Canon Ricking, and his sister, who lived in a part of the right wing, were both away from home. As all three staircases were in ruins, one could only reach the upper storeys by means of ladders. Monsignor Weinand, who in the meantime had hastened to the palace, at once carried the Blessed Sacrament out of the private chapel to the Ludgerianum. Then the furnishings of the chapel and the vestments in the sacristy were stowed away. Besides those, it was possible to save the furniture and paintings in both halls of the middle building, above all the portraits in oil of the bishops of the last centuries. Two croziers were lost and nearly all the Bishop's furniture and books. The salvage was only carried out with great difficulty, as far too little help was available. On Sunday afternoons the centre of the town is usually almost deserted. Besides the inhabitants of the Bishop's Palace and a few sacristans and vergers at the Cathedral, gunners of the flak batteries, men training for ambulance work, a farmer from Gimbte and two men from the parish churches of St. Lambert and the Holy Spirit, made themselves very useful. From 3.30 to 9 p.m. the work went on without a break. A rumour ran round about 6 p.m. that a full alarm was imminent. This drove many people from the middle of the town into the underground shelters, or still further afield. As the hours passed, the fire in the central building of the palace had spread steadily. Gaps had been torn by high-explosive bombs between this central building and those that flanked it on either side and thereby these were spared from burning. About 9 p.m. the first fire-brigade detachment arrived from the Spiegelturm and was able at least to check a further spreading of the fire. An hour later a second detachment came from the Cathedral Square; the firemen continued in action throughout the night. For eight days the detachments from the industrial quarters relieved each other every twenty-four hours; the stores of coke alight in the cellars continually started fresh outbreaks.

*   *   *   *   *

The sight of the burning Cathedral was the Bishop's deepest sorrow. Although he had several times attempted to persuade the fire-brigade to intervene effectually, his efforts led to no result. The tower on the left was wrapped in flames; thence the fire spread to the whole roof of the Cathedral. No one who lived through that evening will ever forget that fearful and awe-inspiring sight. Like a lofty cresset, the tower at intervals shot up pillars of fire against the night sky. A thick shower of sparks rained down all about the west door, and even threatened to set alight the records of the Cathedral, which had been heaped behind the iron railings round the palace forecourt. A huge conflagration had turned the whole roof of the Cathedral into a lake of fire, which, by an untimely and rising storm, was blown wildly hither and thither. Were the prophecies of the Blessed Anna Catharine Emmerick[1] now come to fulfilment? She had foretold a rain of fire and the burning of the Cathedral roof, in the sixtieth year before 2000, when Hell would be let loose. Powerless and helpless, one stood there and beheld the abomination of desolation in the holy places.

Towards 9 p.m. we had found a first refuge in the Ludgerianum. The Auxiliary Bishop had been overtaken by the raid while in the pulpit at Roxel, and had joined us in our shelter. He, too, like nearly all the other clergy of the Cathedral, stood before the grave of his earthly goods. At the Ludgerianum there was no artificial light and no piped water; we could only wash our hands and face in pails. There till 2 a.m. we watched the activities of the fire-brigades on the Cathedral Square. Then the Bishop went down to the cellar, where a capitular of the cathedral, Canon Emmerich, who had been severely injured in his flat, had died the same afternoon. About the same time that he was hit, another bomb, exploding on the Promenade, had killed another member of the chapter, Canon Diekamp, who was well known as a professor of Dogmatic Theology, even beyond the German frontiers. Besides these, two priests, Professor Vrede and Father Hautkappe, tutor to the theological students, had fallen victims to the raid. Quite tired-out, the Bishop laid himself down on an old sofa that stood in a corner of the cellar, and so spent the later hours of the night. In a neighbouring room there were camp-beds belonging to the

[1] Translator's note: An Augustinian nun, stigmatic, and ecstatic, b. 1774 at Flamsche in the diocese of Münster, d. at Dülmen 1824. In 1892 the process of her beatification was introduced by the Bishop of Münster.

ambulance trainees; here we lay down in our clothes: there was no thought of sleep. Spontaneously there welled up from the depths of our hearts a *Te Deum* for our almost miraculous rescue on that afternoon of death. We seemed to behold, looming ghost-like in the blood-red night sky, the threat of Adolf Hitler, 'I will raze out their cities (*Ich werde ihre Städte ausradieren*).' Like a horrible echo rang the voice of the Minister of Propaganda from the Sportpalast in Berlin: 'Do you trust the Führer? Do you want total war?' The fanatic, misguided and maddened crowd had yelled out, 'Yes.' The wireless had borne the songs of hatred through the world. Can one reap love, when one has sown hate? Now the German people saw their cathedrals burn down.

At dawn the work of digging out began again. The Bishop washed his hands in a pail that Father Roth had filled from a watercart. Then, stiff from his night in the cellerage, he climbed slowly up the stairs to the chapel of the Ludgerianum, there to celebrate the Holy Sacrifice. Outside was a picture of desolation. The first rays of the sun broke through the clouds of smoke that still drifted upwards. Dust and sickening stench of burning yet filled the air. The firemen were still busy. Here and there they were rolling up their hoses, or seeking out fresh sources of water; even the Aa was dry. In the small hours, the artistic pediment over the entrance to the episcopal palace, with the carved lions and the date 1732, had fallen headlong into the forecourt. It would have crushed a watchman, had he not had the presence of mind to spring backward into the doorway. During the morning the Bishop spoke with Regent Francken, the Principal of the Theological College, as to removal into that building. The salved furniture was stored, partly in the presbytery at Gimbte, partly with farmers, named Horstmann and Bölling, at Altenberg-Hansell. The population, even outside Münster, took a very cordial interest in the fate of their spiritual ruler. On the Sunday evening foreign broadcasts had already announced the destruction of the Cathedral and of the palace. Thence again and again came anxious enquiries: 'Was the Bishop safe? How was he? Where was he?' Many people, above all, naturally, apprehensive women, insisted that he absolutely must, as soon as a full alarm were sounded, leave Münster by car: that was what the Nazi party-leaders did. It was not always easy to put aside such well-meant advice as inadmissible. In order to inform passers-by quickly and without trouble, a board was hung up on the iron gate of the forecourt with a notice, 'The Bishop is well and is living at the Theological College.' How often during the next few days one heard the exclamation, 'Thank God,' with a sigh of relief. Two louts, belonging to the Hitler Youth, who could not in passing suppress a derogatory remark, narrowly escaped from grown-up passers-by the cuffing they richly deserved.

As by a miracle, the Bishop had been saved. In the funeral sermon for all who died on that 10th of October, he spoke of the moments he had spent in the shadow of death. 'When I stood on that upper floor and the cloud of dust covered me, when everything was clattering down, I could see nothing at all and did not know what the next second might bring, an instinctive prayer rose to my lips, "Lord Jesus, have Mercy!" That is a consolation for us all. Thus will those have prayed whom death has taken from us. The Lord will have been a Merciful Judge to them.' The faithful, who thronged the church, were moved to tears, but also deeply comforted by the Bishop's words.

The ancient and venerable picture of Our Lady of Consolation from the Convent of Vinnenberg, that stood on the Bishop's writing-table, had been hurled into the abyss and destroyed, but had, so his faithful people believed, guarded him from death. That he had received a wound in his left thigh, his household only found out a week later, when the pain and the resulting lameness could no longer be hidden. Then medical help was called in. This again showed that the Bishop paid too little regard to his bodily condition. It had always been his principle, that the body was there to serve, not to dictate.

The two dead capitulars of the cathedral, Diekamp and Emmerich, had been buried; their spiritual chief in a funeral

sermon at St. Ludger's had bidden his friends a last laudatory
farewell. Father Emmerich's body had been carried out of
the cellar of the Ludgerianum into the sacristy of the Cathedral;
only a few clergy followed the coffin through the ruins in the
Cathedral Square; a pathetic cortège. The cathedral-vicars,
Holling and Leiwering, had themselves dug the graves in the
churchyard appropriated to the cathedral-chapter. When the
coffins had been lowered and the vicar of the cathedral-parish
spoke the final words, 'Let us pray for him among us who will
be first to die,' his voice trembled and he burst into tears.

On that Sunday in October the Sisterhood of St. Clement
had drunk the cup of suffering nearly to the dregs. Mothers
Superior from all parts of the diocese were gathered together
for religious exercises and consultation in the Mother-house.
There suddenly death swooped upon more than fifty of them,
among them the Mother Superior of the Province. The
coffins stood open in the Hall on the 16th of October, when
the Bishop knelt there. In a chapel hastily prepared, he had
already celebrated a Requiem Mass and had commemorated
these virgins in an address broken by sobs. 'On Sunday afternoon,' he said, 'a procession of innocent souls entered into
Heaven.' As though to justify himself for so often revealing
compassion and inward emotion, he added that Christ Himself
had wept at the grave of Lazarus, so a mere man need not be
ashamed to shed tears.

When on that same morning the Bishop visited the Vicar-
General, then lodged in the German Students' Hostel, he was
once again oppressed by regret that the bishopric should have
lost so many valuable and irreplaceable documents, and also
that his personal notes on the strife against National Socialism
should have disappeared. The destruction of his furniture and
of objects of artistic, or purely sentimental, value troubled him
far less. How often in the preceding years I had begged him for
leave to take old family portraits or valuable books into some
safer place! He always smiled, said he was old and would not
need that lumber for long. If God willed that it should perish,
well and good. He thought and spoke just the same when the

question was discussed of storing the invaluable works of art in the diocese in places of safety: 'One immortal soul is worth more than all the art that critics and historians worry about so much.' He spoke thus, although, as a Count of the old nobility, he valued history, tradition and culture very highly; but, as a bishop, he held the care of souls infinitely above them. A singular personal experience brought impressively home to the Auxiliary Bishop, Monsignor Roleff, the wisdom of disregarding all that is earthly as transitory and worthless. In the ruins of his chancery he found a charred leaf out of a book. He picked it up and read the first words, 'He to whom nothing is enough, lacks everything; he to whom anything is enough, lacks nothing.' Indeed at times when one has lost everything and must look around for the primary needs of existence, such sayings are a kind of consolatory wisdom.

The days and weeks after Oct. 10th passed by. Almost without a break the autumn sun shone on the episcopal city and the Cathedral Square. This fine weather rendered it much easier to dig out furniture and carry it away when it had been stacked on the pavements. With the help of Ukrainian prisoners, a safe was rescued from the cellars of the palace. The valuable contents were for the most part intact, including a crozier, a typewriter and other objects. The Spiegelturm had been wholly demolished and the water-mains had to be renewed. A way was therefore made for people to pass on foot from the Cathedral Square across the courtyard of the Ludgerianum, thence through the episcopal garden and park, across the bridge over the Aa on to the church square of Überwasser. As the months followed, the Cathedral Square grew quieter and quieter. Nearly all the diocesan offices had been reduced to ruins. The winds blew the dust about among tufts of coarse grass which sprouted through the gaps and fissures of the flagstones. One saw folk come with a sickle and a sack, cut their sackful of herbage and go away. The grass grew tallest among the ruins of the palace, between shattered beams and split blocks of masonry: a few statues stood upright, St. Joseph, St. Paul, St. Ludger. The hallowed centre of the cathedral-city had become a wilderness and a graveyard. The two horses belonging to the ambulance company grazed in the quiet of that strange pasture. Sometimes a soldier lay on the ground and wrote a privileged letter. Then the advancing spring clad and wreathed everything in plants and flowers. The birds sang as they had sung the year before. Nature went on her way and adorned with her gifts the works of men and their graves. The war went on. The city, making atonement with her faithful people, was doomed to drift yet further into the valley of the shadow of death.

CHAPTER 18

THE TWO TOWERS

ON Oct. 11th, the Feast of the Maternity of the Blessed Virgin, the Bishop had gone through the still glowing and smoking ruins of the Cathedral Square and the Spiegelturm to the Church of Überwasser. There, where his revered parents had so often knelt, he thanked the Lord God in silent worship for the almost miraculous saving of his life. In the neighbouring Theological College the new living-rooms stood ready for him, also for his chaplain and the staff of the episcopal palace. On the same storey and only a few yards from the Bishop's rooms, quarters had also been made ready for the Provost, Dr. Donders. We all remember what primitive forms in those weeks life had assumed: no piped water-supply, no artificial light, windows and doors temporarily repaired to keep out the cold. It hurt one's feelings to watch these elderly gentlemen groping about in all this muddle with a candle. When the sirens howled a full alarm, during supper, perhaps, or in the middle of the night, these two, the Bishop and the Provost of his Cathedral, came down into the cellars. The Bishop carried in his hand a large old-fashioned lantern (how scarce pocket-torches had become!); one heard his slow, stiff footsteps strike nearer and nearer on the stone stairs. A neighbour was knocking at the same time on the outer door of the cellar and asking to be let in. Cupboards and stacks of trunks, dragged in from the surrounding buildings, stood against the walls. We clergy sat on chairs and benches in the middle round the Bishop and the Provost; besides, there were Father Höping of Überwasser with his curates, generally also two accountants from the military pay-office, quartered in the College. When the Vice-Principal, Dr. Gleumes, was on furlough from his duties as a military chaplain, he also turned in sometimes, but only shortly before the bombs fell. In an adjoining cellar there were Sisters, lodged in the Theological College, and many neighbours, among them the College Principal. How many a rosary was said there, how much distress and anxiety gone through! The

radio-announcer proclaimed: 'Onset on city precincts. . . .
Go to your shelters. . . . A raid is imminent.'

Then (who will ever forget it?) the uncanny quaking of
the ground, the shaking of the walls, the banging of the doors.
How deeply we breathed again, when, after twenty or thirty
minutes, perhaps an hour, of suspense and fear of death, we
could once more leave the cellar. Through a whole year, till
Oct. 14th, 1944, the Bishop here lived through the raids on
Münster with their nerve-racking alternate depression and
relief. Up till Feb. 1944 the Provost stayed at his side. A
young man of Münster, who felt a deep spiritual debt to these
two great churchmen, compared them with the two soaring
towers of the Cathedral.

Since 1911 Dr. Donders, Sunday after Sunday, had stood
in the pulpit of the Cathedral. His sermons at 11 o'clock,
delivered with a remarkably powerful and flexible voice, had
become an institution. In all those years he was never weary,
as a teacher of truth, of pointing out to the thousands who
flocked to the Cathedral the true way through the perplexities
of the modern world. When National Socialism raised its head,
he was well aware of the mission and responsibility of a cathedral pulpit in such times of strife, and never faltered in telling
the truth openly against the new heathendom. How many who
sat under him were grateful, when, with an intellectual power
which left no possibility of misunderstanding, he set forth the
strength and depth of Christianity against the pinchbeck
glitter of a spurious religion, like the movement towards so-
called Teutonic Beliefs.[1] How many he saved from backsliding
and apostasy! The enemies of the Church also knew that. They
knew (one of their leaders often admitted it) that the Provost,
by his constant and repeated refutation from the pulpit,
provoked as dangerous a wavering in their ranks as the Bishop,
when he struck out with harder, but rarer, blows. They would
therefore have much liked to reduce him to silence, as they had
many another priest in the land; but courage failed them, for
they were quite as well aware how deeply the people loved and

[1] *Vide* Appendix.

revered him, as how dangerous his intellectual opposition was to their opinions.

To people who have lived at Münster there is no need to say that, except the Bishop, none of the diocesan clergy enjoyed such high esteem and such enthusiastic affection as Provost Donders. No less a man than the Bishop said one day that, were he not the Bishop, he would attend every Sunday at Donders' sermon; so great was the respect and regard he felt for that highly gifted preacher. With what reverence and devotion the Provost reciprocated those feelings, everyone must know who had lived for any length of time in the intimate circle of those two great men. A wonderful bond of mutual esteem and loyalty, one may say, bound them to each other through a difficult period. Inspired by a like love for Christ and His Church, each fought in his own way the fight against Satan and his followers; like unbreachable dykes, they held back the rising flood of Anti-Christ. They had the sacred mission to be leaders, and, by their shining example of fearlessness and endurance, to impart trust, sureness and confidence to their flock. That privilege God vouchsafed to them both.

. . . . .

On that fatal Saturday in October the Provost was staying outside Münster, but that afternoon's disaster dealt him a spiritual blow from which he never recovered. When he returned on the morrow, the north tower and his own house adjoining it had been burnt out: only the bare walls were left. He was bereft not only of his personal belongings, his clothes, furniture, books, his large store of manuscripts; far worse, his beloved Cathedral and his pulpit were gone. The days and weeks after that day of horror were for the Provost one long agony of decline. When priests from outside Münster saw him, they were shocked at his altered appearance. How weary and bent his tall and strongly built figure had become! The sight of such barbarism and brutality had stricken to the heart this deep-feeling man, who partook in all the sufferings of his fellows. The faculty of sharing the needs and distresses of others had been the inspiration of his preaching: the imaginative sympathy, which had been his strength, now, in the presence of so much misery and devastation, became his weakness. The pulpit of the Cathedral was shattered and in all that spacious and venerable building lay the abomination of desolation. Nevertheless he would not give up, but pull his strength together and work on, until the Lord Himself bade him to stop. On the Sunday after Oct. 10th, he mounted the pulpit of St. Joseph's and then, when Christmas drew near, he gathered the faithful about him in the Church of the Holy Cross. That was his last pulpit and there his last sermons were delivered. From those sermons he came back with staggering steps and his forehead bathed in sweat. The zeal of the Lord's House had devoured him.

Late in the evening of Feb. 14th, 1944, our revered Provost suffered the stroke which paralysed his left side and took away the power of calling aloud for help. The next morning, when he did not arrive in due time for the celebration of Mass at St. Mary's Church, he was sought for and found lying helpless on the floor of his bedroom at the Theological College. Soon after midday, the Bishop gave his Provost the Last Sacraments. The sick man repeated the prayers for the dying in a calm and clear voice. He was then laid on a stretcher and carried to the Hospital of St. Raphael. In the following days and weeks it became evident, often in a most moving way, how deep the spiritual figure of the Provost lived in the hearts of the people. In the streets men and women of all classes stood still to enquire anxiously after his condition. They went on their way sorrowfully, when they had to hear the tidings that it was God's Will that, with the end of the Cathedral, the earthly life of its great preacher should end also. On a morning in spring, an ambulance bore away the dying Provost from his beloved city. In the little township of Langenhorst, beyond the danger of air-raids, he was welcomed with affection by his nearest kinsfolk. During the following months the Bishop visited him several times in company with the Auxiliary Bishop and Regent Francken. How pathetic was the slow flickering out of this great light, which for so many years had shone so clear before men! The Provost lost his voice. The gifted preacher, from whose lips the words had flowed in so wonderful a stream, became, by the inscrutable decree of Providence, bereft of articulate speech: only an incomprehensible muttering was left. He had wished to be buried in the little churchyard at Langenhorst in the shadow of the old church. When, however, the Bishop expressed a wish that his grave should be near the towers of the cathedral, he at once agreed.

On August 9th, 1944, the Lord took His faithful servant into His Kingdom. Deep sorrow spread through the whole cathedral-city and throughout the diocese. The coffin stood closed in St. Stephen's chapel in the cathedral. On the Sunday before the funeral people filed past it as in a procession. Beside it stood the medieval cross, dedicated as a thankoffering for deliverance from the plague. Those who had passed wrote their names on a register; they wished to record beyond the grave their faithfulness and gratitude to the great man who was dead. On Aug. 14th the Bishop celebrated the Requiem in St. Stephen's chapel. In spite of the constant peril from air-raids, the faithful stood closely crowded up to the steps of the altar, when the Bishop spoke the text of the panegyric: 'He who sows sparingly will reap sparingly; he who sows freely will reap freely, too.' (Cor. II, 9, 6.) 'How often during thirty-three years did this time-honoured building resound to the tones of his voice! On nearly every Sunday and Festival, he proclaimed to the thousands who stood thronged before his pulpit that divine Gospel, which, with unwearied study and prayer, he had searched and meditated. In this venerable Cathedral of St. Paul we have entombed the body of the dead Provost. Alas, in one corner only of this glorious building can we hold his burial service. . . . The frightful disaster that has fallen upon Münster and this Cathedral smote with a deadly wound the heart of this righteous man, weakened already by compassion with the sufferings of our sorely-tried Church in Germany and the sufferings of the German people in war. After twenty-five weeks of severe illness, borne with a heroic spirit of self-sacrifice, the Lord of the harvest called him home to reap his everlasting recompense.'

When the coffin was carried by six priests to the burial ground of the cathedral clergy, the wailing tones of the damaged cathedral organ rang out for the last time. The left tower on that August morning soared, gaunt and fire-scarred, against the sky; a few martins flew twittering around it. It had become a symbol: one of the two human pillars of the Cathedral had likewise been stricken.

The other tower still stood. It stood unharmed till Palm Sunday in 1945. Then that tower likewise was burnt out. The huge bell, dedicated in memory of the Confessor-Bishop, Johann Bernard, fell and melted in the furnace. About a year later, the Cardinal made his entry into his episcopal city. His throne stood on the ruins of the west door, overshadowed by the bare walls of the towers. Three days afterwards, he was driven, dangerously ill, in an ambulance to the hospital. As he lay on the stretcher, he said, 'Perhaps you will have to bury me in one of the Cathedral towers.'

The towers are, as it were, symbols of two men, who lived and strove in a difficult time and then, in a way that men call tragic, were summoned from this world. The towers were burnt out, but their bare walls yet abide and point Heavenward. Abiding, too, is the heritage of those great churchmen. It lays a sacred duty on us all to rise up out of the suffering of our time, and build again bravely in the spirit that moved them.

CHAPTER 19

SENDENHORST

AUTUMN had come in 1944. For a whole year Münster had undergone no air-raid on a large scale. Many people believed that the Allies would keep up the pace of their progress through France and Belgium and seek a decision on land in the heart of Germany. During those breathless weeks of their advance since June, the bombardment of our cities had almost ceased. Then came the turning-point. The enemy halted on our Western frontier and the war from the air entered on its most frightful stage. Here are a few entries taken at random from my diary: Feast of the Holy Name of Mary, Sept. 12th, 1944, 6.30 p.m. 'The greatest air-raid on Münster till now. The presbyteries of St. Anthony, St. Joseph and St. Elizabeth almost wholly burnt down. At 6 p.m. the full alarm had sounded. A few scouting planes could be seen from the front windows of the Theological College. Trails of smoke: a splendid sunset: a squadron of bombers to the south; warning by wireless: "Small flight of fighter planes from neighbourhood of Dülmen making toward provincial capital." Down to the cellar. Anti-aircraft fire. Warning: "Fresh flights of aircraft toward the town from the south-west." The first bombs fall. The women pray out loud and crouch down on the floor. At short intervals over and over again a screeching and whistling down of bombs, many rather near: the doors rattle: the electric light goes out: The raid lasted about twelve minutes: Theological College unharmed. We climbed up the tower of the Überwasser Church. There was still anti-aircraft fire in the distance: Thick smoke over the neighbourhood of the railway-station: all the way from the Church of the Sacred Heart to the Lake of the Aa widespread fires were breaking out: meanwhile a continual succession of explosions: a train laden with ammunition had been hit by incendiary bombs. . . .'

On that evening the south-western quarter of the town had become a landscape of craters. On the 19th of September a Pontifical Requiem Mass was celebrated for those who died on the

143

12th. Bishop Roleff preached the funeral sermon. On the 30th a further raid followed on a large scale. Precisely where the last raid had stopped the work of further destruction now began, so that it looked as if Münster were to be systematically blotted out. On that Saturday afternoon high-explosive bombs struck the chief market place and the Cathedral Square. One of them tore down the west doorway of the cathedral, with the splendid stonework relief of Christ's Entry into Jerusalem. The bombs that fell on the district round the Church of the Holy Cross were mostly incendiaries. On Oct. 5th followed the heaviest attack with high-explosives on the inner city up till then. The Church of Überwasser, in which since Easter divine service had been resumed, was again put out of use. The Borromäum, in whose right wing the office of the Vicar-General was housed, underwent two direct hits. Day after day, the sirens howled the full alarm. Huge squadrons flew over Western Germany as far as Berlin. The Bishop sat for many hours of the day in the cellar of the Theological College. The wireless, owing to the current being repeatedly cut off, was usually not working, so that we got no warning beforehand about what would happen in the air and we had to reckon therefore with possible raids all the time. Even if one chose to disregard the wearing effect on the nerves of continually squatting in a cellar, the administration of the diocese grew quite impossible. A step, which no one had foreseen, became in this crisis an urgent necessity: the official residence of the bishopric had to be transferred elsewhere. After tedious and widespread enquiries and investigations, the Vicar-General, Canon Meis, concluded that the Institute at Sendenhorst, a township lying 22 kms. to the south-east, would be the most suitable site for the diocesan administration. It followed that the Bishop must also now leave Münster. He still withstood strongly the idea of forsaking the city, but Regent Francken brought forward decisive arguments: the cellar of the Theological College afforded too little shelter, the Bishop must no longer take the responsibility of hazarding his life, the welfare of the diocese imperatively required the evacuation. With a heavy heart the Bishop took the resolution to part from his flock.

10. Cardinal von Galen just before he made his journey to Rome

11. Cardinal von Galen at the moment of receiving the Red Hat, kneeling before His Holiness
Pius XII, February 1946

On the general policy of the authorities towards the Church at the time, the following document is very instructive: Lieut.-General Faeckenstedt warrants that it is genuine.

Extract from an official record of Lt.-Gen. Faeckenstedt, C. of General Staff, Military District VI.

Münster. Oct. 2. 1944.

On Sept. 30th a conference was held near Oldenburg on board the armoured train 'Styria', in the compartment of the Commander-in-Chief of the Reserve Army and National Head of the S.S. Heinrich Himmler. At this conference there was a difference of opinion between the Head of the S.S. and Lt.-Gen. Faeckenstedt, whose dismissal from his military appointment was ordered on the ground of political untrustworthiness. In the course of this difference, Himmler expressed himself much as follows:

'Holding that appointment, you cannot cultivate relations with a traitor to his country, like Bishop Count Galen. The whole clique (he meant leading circles in Westphalia) has a way of thinking hostile to the State, as he has. They won't cram that down your throat. The Church alone is to blame that Germany's course was so unfortunate until National Socialism came along. The Führer has met with nothing but opposition, like many Emperors in the Middle Ages, like Bismarck. For 1500 years the Catholic Church has been the chief hindrance to the inner development of Germany.' When I took strong objection to that view, the Head of the S.S. broke me off sharply. 'The whole set are enemies of the State. We couldn't settle accounts with the traitor Galen for reasons of foreign policy. We shall catch up with him later on, and the whole Church with him and the gang that is backing it. There will be a thorough liquidation in that quarter. I cannot put up with your attitude as a general. I have had enough of religious generals and officers in any rank whatever, more especially since that treacherous gang in July were convicted. It was laughable to see how those fellows clung to their church-habits. One general went over to another religion because his wife belonged to it. He believed most likely that he would get a seat on a cloud in heaven by her side. One can't help laughing at the notion a general like that has of God. Stauffenberg even wore a gold cross on a chain round his neck. That murderer! But we shall clear all that out. . . .'

K

Early in the morning of Oct. 14th, a Saturday, the Bishop got up into a delivery-van and drove, unaccompanied, with such light luggage as the hail of bombs had left him, to Sendenhorst, where the offices of the Vicar-General had been accommodated in a few rooms of the hospital. Part of the episcopal staff found quarters in Albersloh, the diocesan officials in Gimbte and Greven. The van stopped at the side-entrance to the St. Joseph Institute. The Marist Father Boesch, who had been deported by the Gestapo and was staying in the hospital, happened to come that way. He led the distinguished guest to his lodging.

First of all the Bishop went to the chapel of the institution. He bore thither in his breast-pocket a relic of St. Ludger, of which he had taken charge the day before. He had given another relic to a priest, who had worked in his immediate circle and now had to part from him. Father Huthmacher, the spiritual director of the St. Joseph Institute, and Father Westermann, the Rector of Sendenhorst, welcomed the Bishop in the two rooms which the Institute, although overcrowded with patients and refugees, had been able to clear for him. Beside the small bedroom, which was also to serve as a study and reception-room, there was a larger room in which the Bishop took his meals together with the Vicar-General and Monsignor Hugenroth and Councillor Gelhaus, who were resident at Sendenhorst.

·   ·   ·   ·   ·

In these rooms the heart of the diocese of Münster was to beat through long and anxious months. Many a priest came there, laden and oppressed by the pain and sorrow of those days, which brought the frightful climax of the War's events. The Bishop reassured them, gave them advice and help, as far as he could; then they went back to the scene of action, the industrial districts or the Lower Rhine. But many, who wished to come, could not owing to the growing difficulty of transport. So in the following weeks and months the Bishop was beset more and more by a kind of isolation and sorrowful loneliness. This was aggravated by uncertainty as to the fate of his brother Franz, who had been arrested in connection with the events of

July and conveyed to the concentration camp at Oranienburg. In July of 1945 the two brothers had the great joy of meeting again at Sendenhorst.

The tidings that reached the Bishop grew ever gloomier and more sinister. The Front drew nearer, the bombardment of the towns became more and more intense. Old men and young girls, equipped with picks and shovels, were driven off to the Western Front, where they were to throw up an impassable barrier of resistance in the guise of tank-traps and suchlike. The armoured Atlantic Wall, built up through many years by a gigantic army, had not held, but these holes in the ground and little heaps of mould were to break the mass onset of the enemy.

This chaos, which was ever growing more dreadful, this flood, in which the German people would inevitably be drowned, the Bishop watched day after day. More and more painfully the cross of these sufferings weighed upon his shoulders, when of an afternoon he walked up and down the silent paths of the hospital garden and said his rosary. He thought of Münster, whither a car took him from time to time. Regent Francken had stayed there in charge of the Theological College and of the Cathedral. He sat through the winter afternoons in the basement of the College, beside an old stove in a kind of lumber-room. Regularly Father Holstein from the Church of the Holy Cross and Father Uppenkamp of St. Lambert's joined him. The River Aa had overflowed its banks in the late autumn and the basement of the College stood wholly under water. The Vice-Rector, Dr. Gleumes, in a bathing costume waded into the cold waters of the cellar to fetch potatoes for cooking. One day, while suchlike depressing pictures were passing through the Bishop's mind, he suddenly looked up: a priest from the Lower Rhine stood before him. He had been compulsorily evacuated from his home-town, together with his parishioners. He was on his way to a place near Magdeburg. How could he there do his duty by his parishioners, how and where could he hold services in a neighbourhood where there were no Catholics?

During those winter months cases with the requisites for celebrating Mass were hastily got ready. Guilds for church embroidery at Emsdetten, Greven, Borghorst, Oelde and

Ibbenbüren worked feverishly to provide the priests with what was indispensable in vestments and sacred vessels. Through snow and ice, young people on bicycles brought what they had gathered together to the Bishop at Sendenhorst. In those months, before one problem could be solved, another took its place.

But, in spite of all, the Bishop did not falter or give way. Even in the last weeks of the War, a steadfast faith and trust in God never forsook him. Sirens howled, enemy squadrons gave forth the sinister roar of their approach, from a clear sky fell the foretokens of attack, pointing like bloodless fingers on the works of man appointed to destruction, low-flying airmen with clattering engines scattered their fire-sowing sheaves, showers of phosphorus poured down on Münster, Hamm and Dortmund, 'the Christmas trees' over the canal at Greven turned night into day with their unholy flame, the burning episcopal city signalled as with murky torches the message of suffering and death, the maimed and sick in the great hospital shook and trembled in their beds, children, waking in terror, prayed and cried, priests, doctors and sisters, nurses, both men and women, gave themselves unsparingly to the work of rescue with self-forgetting devotion, the great building quaked to the foundations from the bursting bombs. Through all this uproar and chaos the Bishop knelt in the chapel before the Blessed Sacrament. God alone could help; men had become mad. In those weeks radiated from that lofty figure on everyone in the hospital a peculiar calm, sureness and serenity. As a priest well said, one saw a saying of Holy Writ literally fulfilled: 'There appeared a man with grey hairs and exceeding glorious, who was of a wonderful and excellent majesty. . . . This is a lover of the brethren, who prayeth much for the people and for the holy city.'

The great well-spring of power in those sorrowful days was the Holy Sacrifice in the morning. A priest, who at that time was an eye-witness at Sendenhorst, wrote: 'It was a striking sight, when, at the ringing of a bell in the sacristy, behind the short-stepping figures of the servers, this giant appeared with

his long strides. The impression deepened, as one grew aware
of the halo of manly devotion which seemed to enfold the
Bishop yet more solemnly than his liturgical vestments. To
such shoulders as that one could attribute the strength to bear a
heavy cross, such hands as that could be entrusted with a cup
of bitter sacrifice. The atmosphere, which the celebrating
Bishop by his bearing alone could diffuse, drew more and
more of the faithful to the morning Mystery.'

In those weeks, which often seemed to him like banishment
to a desert island, the chapel was the Bishop's favourite spot.
Everyone at St. Joseph's knew that, if the Bishop were wanted
and were not found in his room, he would certainly be found
in the chapel. This emphatic orientation of spirit toward God
and Eternity in no wise impaired his human kindliness to those
about him: to the children, whom his great bulk did not
frighten, because his friendly smile drew them towards him,
to the sick, for whom he always added an affectionate word to
his blessing, to the Sisters of the Good Shepherd from Münster,
to the Sisters of the Visitation from Uedem, who were staying
at St. Joseph's as fugitives. In the scullery of the hospital there
was a female factotum, known as Aunt Agnes, whose limited
intellect was a source of amusement, not only to others, but
even to herself. One afternoon Aunt Agnes turned up at the
Bishop's room to put up a new black-out contrivance. As this
was rather hard to fix up, she could think of no better plan than
to rope in the Bishop himself and addressed him as follows in
the Westphalian dialect. 'Bishop, can't you help me with the
black-out? It's so hard to do it alone.' The Bishop answered in
the same dialect, 'Yes, Agnes, I'll willingly help you with it.'
(*'Bischof, kannst du mi nich es helpen bi de Verdunkelung; dat geiht
sau slecht allene?' Der Bischof: 'Jau, Agnes, gän well ich di dobi
helpen.'*)

Many times in the parish church of Sendenhorst the Bishop
celebrated Mass and preached, addressing special words of
comfort to the fugitives from Münster. During Passion-week,
shortly before the Allies marched in, that church witnessed on
Maundy Thursday a ceremony peculiarly moving in those

hours of anxiety, the consecration of the Holy Oils for the whole diocese. On that morning priests had come from many parts of it to fetch the Oils, when they had been consecrated. They brought the alarming news with them, 'They are already at Dülmen, at Coesfeld.' People stood in knots in the streets. They saw our weary soldiers drive past on primitive vehicles; they saw the depressed and irresolute looks of the men called up from the Last Reserve (*Volkssturm*). The confusion grew worse and worse. Conflicting streams of emotion coursed through men's minds; at the same hour they were racked with anxiety and breathed a sigh of relief: 'Let us hope things will go quickly and well.' What of the Bishop? Some words he had spoken on Maundy Thursday were prophetic. When he was told that soon the hour of liberation would strike, he only answered: 'Ah, and when will our poor prisoners come home? And how many won't be there! This is only a turn in the road, not the end of it.' When we parted at noon on that day, tears stood in his eyes.

On Easter Sunday, March 31st, at two o'clock in the afternoon, the first heavy American tanks rolled slowly past the front of St. Joseph's at Sendenhorst. It was an unforgettable hour, full of the utmost tension; men hoped and feared and breathed again. Patients too ill to walk had been carried down into the cellars. Those who could move about lined the doors and windows, or ventured into the forecourt, into the vicinity of that rolling destiny. They were freed from the fear of death, but seemed as if paralysed by this unwonted and sinister sight. The Bishop had looked for a moment or two through the windows onto the street. Then, says an eye-witness, he turned pale, walked silently to the chapel, knelt down there and covered his face with his hands. On the Sunday morning that England and France declared war against Hitler's Germany, when the wireless broadcast these shattering tidings to the world, he had uttered the foreseeing words: '*Finis Germaniae* (Germany's End).' For the Bishop, whose love for his country and countrymen stood beyond all doubt, it was a true *via dolorosa*, to watch through all those years, how the criminal followers of a tyrant with no true patriotism, by their systematic and consistent brutality, dragged Germany down into the abyss. How he, of all men, suffered from the rift which clove the spirit of all honourable men; on the one hand the patriotic duty in war of military service for the safety and protection of the home-country and, on the other hand, to have to say to themselves, on sober reflection, that the fulfilment of that moral obligation brought daily renewed strength to a criminal administration and supplied the foundations on which to consolidate a satanic rule and spread its dreadful abuses over guiltless neighbours! Here lay the appalling tragedy. Men who offered up in honourable intent all that was good, great, nay heroic in them, indeed sacrificed their own lives, on the altar of their fatherland, inevitably raised up the leaders of National Socialism, which they hated in their inmost souls, to victory and success. How many a soldier marched to the Front with his spirit thus cloven! How many a soldier-priest could on this very ground never be content with his military life: he was aware that he was helping to load the pistols that would some day be pointed at Christians. The Bishop, in order to restore the moral balance of priests with that outlook, always affirmed that their vocation was to help their comrades by their spiritual and medical ministrations. During the early years of the War, he cherished the unexpressed wish that some day the National-Socialist leadership might be swept aside by a military government and thus that Germany, by a compromise peace, might be preserved from total downfall. For him there could be no question that Germany and Europe must be freed from Hitler and his satellites. But how? When people about him put forward the view that Hitler could only be displaced from outside, i.e. by the complete overthrow of Germany, the Bishop always pointed out that an unconditional capitulation and surrender would have unthinkable consequences: 'Not for a handful of Nazis, the real culprits, but for the whole unhappy German people.' How often he spoke in that strain, or at least to that effect! After the Idealists of July 1944 had paid for their patriotism by their death, it seemed clear that Hitler could only be deposed from power by the action of foreign armies.

These days for the Bishop grew more and more gloomy. He did not consider that our soldiers ought to withstand the

enemy's advance even in the last ditch; on the contrary he
wished for as rapid an end as possible. But he foresaw that
end as the beginning of long and bitter years of hardship. Woe
to the conquered! How could one expect the enemy Powers to
act otherwise? The Germany of Hitler had sown nothing but
hatred. How could one hope to reap a harvest of love from its
opponents? They moreover had also been weakened to the
uttermost by their sacrifices in the war. He did not attach much
weight to the amiable words of the foreign wireless propaganda.
It did not veil from his sight the fearful judgment falling on
Germany. Only the principles of Christianity, Righteousness,
Compassion, Charity, could keep the conduct of the visitors
within bounds. As a Bishop, he had warned the holders of
power in the Third Reich of the limits God had set to its use:
now he would not fear to utter the same warning in the sight of
those who had newly acquired it. Thus on that Saturday before
Easter, earnest thoughts of his grave responsibility passed
through his mind. Full of trust, he looked to the altar, the
abode of Him who had been his strength in the past. Now once
more, in the downfall of his fatherland, the Lord would be
with him. . . . And outside the heavy tanks rolled on.

CHAPTER 20

FATHER AND DEFENDER OF THE FATHERLAND

LATE that afternoon rumours reached Sendenhorst that the Bishop was already treating with senior American officers. He was intensely annoyed by this gossip. On that evening of Holy Saturday lurid flames shot up into the Easter sky: they came from burning houses and illumined the Easter night like some uncanny Paschal Fire. . . .

The Bishop retired to his room and wrote the following words (the holograph note was found among his papers after his death. On Easter morning he brought it to the notice of his congregation in the church at Sendenhorst): 'Yesterday the advance troops of our enemies passed through the locality. We must thank God that this city has not suffered any great damage as it did throughout the long years of war. But for me as well as for all of you the memory of this occurrence will long remain a dreadful experience—namely the sight of hostile forces here in our German homeland. It is neither the time nor is here the place to speak of this event, of how our hearts bleed at the dire peril of our people; but necessity demands that I should say this publicly: It has come to my ears that deliberate lies are being spread around to the effect that the Bishop of Münster, together with the head doctor of St. Joseph's Hospital, have established contact with the troops passing through, and have held consultations with them. To this calumny I categorically state that whoever says this or anything approaching it is guilty of deliberate lies. I have neither held nor sought any kind of liaison with them. Should, however, I find that it is in the interests of the Church . . .'. Here the document breaks off.

At about this time a similar false report found its way into the bunker of the Reichs Chancellery affirming that Münster had been handed over to the Allies by its Bishop—an announcement which threw Hitler into a frenzy. 'If I could only catch the fellow I would have him hanged.'

A few days afterwards British and American Press representatives made their appearance. To a Reuter report apropos of this and of some fantastic story of the Bishop's arrest by Himmler's agents the Bishop made his position clear in a public statement of the 9th of April. 'I have announced formally to the gentlemen of the British and American Press visiting me, that as a German bishop, I feel and suffer with my German people, and that I refuse, as long as hostilities continue, to discuss political questions with them, or make any statements. Moreover, it is my express wish that my name should not be mentioned either in the Press or on the Radio. The statements made about me in the Reuter report have no foundation whatsoever, and the tale about the attempt to arrest me is a complete fabrication.'

Owing to the fact that the short conferences which took place at Eastertide were reported in a melodramatic or sensational way, or were distorted and abused, the Bishop from then on refused to receive most of the Pressmen or V.I.P.s coming from the Allied H.Q. in Paris. The well-known emigrant writer, Thomas Mann, expressed his anger against the Bishop for speaking of the Allies as enemies (noch Feinde)—as yet no truce had been concluded—hence, so ran the report, the Bishop must needs also be numbered among the Boeotians. The Germans were not the only ones to take offence at Thomas Mann's attack: they looked upon it as both boorish and tactless, as did also American officers who came to Sendenhorst; they invited the Bishop to give the riposte to the emigré, who (they said) had been able to enjoy life all these years in the safety of the U.S.A. so far from the scene of the shooting. The Bishop discharged himself from this suggestion, which was supported by priests in his immediate circle, with a generous smile, saying that it was not necessary as the affair would settle itself in its own good time; if, however, the fine gentleman on the other side of the Atlantic went on in the same strain the German people could not be blamed for their answer!

As the great host of tanks rolled unceasingly towards the East and the fighting grew less severe round Münster, the Bishop felt more disposed to receive the American Catholic chaplains. Their appearance was an unequivocal and sincere expression of homage to the great Prelate. They brought him various items of news about ecclesiastical affairs in the invaded territories in which they promised to afford all the help they could to German priests who were now prisoners, and were in immediate need of vestments and the sacred vessels necessary for the celebration of Mass. They would also take the Holy Chrism,[1] blessed on Maundy Thursday, to the parish priests of the devastated areas of the Lower Rhine.

On April 12th the Bishop went to Münster for the first time since it had been occupied by the Americans. The object of the visitation was to make a public protest against the excesses of the Russian and Polish workers who, unrestrained by the military, were plundering, torturing and murdering the inhabitants.

The following notes, again in the Cardinal's handwriting, were found among his documents dated April 13th, 1945:

Orally communicated to Colonel Leadenham, Chief of Military Government in Westphalia in Army Administration District Command, Münster:

'I take it for granted that my name is known to you: it appeared often enough on British leaflets and radio. I fought against the German Government on the side of truth, freedom and justice, and I am doing the same now against the Occupying Forces. You have entered a Christian country and we intend to obey your authority. But it is the fundamental task and duty of the said military authority to maintain public safety and to protect life and property from unnecessary outrage, destruction and plunder. *First: The Foreign Workers.* They steal out of necessity. A difficult problem to procure shelter and food for them; but obviously a preliminary measure was feasible, viz., they should not be allowed to leave their quarters at night. *Second: American soldiers (Negroes).* They plunder wantonly. It is incomprehensible that so little discipline is exercised, especially at night. On April 10th, four girls were raped in Sendenhorst. *Profanation of Churches.* More control must be exerted during leave time, especially during the hours of darkness; there are not

[1] Translator's note: A mixture of oil of olives and balsam consecrated on Holy Thursday by the bishop and used for the administration of certain sacraments, etc.

enough sentries and pickets. We did not believe German spokesmen when they assured us there was neither rape nor plunder in the East and West during the war; but we did believe the British Radio when it said that Allied troops were coming to restore justice and freedom in Germany and that its inhabitants would be decently treated. If vigorous steps are not immediately taken to stop the violation of women and wholesale looting then we shall be forced to believe the warnings of Nazi propaganda. Our people will be driven to hate and adopt retaliatory measures (e.g. werewolves); In despair they will turn to Bolshevism.'

In the time to come the Bishop made repeated visits of this sort to the Allied commanders. He looked upon himself not only as a shepherd of souls, but also as the appointed protector of his fellow citizens and countrymen—a veritable *Landesvater*[1] —there being no one else who seemed willing to play such a role. Military Government respected the Bishop and did not press their restrictions too severely: they honoured him for his fight against the Nazi criminals. On April 19th the American Military Governor came to see him at the St. Joseph Hospital, and a few hours later the American Commandant in Sendenhorst paid a similar courtesy visit.

During the early part of summer the Americans were replaced by the Belgians and British respectively. Sudden attacks and looting raids by Russians and Poles increased and often took place in broad daylight. They were the terror of the Münster area. On June 12th when the newly appointed parish priest of Haldern in Niederrhein was cycling to Sendenhorst he was set upon by Russians, robbed and beaten-up. He arrived at the St. Joseph Hospital, bleeding profusely from a deep knife-wound in the back, and was at once treated by Dr. Lintel-Höping. In the meantime Father Boesch had lodged a complaint with the Belgian officers of the guard and the delinquents were taken in charge. After a short interval a Belgian officer appeared, announced the arrest and punishment of the Russian bandits, and returned the stolen property. The lieutenant conducted himself with military correctness, and as a Catholic showed a proper respect for the Bishop who expressed his thanks for the prompt action taken. He took the opportunity of urging stronger protective measures for the populace

[1] Translator's note: A father of his people. Students' song.

and the confiscation of all weapons from the Russians. When the lieutenant replied with some embarrassment that he thought it useless to search Russian camps the Bishop retorted sternly and not without irony, 'When the Germans have only a toy pistol you ferret it out, but with the Russians not even a tommy-gun can be found.' After this the Belgian officer smiled ruefully, kissed the Bishop's ring and took his leave.

Another incident illustrates how conscientiously he performed his self-imposed duties as *Landesvater*. In an interview at Sendenhorst with a senior British officer the latter made some excuses about the difficulty of preventing the atrocities committed by the foreign workers who were given a free hand by the military. The conversation became very heated and ended like this:

'You know my name?'

'Yes, von Galen.'

'You know how I have stood out against Nazi crimes? Very well, then: I shall continue to fight against every injustice and wrongdoing no matter who does it. Tell that to your superiors.' With these words the clenched Galen fist swished down on to the small writing-desk with such force that pencil, pen and ruler jumped into the air in fright. What the officer muttered as he bowed and departed—whether in agreement, excuse or protest—not even the interpreter could make out.

As can well be imagined cold douches of this sort somewhat dampened the atmosphere. The Bishop's dauntless energy which had at first impressed the new masters began by this time to irritate them. A summer sultriness arose that presaged an explosion. On Sunday, July 1st, the Bishop accompanied his flock on their yearly pilgrimage from Münster to Telgte; he now chose the same place where previously he had inveighed against the tyranny of the past to indict the new rulers for their supine attitude to the crimes being committed up and down the land. Up to now, his repeated complaints, petitions and conferences had brought no tangible results; he therefore conceived it his bounden duty as bishop of the diocese where the Catholics entrusted to his care were undergoing terrible hardships to raise his voice on their behalf. It had been the same with Hitler, who relegated his complaints and requests to the waste-paper basket. Very well then; he would again dare to step out into the open. In that Telgte sermon he referred to events which 'can only be explained as acts of hate and a desire for revenge on the part of our former enemies; to the attacks and robberies perpetrated by Russians and Poles in Münsterland; to the rape of women and girls—and all this with the connivance and under the very eyes of the occupation authorities. Those responsible and those who now wield power must realize that I plead for the same principles as heretofore and make the same demands for rectitude and justice. I only hope and pray that today my words may reach the ears of our former foes and there receive consideration and understanding.' Once again the news of this sermon spread through all Germany like a forest fire. Once more, as in 1941, the Bishop's utterances were passed from hand to hand in leaflets duplicated in thousands. From all parts of the Fatherland letters of thanks and expressions of gratitude poured into Münster. In the huge P.O.W. and De-Nazification camps, which had been set up on German soil, groups of prisoners seized the worn and tattered pages, and hope was born again. The Telgte message soon reached the other side as well, but it received neither the understanding nor the sympathy for which the Bishop hoped.

At midday on July 25th the Telgte sermon was the subject of a serious but dignified conference lasting some two hours. A Polish officer acted as interpreter. After a few introductory remarks the British colonel handed the Bishop a typewritten copy of his Telgte address, many parts of which had been crossed out in red. The Bishop immediately handed back the document with the remark that it was, in point of fact, a copy of the sermon in question. The discussion which followed resolved itself round three main points: *Firstly, War Guilt.* According to the colonel's interpretation the German race was collectively guilty. Since the Bishop denied this in his address he thereby made it impossible for Military Government to re-educate the nation as a whole. The colonel was of the opinion that the attachment of blame was not so much a question of punishment as a means of instruction and education. The Bishop fiercely opposed this view. Entering the lists he vigorously demonstrated that any form of resistance had ended either in death or the worst form of concentration camp; one could neither ask nor expect such kinds of heroism from an entire nation. He alluded to the devilish power of propaganda: the fact that the Bishop of Münster had not been imprisoned, let alone hanged, certainly showed how strong the latent resistance of the people had been. *Secondly, Looting.* According to the Bishop's view this was caused by a concerted Press and wireless campaign of hatred and revenge against Germany. The same thing applied to the food problem which would develop into a catastrophic famine if the Allies did nothing about it. All this the colonel contradicted. The Bishop must either withdraw completely or tone down what he had said in Telgte against the wretched situation and relations *vis-à-vis* the Occupying Powers. Correctly, and making every effort to keep his temper, the colonel insisted that the Bishop should make a public recantation or modification of his Telgte sermon, especially those passages which disparaged the authority of Military Government, and which he considered aggravated occupational problems. The Bishop would not swerve one iota from what he had said, but was prepared to make the following statement which appeared a few months later in the diocesan journal: 'British Military Government has made it clear to me that it has no intention of allowing its policy and mode of acting to be dictated by motives of either hatred or revenge, and that it will neither connive at the excesses and outrages to which I have referred, nor ignore the problem of famine. In order to remove misunderstandings which have arisen, I willingly communicate this declaration to the faithful of my diocese.'

The day after this interview at Warendorf the Bishop received a letter from the British colonel conciliatory in tone and which is here reproduced in full because it throws some light on the situation then prevailing:

I am writing Your Lordship a private letter because I feel that in our conversation of yesterday I did not make myself clear on a certain point. Nevertheless I am convinced that in the wider issues we are both moving towards the same goal, namely a lasting peace. The point in question concerns the difficulties connected with the supervision of the lawless element among the foreign workers still in this country. In Your Lordship's deep sympathy for your suffering people, and the fact that you think that this trouble can be easily put right, I fear that you fail to understand clearly enough the other side of the picture. There are in your diocese some hundred thousand human beings who were brought forcibly to this country; they have already spent some years here where they have been forced to work for the country which violently imported them, and which was fighting against their own homeland. During their sojourn here, many have been terribly ill-treated. From the cruel thraldom they have experienced, they have assimilated the principle that might is right. Many have lost relations and country; many have absolutely nothing left in the world on which to build their future even supposing they could reach home; they have heard, and in many cases seen, the frightful crimes the Germans have committed against them, their countrymen, or their allies. It is not then surprising that some of them look upon Germans as their enemies and seize every opportunity of paying off part of the score. Is it to be wondered at if they have lost every vestige of Christian sentiment or restraint they may have possessed previously? The element, however, which perpetrates these crimes of reprisal is in the minority: the greater part conduct themselves in a proper way. It is hardly astonishing that we should not regard it as being only right and just to keep these people, who are still our allies, in concentration camps behind barbed wire. Of course we must grant them the freedom which they have been so long denied even if some of them are undisciplined. Think then of the thousands of scattered farms and villages in our jurisdiction. Remember too that our first commitment is that we must still wage a major war against Japan. Further, that we also, as a result of the ruin and devastation of war, have the second problem of rebuilding and recovery in our own country. It is still then not surprising that we maintain here in Germany an army only large enough to preserve order. We cannot impair our two primary objectives. The preservation of law and order is the first duty of our army, whether the threat comes from Germans or elsewhere. We deplore all crimes committed here as we deprecate the still worse crimes perpetrated by the Germans in the last few years. We hope we have put an end to the latter for ever. We hope soon to end the former, and we are taking all possible steps to bring this about. It is idle and foolish to imagine that they have never happened or could have been at once prevented. We shall earnestly endeavour to return these unfortunate men to their homes from which they were forcibly dragged, and

12. (*Top*) Cardinal von Galen on his return from Rome to Munster: picture taken the day before his fatal illness March 16th, 1946

13. (*Bottom*) Cardinal von Galen, tallest in left background, with the Holy Father in the Vatican on his elevation to the Cardinalate

14. The home-coming from Rome, March 16th, 1946, in front of the Church of St. Lambert

which, in many cases, have been damaged or destroyed. My
Lord, I understand perfectly the agitation and emotion which
you showed during our discussion. But I wonder much more at
the restraint of our interpreter, the Polish Lieutenant Klink,
who himself, as a prisoner of war, has undergone far more
physical and psychological suffering than has any unfortunate
German in the recent events under discussion. I myself freed
him from Belsen. If the crimes committed during the last two
months in Münster were added to the horrors perpetrated there,
no appreciable difference would be noticed. It can easily be understood that he holds all Germans responsible for the inhuman
treatment meted out to the inmates of Belsen in the name of the
whole nation. But I repeat we deplore all violation of human
rights, and are doing our utmost to prevent them, and to punish
offenders as far as circumstances permit. I beg Your Lordship
to take these facts into consideration.

(signed) Spottiswood.

Naturally the Bishop received this letter with satisfaction,
for, together with defence and exculpation, there was also good-
will expressed in it. As a witness of the long discussion at
Warendorf, I can only confirm the correct behaviour of the
English colonel and of his Polish interpreter. It is also true that
the Bishop at times grew very excited and that the other two
kept thorough self-possession, though I could see that they found
it difficult. Understandably enough, that letter was intended
particularly to have a calming effect on the Bishop: if possible
a renewal of open episcopal protest was to be avoided. In the
following months, in spite of perfectly correct relations, an
impassable barrier grew up between the Bishop and the military
authorities. We can read this in his Lenten Pastoral for 1946:
'You may believe me that it is a bitter sorrow to me and often
causes me deep sadness that I can help you so little, and
indeed hardly at all. I have no power, and no influence on
those who have any. It is not even possible for me to put forward our needs and our grievances in quarters which could
give a decisive answer.'
Although through the summer and autumn of 1945 the
Bishop had grown every day more and more clearly aware of

L

this position, he never ceased knocking on the doors of the British authorities, petitioning, complaining, protesting. For him, those approaches were not easy. He certainly always met with courtesy and gentlemanly manners. He never entered the officers' room without their rising to greet him. The same happened when he left, even when the discussions had lasted a long time and could only be brought to an end after many differences of opinion had been thrashed out. The Bishop's temperament was combative rather than diplomatic. Though this never misled him into forgetting the forms of politeness, it sometimes induced him to use vivid figures of speech, which were embarrassing to an interpreter, if he was to render them with the living homeliness of Westphalian usage.

Till late into the night, sometimes even into the small hours of the morning, the Bishop sat at his writing-desk, either at Sendenhorst or at Münster, where he spent most of the week at the Borromäum, in order to answer personally the petitions which reached him from all parts of Germany and were piled in heaps beside him. In the afternoon after lunch he sat in his chair reading these long effusions. Sometimes, from utter weariness, his eyes would close and the letters slip out of his hands. People could come into the Borromäum whenever they liked. At all hours of the day visitors were waiting, sometimes in regular queues, in the long roofless corridor, where rain, wind and sunshine mingled unhindered with their ranks. What anxieties and problems all these folk brought with them! All this worked fearful ravages on his health, hitherto unassailable. Apart from anxieties common to the country at large, there were the troubles of single families and individuals. All these were submitted to the Bishop and required a discussion with the military authorities. As often as six times in the week he went on foot through the ruins of the Spiegelturm and the Katthagen and clambered over the mounds of rubble which had been the Hollenbeckerstrasse and the Jüdefelderstrasse, in order to bring these grievances before the British officers. As a sample of his fatherly carefulness, which did not overlook even the smallest matters, I may tell the following incident, insignificant as it may appear. At a street corner the lid of the man-hole giving access to the drainage was missing and the gaping hole might in the dark have proved the undoing of many a passer-by. He and his companion, Dr. Kamp, dragged some planks out of the ruins, to cover this opening with them.

. . . . .

Reporters from all parts of the world were a persistent nuisance. They always knew how, by some trick or other, to work an interview. Among others there was the interview, which became so widely known to the public, with two reporters, Anderson from Sweden and Allemann from Switzerland. He asked the British officer who was present whether he was free to tell these two gentlemen everything he found to criticize in the measures of the military authorities. The question was evidence of his honourable and straightforward attitude towards those authorities, as the officer knew no German. This permission was then given; the British authorities had found out that his criticisms did not spring from an irresponsible wish to find fault, but from his very decided sense of what was just and fair. Here follows the interview published in a Zürich newspaper, which drew widespread attention at the time:

A bishop says 'no'. It cannot be concealed that the methods of the British Occupation meet with criticism, which sometimes is very sharp and bitter. There are certain aspects in the English rule to which the Germans find it difficult to adapt themselves. Of all those whom I met on my tour, no one described these aspects in such sharp and uncompromising terms as an old opponent of National Socialism, Count von Galen, the Catholic Bishop of Münster, whose exceptional public opposition to Hitler's erroneous doctrine in 1941 (i.e. considerably before the fortunes of war turned against Germany) gave him in the eyes of the English and the German people a moral authority similar to that possessed by his Protestant fellow-worker in the opposite camp, Pastor Niemöller. Count von Galen at the present day expresses his opinions in matters where the English are concerned with the same disregard of the consequences as at one time he did where the rulers of the Third Reich were concerned. One might indeed say, with a greater disregard of consequences, as today it is less necessary for him to weigh his words. In spite of this, he at first appeared unwilling to talk to neutrals upon matters which he had at heart, not through fear, but because he held that criticism of the English should be put upon the assize

of British and not foreign public opinion. I have myself heard
Englishmen say that von Galen does not mince matters as
regards themselves. It was the invitation of our British conducting officer to speak freely and without regard for consequences which led him to speak out. Upon the subject of
National Socialism as a form of foreign domination the Bishop
spoke as follows: 'The war and the defeat of our people has been
a bitter experience and we suffer greatly under it. We have for
years suffered greatly under the foreign domination of National
Socialism and we had hoped and expected that we should be
free from it. We now see that we can only win freedom through
very bitter suffering and that we must hold on in patience. The
fact that we are held responsible to the victorious powers for the
acts of those who have enslaved and dominated us is very
bitterly felt.'

The Bishop admitted that many things were certainly better.
The persecution of the Church had ceased, religious freedom was
largely restored. But even here he had some criticism to make.
The control which is still exercised over the churches by the
occupying authorities seemed to him to go beyond what was
strictly necessary. As regards education he thinks that there is a
long delay in satisfying the well-grounded claims of Catholics
in respect of Christian denominational schools. The prohib-
ition of Corpus Christi processions of the Blessed Sacrament
and still more the translation of that great Church festival to
the Sunday following it, reminds him of National Socialist
methods.

But these objections on particular ecclesiastical matters did
not go to the root of the Bishop's criticisms. He made the much
wider charge that in many respects the British régime was an
imitation of National Socialism.

Concentration camps worse than those of the Nazis! 'I must say
plainly,' said the Bishop, 'that in some respects we have the same
complaints to put forward as we had against National Socialism.
We can only regard with anxiety the methods with which men
alleged to be politically tainted are treated. I am indeed convinced that those responsible for the National Socialist régime
should be removed and punished. But that the many persons
who, merely to avoid worse consequences, accepted some rank
in the party and undertook some work of a party character, are
arrested in hundreds and confined to concentration camps,
where they for weeks and months are not even examined and
have no opportunity to defend themselves, amounts to a denial

of justice which we cannot understand in Englishmen. The poison of National Socialistic error has, as is notorious, infected other nations than our own, including some who used to boast of their attachment to democracy. Even the National Socialists allowed the prisoners in the concentration camps to correspond twice a month with their families and to receive food packets from them.

'These concessions are not to be had from the English. And when I say this to the English and get the answer that even the Nazis did not everywhere make those concessions to the people in concentration camps, I can only put this question to them: "If you English must imitate the camps, why follow the worst pattern?" And so on in other spheres. When the National Socialists came into power, they indeed remorselessly removed their opponents from public positions under the law providing for the reconstitution of the permanent Civil Service, but they did at least pension them or compensated them in some way. Today men are thrown out without compensation and not only they but also their innocent families, their wives and children are reduced to penury.'

The greatest anxiety. His greatest anxiety, the Bishop said, was that action on these lines and the destitution which it caused might lead to the elimination of fixed principles in the people and conjure up the danger of hostility to all reasonable social order, that is, the danger of nihilism and bolshevism. This applies in his view to living conditions generally. Count von Galen cannot understand why the English do not release in winter even the smallest quantity of heating fuel for the civil population, although the coal in the Ruhr is being stacked at the pithead and the production of three days' mining would cover the needs of civilians. This, he thinks, cannot be defended. My comment that last winter France was left almost without any coal at all caused him to look astonished and somewhat angry. 'Certainly, that is wrong too, the Americans and the English should have made deliveries to them.'

A final comment. 'The quite inconceivable Eastern boundary' and the expulsion of Germans from the areas recently added to Poland. 'This too is a thing hitherto without precedent in history: ever since Christianity came into the world, such action was never taken until the Allies and National Socialists made a start. That the latter should act thus has not surprised us: what has surprised us is that the Christian peoples of the

West give their approval to such methods, that they tacitly or
even by formal agreement (as at Potsdam) assume a joint
responsibility for such things happening.'

Why are we not informed? The Bishop rejected the proposition
that he as a priest should be silent on these matters because they
related to material interest. 'I am not only the bishop but I am
also a German, a Christian who feels pity for poor men. I am a
pastor of souls. . . .'

Of peculiar importance was the meeting with the Anglican
Bishop of Chichester, Dr. Bell, in October of 1945, in the presence of Brigadier Chadwick, Head of the Military Authority in
Westphalia. After the Cardinal's death, Dr. Bell wrote about
this meeting: 'I was very deeply impressed by the decision and
ardour with which he defended right and justice in all circumstances and against every Government. He was a man whose
outstanding bodily stature was matched by an equally outstanding moral power. He dominated every gathering where he
came by his striking appearance and distinguished bearing. He
was unwearied in his care for his people. He believed firmly
that Catholics and Protestants would work together. He said
to me that it was clearly imperative that all who were at one
in their belief in God, in their faithfulness to Christ and in their
conviction of the soul's immortality should come forward
strongly on behalf of righteousness and peace.'
A few months later, General Templer had invited the
bishops of the British Zone to a conference at Lübbecke. According to an 'Information Report' the bishops had the opportunity
to bring forward their requests, among others the Bishop of
Münster. In some respects he put forward criticisms of general
policy: the military authorities ought to restore to the German
people a trust in Right and Justice; they ought to make evident
that the National-Socialist principle of Might before Right no
longer prevailed, but Right before Might. At the conclusion
of the conference, General Templer expressed himself to
Brigadier Sedgwick, the Controller-General for Religious Affairs
at Headquarters, to the effect that he had supposed that in the
Bishop of Münster he would meet with a fire-eating dragon,

but he had been pleased to find in him an honourable and straightforward opponent.

· · · · ·

One day in October, 1945, all Mércèdes-Benz cars were confiscated. In the course of the summer the Bishop had been able to obtain one of these cars; before that he had been compelled to take many journeys on foot. An hour before he was to start for the rural deanery of Bottrop, to administer Confirmation, an English officer appeared at the Borromäum to confiscate the episcopal car. Through his interpreter, Dr. Kamp, the Bishop expressed his astonishment and indignation at such a step. In the end the officer declared himself ready to put in a word with higher authority for the release of the car, but meanwhile insisted on confiscating it according to his orders. After an hour, he brought it back with instructions that the Bishop could use it for travelling to the Confirmation, which could not be put off. The impression that this scene made on the officer charged with the confiscation was perceptible many weeks afterwards from the look that came over the faces of some other officers, when the Bishop's car was mentioned. He was allowed to keep it until his death.

A Scottish paper, the *Glasgow Observer*, on Jan. 4th, 1946, published the following comment on this incident by a correspondent:

> When I left that plainly furnished room, I could not get rid of the feeling that the military authorities had shown themselves unusually narrow-minded and lacking in imagination in their behaviour towards this great bishop and popular leader. A fortnight later I learnt that those authorities had thought needful to confiscate the car of Bishop von Galen. Perhaps it will be given back to the Cardinal.

Anyhow, on people who went about for ten years in Nazi Germany with their mouths muzzled, such words of democratic criticism produced an effect which is not only refreshing but educative.

As a conclusion to this chapter, I should like to mention a British officer, the Jesuit Father Murphy, who as a chaplain attached to the garrison at Münster, and to the local military hospital, had been appointed as a liaison officer between the Bishop and the military authorities. In a most obliging way, he spared the Bishop much trudging to and fro and greatly eased the negotiations with the British officers. He did it willingly, for he learnt from daily observation what a huge burden of work the spiritual leader of Münster had to cope with.

One Saturday evening he grew so strongly aware of the bond of a common humanity between them, that he made free to offer the Bishop 'a little medicine' in the form of a bottle of whisky. It touched the Bishop very much that in the midst of this tiring and exacting work such very human sympathy was shown him. He asked Father Murphy to drink a first glass with him. When however he did not succeed in persuading him, he had recourse to a stratagem and declared with a slight smile: 'Father, I cannot accept your remedy, unless you drink the first glass. Since we are "enemies", you must convince me, before I do so, that the drink is not dangerous or poisonous.' Amidst a hearty laugh on both sides, the Bishop poured out the whisky and Father Murphy raised the glass.

CARDINAL

AUTUMN had come round again—the first after the cessation of hostilities. All over the world, including Japan, the guns were now silent. But peace, in the true sense of the word, was still far off. How battered was the face of the homeland with its burnt-out towns to which the men returned to find shelter only in cellars or ruins! In the streets of the Münster province one saw wretched people from the great industrial areas trekking out into the countryside in long columns (as a protection against the foreign workers) to try and find there the barest necessities to keep body and soul together. During the course of the summer people began to use the railways again in their thousands, and all these 'hamsters' hung about the stations or packed themselves into goods trucks; passenger coaches no longer existed. Hordes of evacuees poured back into the west of the Fatherland from south and central Germany. Despite the fact the country bled from a thousand wounds it was and remained the homeland. In Münster itself the inhabitants collected together during the hours of evening, and armed with picks and shovels cleared a way for pedestrians and traffic. Under the leadership of Canon Leiwering a group of volunteers were able to move some of the rubble from the interior of the cathedral, and on the Feast of the Dedication the first High Mass was celebrated in the ruins of the quire.

The last weeks of the Bishop's stay in Sendenhorst drew near. Relations with the Belgian occupying forces were becoming daily more favourable. Led by an officer, Belgian soldiers acted as guards of honour to the Bishop on the occasion of various Church festivals and similar functions. On September 6th a Belgian military chaplain brought two of his men to the chapel of the St. Joseph Sodality to receive the sacrament of Confirmation at the hands of the Bishop. On the morning of the day appointed for the ceremony one of these soldiers, who had been baptized the evening before, made his first Holy Communion accompanied by his battalion commander and his friend. 'If there is one German to whom I would take off my hat, it's this Count von Galen,' said the Belgian major. After the ceremony the chaplain came out of the historic little audience chamber beaming with delight; with a laughing countenance and revealing gestures he said: 'At the end of the interview the Bishop held out his gigantic hand—big enough for me to sleep in—and with a flash in those bushy, brown eyes, and a quiver at the corners of his mouth, said: "Well, and now I wish you and your whole company the quickest possible return home!"' This engaging hint was received with appreciative laughter.

Some time before this the Bishop had also confirmed nine American soldiers in the chapel of the Collegium Borromäum. When the solemnity, carried out under somewhat unusual circumstances, was over, they paid tribute not only to the great impression the Bishop's personality and outward appearance had made on them, but also to the simple and deep piety with which he had celebrated both Mass and the rite of Confirmation. Curiosity frequently brought soldiers to the Cathedral Square to stare at the building where 'the giant bishop' lived; they did not venture to enter, but it was apparently enough to have seen for themselves the place where worked and prayed the man of whom the whole world spoke. One day an English soldier, the father of six children, called on the Bishop's interpreter, Dr. Kamp, and in order to prove his faith and orthodoxy begged that he should be put through his paces in the catechism. He had known all the answers to the 370 questions since his childhood.

The November storms blustered over the land. For weeks on end the Bishop made his rounds to priests and laity alike, especially to those living in the distressed industrial areas and those who, during the war, had migrated to the provinces of West Münster, Niederrhein and North Oldenburg. In the meantime the Vicariate-General at Sendenhorst, now that the bombing of Münster was over, began to pack newly arrived documents and furniture and make all preparations for the final return to the Bishop's see. Thanks to the strenuous and successful efforts of Monsignor Tenspolde adequate rooms had been found in the Caritas House for accommodating the Vicariate-General. It was not, however, found suitable to house the Bishop in the same building and the Borromäum was to be used instead.

On the 18th of December the farewells to Sendenhorst were made. In warm terms the Bishop expressed his gratitude to all those who had made his stay there possible during those long, dark weeks. Quietly and unobtrusively the car moved away as it had fourteen months before. 'He sat bolt upright in the car,' an eye-witness wrote, 'with shoulders squared to face fresh events, the striking and characteristic Galen features set grimly for whatever lay ahead: the strong lips compressed in emotion. But on the lashes of those large eyes hung a tear.'

Christmas stood at the threshold. Three priests sat in the presbytery of St. Lambert's. The conversation turned on the *Sturm und Drang* of the times and on the Bishop's exploits. A newly discovered document emanating from the Ministry of Propaganda in the summer of 1941 made it clear that the Nazis had wanted to hang him but did not dare to carry out their intention. Suddenly the question was raised as to whether the Pope might not offer some tangible reward to his brave German bishop. Words like 'titular Archbishop' were used and even the word 'Cardinal' was mentioned but soon rejected as impossible: such a nomination was against all custom, and was out of the question. . . . Thus ran the thoughts of those three Münster priests on that autumn afternoon.

Then, on the last Sunday before Christmas, at eight o'clock in the evening, the radio announced the surprising news of the appointment of thirty-two new Cardinals. It was an unforgettable moment. We were sitting in front of the wireless in the Students' Hostel—Dr. Tenspolde and myself. When suddenly the name of our Bishop fell on our ears we both sprang up electrified. Snatching our hats and coats we made for the Borromäum in double quick time. The Bishop had no radio. We wanted to be the first to tell him. As we knocked at the door we could hear him pacing up and down in his room. We greeted him as befitted a Prince of the Church. 'Your Eminence, have you heard the news?' He smiled and said, '*Ach*, that's all my eye and Betty Martin!' 'Then you already know?' 'Yes,

Berghaus has just telephoned, but I didn't believe him; the radio has tricked us before, and it's not much better nowadays.' This observation could neither shake our belief nor damp our enthusiasm. We had to sit down, and even in those days there were cigars. And then we chatted about it all. . . . Was it true or not? From time to time a smile hovered over the Bishop's face; he was humorous and ironical in turn or spoke words of deep humility tinged with anguish. Deep down in him lay a quiet composure but with us dreams and reality conflicted.

When, on the following morning, the Cathedral chapter appeared, and the Auxiliary Bishop, in felicitous words, had expressed the tempestuous joy of the clergy and faithful of the entire diocese, the Bishop still could not restrain his laughter. He simply did not believe it. But doubts of this sort in no way affected the long chain of well-wishers who came in unbroken succession to knock on the door and express their heartfelt felicitations. Waiting on the Bishop that morning were the Rector and Dean of the university, the Chief Burgomaster and all the parish priests of the city. One of the latter, who was waiting in an ante-room, gave utterance to the delight he felt with emphatic gestures. 'I saw this coming—I've always said that——' A Canon interrupted: 'He is the first Cardinal ever to sit on the episcopal throne of Münster.' And a third: 'He has really earned it! *Grossartig*, this act of the Holy Father!'

The wonderful news from Rome came as a complete surprise to everybody. Enthusiasm in Germany knew no bounds. The tidings ran like wildfire from house to house, and was bruited from mouth to mouth. As in 1941, the name of Münster was on everyone's lips. But what of the prelate who wore the laurel? His evening hours were spent alone in the quiet of his study; and there the past came before him in retrospect. If only his parents were alive! No von Galen had ever before won the Sacred Purple! He thought of his years as a bishop—years so often full of difficult and bitter hours. But God had always been at his side. Making allowances for human frailty he had ever striven for the rights and property of Holy Church and its Chief Shepherd. The words of St. Cyprian:

Ubi Petrus, ibi Ecclesia—the *Sentire cum Petro* were to him not only the claims and demands of the Faith but vital roots deeply embedded in his heart. On the 14th of February he had preached the panegyric at the Requiem for Pius XI. In it he outlined the life-work of that illustrious Pontiff whose actions and policy he staunchly defended. His reverent loyalty to the Holy See found expression in the following words: 'Today I have to speak on a very sad occasion. It is a duty which I owe to our dear Holy Father, Pius XI, to my own knightly honour, and to all members of my diocese whose elected representative and spokesman I am. . . . Indeed, I owe it to the honour of all Catholics, not only in Germany, but throughout the world, to raise my protest and indictment against that abuse to which our beloved Holy Father has been subjected recently in official German quarters. . . . We are no true German men but rather base wretches if we do not feel deeply and utterly condemn such infamous derision which is aimed at our Spiritual Father; to take advantage of the defencelessness of the Pope is a symptom of the vile disease which is ravaging our reputation, and is a renunciation of the best aspects of our German way of life. Let this be spoken today for all to hear as we stand in spirit to mourn with awe and respect at the catafalque of our late Holy Father. . . . Today I want to confirm once more our confession of faith and our irrevocable resolve in the words spoken by our Westphalian countryman, Freiherr Burghard von Schorlemer-Alst, whose bronze monument was erected here in the Warendorferstrasse by a grateful people. On the 16th April, 1875, he spoke out openly against slandering the Pope: "You can annihilate us; tear our hearts from our bodies. But I say this to you. You will never rend asunder this Catholic people from its allegiance to the Vicar of Christ! Amen."'

Under the date of that memorable day there is the following entry in my diary: 'Despite it being a week-day the Cathedral was packed as at the eleven o'clock Mass on Sundays. The Bishop spoke out strongly, like a German knight, in defence of Pope and Papacy against the vulgar and cowardly attacks. The Auxiliary Bishop remarked to Canon Albers: "He spoke like an Ambrosian. . . . Most moving was the fact that afterwards both the Provost and the Archpriest came into the sacristy to express the deep gratitude of all the clergy present."'

Two weeks later in the same year, shortly before the outbreak of the war, I wrote this account in my diary recording those stirring hours:

> On Thursday, March 2nd, Eugenio Pacelli was elected Pope at the third scrutiny on the first day of the voting. It was his sixty-third birthday. It would have been about 5.30 p.m. when suddenly the bishop came running across the hall and called everybody to the Radio. Speaking in Italian the announcer said: 'The historic hour is here—a puff of white smoke (the *sfumata*) shoots at this moment into the clear air.' The new Pope had been chosen. In rapid, animated, almost nervous succession the announcers who were stationed under the Bernini Colonnade began broadcasting. First came the German spokesman, then French, English, Dutch, and so on. At approximately 6.30 p.m. the great crowd in the Square (which had not ceased singing the *Te Deum*) raised a shout of joy to herald the news that the procession, with the senior Cardinal Deacon Caccia Dominioni, was approaching—the doors of the Loggia above St. Peter's were already open—and the great *tappezzeria* was let down. A moment of strange, tense silence ensued. . . .
>
> We were sitting in the bishop's ante-room—then came the Cardinal-Deacon's voice: '*Annuntio vobis gaudium magnum, habemus Papam, Eminentissimum ac Excellentissimum Eugenium* (here a great roar from the Piazza)—much acclamation, hand-clapping—our bishop was deeply stirred—) *Sanctae Romanae Ecclesiae Cardinalem Pacelli, nomine Pium XII.*' We were overjoyed. The Bishop took out his rosary and we began to pray. The Holy Hour in the cathedral had just begun. At half past eight the Radio announced that the Holy Father's procession was approaching the central balcony. At the words, '*Benedicat vos Omnipotens Deus . . .*' we knelt down. The voice of the *Pastor Angelicus* sounded strong at first, becoming slower and softer with emotion.

Thus I read in my diary. A few months later the Bishop of Münster was kneeling in front of the new Holy Father.

Came the war. Year in year out the Bishop reported the events in his diocese to the Vicar of Christ, and his heart was gladdened by the personal replies he received from the Pope. These letters afforded him the greatest consolation during those long years of persecution. He knew well the Holy Father's love for Germany and because of this was moved to heights of anger whenever this Pontiff was slandered and calumniated in Germany. On the Feast of St. Peter and St. Paul in 1943 he preached in defence of the Pope, and again in September of the same year. Here is an extract from the sermon, the last to be preached in the cathedral pulpit before the destruction of the building on October 10th, 1943: 'We know our Holy Father, Pius XII, as the former Apostolic Nuncio who lived for so many years in this country—here in our midst. Only last year, in his letter to the German bishops of October 26th, 1942, he gave positive expression of his esteem for the German people among whom he had moved for so many years. It is nothing short of disgraceful, and it reflects the greatest shame on us, that such nonsensical and wicked slanders on the Pope should be hawked round the streets to the effect that the Pope holds shares in the Italian fleet, and has forbidden or hindered its attempts to rescue German soldiers fighting in Africa. So the war fleet of Mussolini's Fascist Italy has become a business undertaking—a matter of stocks and shares! Or again: The Pope has supported the war effort of our opponents by financial gifts! Brethren, I do not propose to insult your intelligence by saying, "Don't believe such rubbish." But I urge you to counter these infamous lies! Ask for proof, real proof; despise and reject rumour and mere statement so often made by the enemies of the Church, whose sole delight it is to smirch and denigrate it. Our delight in children, our love and pride for the family must rise up against this black business of casting suspicion on our common Father. Shame on a child who is silent in the presence of its father's detractors! He who attacks the Pope, attacks us, and impugns the honour of 40 million German Catholics and hundreds of thousands of Catholic soldiers.'

Two years later, after unconditional surrender, the German Fatherland lay prostrate, bleeding and despoiled. Who, in the whole world, had one single word of mercy for her? In his Christmas Allocution of 1945 Pius XII included these words: 'He who seeks to punish those who have committed crimes must take care that he has not done the same. He who demands reparations must do so on the foundations of moral principles nor forget that natural rights are also valid for those who surrendered unconditionally. . . .'

At Pontifical High Mass on the feast of the Epiphany which the Bishop celebrated in the Church of the Holy Cross, he read extracts from the Pope's Christmas message, adding the following remarks of his own: 'We rejoice that the Holy Father has acknowledged before the whole world the sanctity and inviolability of the rights of men on this earth—not forgetting the vanquished. We deplore the fact that in the Eastern territories of our Fatherland Germans are being driven out into the streets from hearth and home, and perish miserably. We must demand justice for our prisoners who must not be incarcerated longer than is necessary. We intercede also for those, who in past years were forced to become members of the Party or its affiliations, such as the N.S.V., and did so only nominally and under duress. Often they were able to do much good. But we have neither strength nor means left to give expression to our rights. In its proper place and time I stood up for the primitive rights of man. I said then: "Righteousness is the foundation of the State; if justice is not re-established our people will perish from an internal rottenness." I must again say today that if justice is not respected by the nations there will never be true peace and harmony among us. May God grant the German nation and all peoples a real and lasting peace!'

.   .   .   .   .

St. Paul wrote to his disciple Timothy, 'It is for thee to be on the watch, to accept every hardship, to employ thyself in preaching the gospel, and perform every duty of thy office, keeping a sober mind' (Tim. 4, 5).[1] During all those years from 1933 when Pius XI entrusted the diocese of Münster to him, Clemens August administered his sacred fief faithfully and holily. He applied his whole strength to this task, and would go on doing so unassumingly. On the afternoon of Epiphany, with the Holy Father's words fresh on his lips in that great plea for justice, his thoughts turned towards Rome, and he wrote the following letter to the Father of Christendom:

Holy Father,
    Humbly prostrate in spirit at the feet of Your Holiness, I seek in vain to find words to express what is in my heart. Both Radio and Press have announced that it has pleased Your

[1] Translator's note: Knox Version.

Holiness to make up the deficiency in the Sacred College by naming a large number of new members. In doing this Your Holiness has demonstrated to the whole world in an incomparable way the supranationality of the Holy Catholic Church, the unity and concord of its people, since men from every continent, race and nation have been called to the highest Senate and Council of the Church's sovereign. That our poor German nation, trampled under foot and devastated by war, humiliated by defeat, and today beset on all sides by hatred and revenge has not been passed over but has been honoured by the appointment of three German bishops to the College of Cardinals evokes our heartfelt gratitude. For this the German Catholics with their bishops and priests, as also many non-Catholic Germans, thank the Vicar of Christ. If however, Your Holiness has decided that my humble self is to be numbered among the new Cardinals, I can only say that this unexpected and undeserved distinction has so deeply moved and disconcerted my unworthy self that I must say with St. Peter, '*Exi a me, quia homo peccator sum, Domine.*' Only the principle, which I have held steadfastly all through my life, namely that I should regard every wish of the Pope as a command, coming as it does from the Shepherd of the whole flock, determines me in all humility to accept this honour and office entrusted to me, in the same spirit of obedience as when I spoke my '*Adsum*' on the day of my ordination.[1] It is a solace to me if I may see in this nomination a recognition of the brave steadfastness shown by the majority of the Catholics in my diocese of Münster, of their loyalty to Christ, His Holy Church, and to the Holy Father during those years of persecution and oppression, and of their public witness to the rights of God and His Church, and for the stand which they made on behalf of the God-given rights of the human individual. The unrestrained manifestations of joy shown in my diocese when the news of my appointment became known, and the countless congratulations from all parts of Germany which I have received, would seem to give me the right to accept this mark of Your Holiness' favour. Therefore I beg leave to convey to Your Holiness in the name of my diocesans, and at the same time all German Catholics, the humble and devoted expression of our respectful thanks for this renewed and un-

---

[1] Translator's note: Candidates for Ordination present themselves in the church with tonsure and in clerical dress, carrying the vestments of the order to which they are to be raised, and lighted candles. They are all summoned by name, each candidate answering, '*Adsum*'.

M

merited proof of Your favour and fatherly love. At the same time
I renew the vow of our unchangeable loyalty, constant obedience and humble love to the Sovereign Pontiff, the Vicar of
Christ on earth, and to the august person of Your Holiness for
whom in our daily prayers we implore the continuance of God's
mercy and protection. In the glad hope of being able to kneel
soon at the feet of Your Holiness, and humbly begging the
apostolic blessing for myself and the people of my diocese,
I remain, with the greatest respect, Your Holiness' most obedient
son and servant,

✠ Clemens August.

Three days later, on the 9th of January, he wrote to his
sister-in-law, Countess Paula von Galen (*née* Freiin von Wendt),
in Haus Essen:

Dear Paula,

How moved and pleased I am by the love and goodness of
the Holy Father in raising three German bishops to the Cardinalate! By this action he has proved to the whole world not only
that he is the father of all nations but also of our poor reviled
German people. It is also manifest that he wished to reward my
brave diocese for making it possible for me by their support to
speak the truth openly however unpleasant it may have been.
At the same time I must admit that this event distresses and
embarrasses me. . . . I beg you to pray that I may be worthy of
the increased responsibility, and that I may not be affected by
external honour and look for earthly rather than heavenly
reward. I know only too well from the closest observation that
many other German bishops have laboured more than I have.
You will feel with me, I know, how much it worries me to have
taken away the preferment from them. *In Gottes Namen!* At the
time of writing I am overwhelmed by the pressure of well-
wishers, petitions and emergency calls from all over Germany.
Innumerable people believe or at least hope that I can help
them in some way, or at least intercede for them with the occupying powers, or the Holy Father, etc. Up to now it has been
pretty bad, but candidly it is getting out of hand, and I feel I
can do nothing else but ignore the post completely. Nor can I
cope with the endless visits. I feel very sad when I have to refuse
these poor people or protest that I cannot really do much for
them. Forgive me, I have no right to complain, and am sorry
I wrote the last few sentences. Please take care of yourself. . . .

After the great sermons of the summer of 1941 hundreds of letters arrived at the Bishop's Palace: the far-voiced echo of indignation and gratitude deeply felt. When the Bishop was created cardinal a fresh collection of letters accumulated, no longer in hundreds but in their thousands, rejoicing in the Almighty's victory at the triumph of right, and in the green of the laurel with which the Pope had crowned the chief shepherd of Münster. True, it was no longer a brave deed nor a risky undertaking to write such letters. The Gestapo had ceased to exist. During that time between the end of the old year and the beginning of the new, the diocese, the whole of Germany and a part of the world genuinely shared the joy of Münster. Therefore these letters must be regarded as important documents of their time. After the Cardinal's death they were classified and bound under the following headings: Bishops, diocesan priests, clergy regular and secular outside the diocese, government representatives, relations, friends, nobility, intelligentsia, the academic world, soldiers, non-Catholics, Germans abroad, foreigners, free-thinkers in and out of the diocese, children and juveniles.

CHAPTER 22

TO ROME VIA PARIS

IN THE middle of January the Bishop returned from a visit to the Archbishop of Cologne and as a result of a conversation held there he expressed the view that the difficulties connected with a journey to Rome were not insurmountable. And so began those days and months which were appointed to close the life of the great Cardinal in a dramatic series of events. The English Brigadier R. L. Sedgwick, Controller-General for Religious Affairs in the British Zone, obtained the necessary permission from the Foreign Office in London for the two cardinals and their suites to leave the country, and had the necessary passports prepared. The time fixed for the start of the trip was between Feb. 3rd–10th.

On the previous Wednesday it became known that the flight would start from Bückeburg and would be via Frankfurt and Vienna; but some days after a change in the route was announced, namely that München-Gladbach would be the starting-point, and that we should be flying direct across the Alps with no intermediate stop. Again a day later—and this caused the first doubts—we were informed that we would be leaving from Handorf aerodrome, near Münster, on Thursday, Feb. 7th, and that our course would be via Frankfurt and Vienna.

On the afternoon of Feb. 6th, the Archbishop of Cologne (Dr. Frings), accompanied by his Vicar-General, Dr. David, and by his secretary, Dr. Hürtgen, set out for Münster. Owing to a breakdown, their car did not reach Münster until nearly midnight. They traversed the ruins of the city for more than an hour but were unable to locate the Borromäum where the Bishop resided, and they found no one from whom to enquire the way owing to the curfew—nobody being allowed on the streets after sunset. They therefore drove to the Hiltruper Convent and passed the remainder of the night there. On the next morning three British cars arrived in the courtyard of the Borromäum and, as they drew up, Archbishop Fring's car

turned into the gates. At a fast pace we all drove to the Handorf aerodrome in the pleasant expectation of boarding an
English plane and taking off for Rome. An anxious scrutiny of
the airfield showed us a solitary plane on the runway and a
somewhat small one at that, whereupon our exuberance was
considerably diminished and became more so when the officer
commanding the station informed us there would be no flight
owing to bad weather over Austria; but at all events passengers
and luggage were to be weighed. We entered a roomy canteen
and went through the business of being weighed with much
joking and everything was done to make us as comfortable as
possible. When it was over we were told that our total load with
baggage was too heavy for the machine at our disposal. Brigadier Sedgwick, the born court-courier owing to his proficiency
in German, French and Italian, with the sincerest solicitude
for our plight at once established telephonic communication
with American Headquarters in Frankfurt to find out if we
might proceed from there. Should the news be favourable he
proposed an immediate start by car.

In the meantime we had found seats round the warm stove
and settled down in army style in the canteen. Breakfast, with
real English tea, was served by three Irishmen who had been
looking on. They knew instinctively how to behave to the two
prelates, which was immediately noticed by the Bishop, who
rightly guessed their nationality. We knew that about this time
many a window in the Münster houses of our clerical *confrères*
had now been thrown open to listen to the roar of our plane
on its way to Rome; such had been their promise in the great
enthusiasm that prevailed in the city. Two hours passed during
which Brigadier Sedgwick did everything possible to expedite
matters, telephoning to British and American Headquarters to
no avail. Downcast, he came to us and suggested we should
return to the Borromäum, there to await developments while
he made further negotiations. His good humour made us all
laugh and the Bishop rejoined that it would seem the wind that
blew through the Foreign Office windows in London was no
more favourable than that which blew over Austria.

That we might spend the interim profitably we drove to
nearby Telgte and there that morning amidst all this trying
doubt and delay the two new cardinals knelt side by side

before the age-long venerated statue of Our Lady of Münster-land. Back in Münster we remained in the Borromäum until evening when the news came that we should hold ourselves in readiness the following day. We were all a bit depressed, I must admit, but each took up his suitcase and endured with good humour the gentle *badinage* of those around us.

Friday morning (my diary). It has rained unceasingly for twenty-four hours. Two English cars were waiting below out-side the Borromäum. The two prelates, the Vicar-General of Cologne and Brigadier Sedgwick were to ride in the first which was large and roomy; the second was to accommodate Canon Professor Bierbaum and the two secretaries, and had ample room for luggage besides being remarkable for its high clearance. Our way lay through Telgte, Warendorf, Paderborn and Frank-furt. The Ems had flooded the countryside over a wide area so that in places the water streamed over the road in rivulets. The sky was heavy with cloud; the windscreen-wipers clicked un-ceasingly, and the deeper we penetrated the mountain ranges above Paderborn the more threatening the weather became. When we reached the Waldeck territory and came to the boundary village of Wrexen which lies deep in the valley, we found everything in full flood. Our two cars attempted a passage through the torrent. Whilst the station-wagon with its high clearance reached the further bank safely, the car carrying the two cardinals remained stuck in the middle of the stream, its engine hissing and steaming. Brigadier Sedgwick opened the door and called loudly to the country folk, who peered anxiously from their cottage windows, and to others who stood at the top of their steps watching the wild game of the elements, to come and help us.

In the car, he explained, were some V.I.P.s, two German cardinals and an English general. At his appeal the good people waded through the water booted and spurred against the tide and succeeded in pushing the cardinals' car on to dry ground. As no repair facilities were to hand nothing else remained but to borrow a chain and hitch the cardinals' car to that of the humbler clerics! Had the land been flat such a method of progression would not have been too difficult. Since, however, the district became increasingly more mountainous a good deal of jerking on the connecting chain occurred as we climbed

and descended the hills and valleys. Three times the chain
broke, so great was the strain. On the third occasion the
Brigadier's patience snapped, too. Leaping from the cardinals'
car he came over to mine where I sat next to the English
driver and bade me change places with him. He proposed to
go off in the first car to the nearest large town called Korbach
and get help. For a whole hour the damaged car of the cardinals remained on the lonely mountain road while its occupants
joked and the delinquent waters swirled round it. Help came
at last in the form of a German car mechanic who soon put the
trouble right. Then on we sped through the fading light of
evening, through Frankenburg past the blocked Edertal. We
recalled a letter, which the Bishop had received eight days
earlier from an elderly maiden lady, in which she urged that
the Cardinal should in no circumstances make the journey to
Rome by plane as she knew for certain that the air was unlucky
for him. We had to admit that the prophecy was in the very act
of coming true not only in the air but by land and water, too!

As we were about to pass through a place called Wetter the
depth of the water became more and more alarming; the
cardinals' car, which was leading the way, suddenly stopped and
the Brigadier called to us to go in front and test the terrain.
This we did until some anxious cries from a cottage nearby
stopped us, 'Don't drive on or you'll be drowned—there's a
precipice in front!' Eventually, by difficult detours, we succeeded in regaining the main road to Marburg where the
Americans provided us with further supplies of petrol and oil.
Jeeps driven by laughing negroes piloted us through the dimly
lit streets of the villages and market towns.

At 10.30 p.m. we came to a hamlet lying between Marburg
and Giessen called Sichardshausen. The Cardinals' car came
to a sudden stop beneath the lamp-posts of a street crossing.
The engine had failed. The rain streamed down in torrents.
People came up to help but it was no good. Brigadier Sedgwick,
whose lips were quivering with irritation and embarrassment,
asked me to change over to the other car. The Bishop,
astonished, received me with the words, 'You here again so
soon?' 'English orders,' I replied, 'the Brigadier is going on to
Frankfurt in my car to get help from the Americans.' The
Bishop replied, 'Without consulting us, and with our baggage?'

Even as he said this the rear light of the station-wagon was disappearing into the dark night. It was striking eleven, and Frankfurt was more than a hundred kilometres away. Some people came and pushed our car to the side of the road and then returned to the shelter of their houses. The lights in the windows went out followed by the street lamps overhead; the unyielding rain beat inexorably against the windows of our dark and deserted car. We tried to sleep. During the rest of the night American soldiers frequently flashed their torches into the strange automobile,[1] but when they saw peaceful-looking people inside they went away. When it began to grow light we looked at our watches and said to the driver in English, 'It's seven o'clock now.' 'Yes, sir.' Wiping the sleep from his eyes he got out, opened the bonnet, looked at the engine with a yawn, and pressed the starter. It broke into life. One of our party thought there was something fishy about this: it seemed to prove that someone was trying to prevent the German cardinals from arriving in Rome before the British and American prelates; but another voice retorted that the facts of the case were a good deal simpler: the sodden batteries had dried during the night. Then the difficult question arose: should we drive on with our newly gained power or wait for help to come from Frankfurt? If we went on we should have to reckon with the danger of missing each other en route. After some discussion their Eminences decided on going forward with the proviso that arm signals should be given to any approaching car. Sure enough the hoped-for meeting took place on the Giessen-Frankfurt Autobahn. From some distance off we saw the Brigadier waving from the first of two American cars as they slowed down ahead. He was both relieved and delighted to see his charges safe and sound, and told us how he had driven all night and had only reached the quarters provided at Frankfurt at about 3 a.m.

An hour later we drew up in front of the Hospital of Our Lady in Frankfurt. The day before our arrival American officers had personally supervised the arrangement of the room we were to occupy there. During the afternoon we visited the

---

[1] Translator's note: The car placed at the Cardinal's disposal by Military Government was an ancient Daimler which had once belonged to the late Queen Mary.

cathedral which though severely damaged still stood in contrast to the old part of the city which had been utterly destroyed. On Sunday morning our Bishop occupied the pulpit of the parish church of St. Bernard, filled to overflowing by the faithful; clearly deeply stirred they looked up—especially the young folk—at the great pastor about whom they had heard so much and drank in his fine, simple words which comforted them in those dark days. When Mass was finished he received a tumultuous ovation from the crowd outside. This Mass, celebrated *coram cardinalibus*, had been in a Trappist church of which there are so few in Germany. The Cardinal's titular church in Rome was dedicated to St. Bernard. By a peculiar dispensation—so one may think today—the great Cistercian saint wished to take leave of our Bishop in Germany in order to greet him afresh on the soil of the Eternal City as though giving him a second home there.

Sunday afternoon saw us again on our way, this time with three cars at our service. Our objective was now Karlsruhe, lying 150 km. to the south. We drove fast through Darmstadt and Mannheim; away in the distance the dreaming towers and spires of Heidelberg spoke a Godspeed to us. Mild weather, harbinger of the spring, touched both mountain and valley. At about 4 p.m. we pulled up outside the station at Karlsruhe. In a little while Brigadier Sedgwick emerged from the American Commandant's office with the cheerful news that the British leave-train from Calais would arrive at 18.00 hours, and that six compartments had been reserved in it for our party; the overnight journey to Villach in Austria would, therefore, be spent comfortably. From there we were to fly direct to Rome in an American plane. After waiting anxiously in the car for some two hours our courier-plenipotentiary appeared, a troubled expression on his face, and announced: 'Bad news, Your Eminences! The leave-train from Great Britain has been cancelled. Storms in the English Channel have prevented the boat from sailing.' A perplexed silence followed this statement. There were stern faces, and for the first time an atmosphere of real crisis. The two Princes of the Church then told the Brigadier that they were immensely grateful for his aid: he had, they fully realized, done all that lay in his power to help them; by day and night he had telephoned and sent signals on their behalf. All honour was due to him for his efforts and they thanked him from the bottom of their hearts. If, however, by the following afternoon no clear plan for the continuance of the journey to Rome was forthcoming they, as German bishops, would be compelled, in the light of the events, to demand an immediate return to their homes.

Force majeure we had to retrace our way to Frankfurt, and it was with downcast faces that we surveyed from the windows the dull and tedious flatness of the countryside. Connection with the outside world could now be made only from Frankfurt. Midnight struck as we pulled at the night bell of the Hospital of Our Lady, and saw yet again the familiar but astounded faces of the good Sisters who opened the door to their exhausted guests. The Mother Superior came running up and laughingly declared they had heard on the radio in the German news service from London that the German cardinals had landed safely in Rome that afternoon. It's an ill wind that blows nobody any good. The mother of one of the priests of our party heard the same announcement, and said later that at the moment of hearing this a weight had fallen from her shoulders as she declared, 'Thank God he's safely out of that wretched plane.'

On Monday morning Brigadier Sedgwick appeared with an entirely new plan. He had now arranged for us to travel by train via Paris and through Switzerland to Rome. Met with much headshaking he assured us that it was by this route that the Bishop of Berlin, Cardinal von Preysing, had reached his goal and had already been in Paris for some days. He had been informed of this for the first time that morning by the American Religious Affairs colonel.

At noon the radio gave out that all railway bridges over the Rhine were endangered by flooding and thus a new and yet another obstacle blocked our path. How were we to cross the Rhine at Mainz? Happily it proved to be a false alarm, and towards evening four cars arrived and took us to the station. Porters grasped our luggage, we were filmed, and a sense of buoyancy came over us all. Surely the French route must turn out all right! Two American leave-trains were standing ready, one for high-ranking officers in which both prelates and Brigadier Sedgwick had reserved compartments, the other was for less senior officers, and a compartment with four *couchettes* had been earmarked for the *entourage*. Our newly gained confidence was somewhat damped by a gloomy uncertainty when we learnt that our train was scheduled to start fifteen minutes after the first. Would we miss each other in Paris? The train began to move out and soon a bell rang in the corridor, calling us to dinner. We felt like children at the approach of Christmas, and hours of pleasantry followed and the *Stimmung* could not have been happier.

After a comfortable night's sleep the morning sun greeted us, emerging slowly through clouds and banks of light fog. Round us lay the land between Metz and Paris: fateful country for all. Our thoughts went out to our prisoners of war whose camps we thought we could recognize on the outskirts of the towns. At approximately ten in the morning our train steamed slowly into the Paris station. A minute or two of tense anxiety for us ensued; but before the train came to its final halt we saw the massive figure of our Brigadier waiting on the platform; at his side were two officials of the Quai d'Orsay who assured us in fluent German that as long as we were on French soil we could rely on the protection and assistance of the French Government. Waiting cars took us to the Grand Hotel in the centre of Paris where shortly before us the two prelates had arrived, and where they had found an invitation waiting for them to take luncheon with the Papal Nuncio.

When the two German cardinals with their suite and Brigadier Sedgwick arrived at the *Nunziatura* they were met by the Cardinal Archbishop of Paris, the Cardinal Archbishop of Rouen, the Auxiliary Bishop of Toulouse and many other prelates. We were much struck by the attention and brotherly love they extended to the two German Princes of the Church. For the first time one experienced directly some echo in the Christian world outside Germany of the Bishop of Münster's fight. They looked at him with admiration and sympathy, pressing for details of the events of those dismal days. It was consoling to learn that the bishops abroad thought exactly as we did about the repatriation of P.O.W.s and the dreadful plight of the refugees in the East of Germany. Later, similar sentiments were expressed by all the cardinals assembled round the Father of Christendom in the Eternal City. The

German bishops had the opportunity of expressing their anxiety to almost every one of them during the weeks that followed, and one and all promised to do their utmost for the prisoners and the victims of the diaspora when they returned to their own countries.

In the afternoon the French Foreign Office placed cars at our disposal so that we could visit the more important ecclesiastical places of interest in the metropolis. In the evening Brigadier Sedgwick conducted us to the Gare de Lyon where the Orient express stood ready to depart at 19.00 hours. He made all the necessary arrangements and formalities for the remainder of our journey through Switzerland and Italy. He took leave of the cardinals in their compartment and then left us to fly to London. The French cardinals, surrounded by gaily gesticulating priests and relations, then took their seats. Owing to the short notice it had not been possible to reserve a compartment in their *voiture*, and our bishops had to share one sleeper. This carriage stayed with the train only as far as Milan—a fact which occasioned a series of mishaps when it came to changing trains at Milan. The four members of the suites found seats reserved for them in a first-class non-sleeper. There was no truth whatsoever in the fantastic reports issued in both German and foreign newspapers in the following weeks that the journey had been made in goods trucks with wooden seats, etc. The French Foreign Office had defrayed all the costs of the tickets to Rome, and what is more, had detailed two officials to accompany us as far as the Swiss frontier. They begged the French prelates to look after their German *confrères* through Switzerland. Before these friendly officials left us they had telephoned to both Swiss and Italian frontier officers to facilitate all formalities and established liaison with the Cardinal of Milan.

At no frontier station was the baggage of the German cardinals or that of their suite examined: they were treated as diplomats and were able to take to Rome for the Pope's inspection documents and photographs of conditions in Germany. It must be realized that owing to the international situation then prevailing in Europe travelling was a hazardous business; one had constantly to pass through military zones and cross frontiers under totally different conditions as normally prevailed. We learnt later that it took a certain English officer five days to reach Rome from Münster, travelling first up to Calais and from there via Paris and Switzerland. In the light of this, malicious reports, which were then current about the alleged delay and annoyance caused to the German cardinals by the British authorities, must be completely discountenanced.

We had set out from Münster on the Friday afternoon and reached the Swiss border on Wednesday morning. A beautiful, early spring morning rose over the Alps as our train thundered through the impressive mountain scenery and, plunging in and out of the numerous tunnels, was soon skirting the lake of Geneva; the giant snow-capped mountains towered up into the pure world of heaven; here and there chaplets of mist hung over the wooded slopes. How bright were the Bishop's eyes! The carefree, unburdened years of his youth came back to him, and he spoke of that happy time in Freiburg as he pointed in its direction, remembering how often he had scaled those Alpine giants. The roof and castles of Montreux, so gloriously situated, passed us by. It was in the walls of this town (for so we learnt in Rome) that the Jesuit Father Friedrich Muckermann, who was so closely associated with Münster, had prepared himself for death. The inexorable opponent of National Socialism, he had been chased through every country in Europe, finally escaping to the U.S.A. But in the end he had chosen to return to Germany and death.

At last we were in Italy, the country which for a thousand years all Germans have longed to see. Dusk had already fallen when the Orient train drew in to the vast station of Milan. A prelate was waiting on the platform to welcome us in the name of the Cardinal Archbishop. Round him was grouped a happy bevy of German nuns: the Grey Sisters and the nuns *Unserer Lieben Frau*. They carried baskets of delicious food specially prepared for us and we spied in them the gleaming gold of the famous local oranges. But as it turned out they were not to be used as proviant that night. At the nearby platform stood the train which was to go on to Rome that evening; the French cardinals' sleeping *voiture* had already been coupled to it. There was a quick rush. Trunks were dragged out and carried over, but the station-master, who had been informed of our coming earlier in the evening, would not allow us to get in; he said that Eminences of the Church should under no circumstances occupy unreserved seats, and then perhaps later be compelled to move into the corridor. *Ma che!* Two special compartments were to be provided for us next morning. Smiling ruefully our Bishop remarked that the tailor in Rome would never have the time to get the 'red things' ready for the consistory! True, the train bearing the French prelates thereupon drew out of the station, but they had to remain for seven hours on the following morning in the station at Bologna before continuing the journey to Rome with us.

On the other hand, we Germans who had been left behind had the good fortune to experience unforgettable hours in the shadow of the Milan *Duomo*, on ground saturated with history. We entered the two waiting cars and were soon speeding through the brilliantly lighted streets on our way to the Arch-bishop's palace, the foundations of which went back to the time of the holy St. Ambrose, and where St. Charles Borromeus, the great cardinal of the Counter-Reformation, had lived. The hallowed atmosphere of age-old stories fell upon us as we climbed the outer staircase of the courtyard, and passing through the high portal, we went through the dimly lit rooms. In that peaceful silence we felt the impact of the classical world as our eyes fell on the noble statuary and the dark tapestries— half monastery, half museum.

Cardinal Schuster greeted his German brothers most warmly; he himself was the child of south Tyrolean parents, though born and bred in Rome. He had been Abbot of the famous Benedictine monastery of St. Paul Outside-The-Walls in Rome, and then Archbishop of Milan, the largest diocese in the world. That evening he told us fascinating details of Mussolini's end. During the last few days of his life, he had come to the Cardinal's palace when the latter was negotiating with the allies on the Duce's behalf in the event of his giving himself up. At first Mussolini was willing that the Cardinal should act in this way, but later his pride was too great and he fled secretly towards the Swiss frontier taking his mistress, Claretta Petacci, with him. Crouching and in disguise he was dragged from a German truck, swiftly condemned to death and shot with his paramour. Their bodies were brought back to Milan and hung up in the market square with the corpses of fifteen other Fascist leaders. The fury of the mob knew no bounds and their bodies were hideously desecrated. They were buried without rites in a nearby cemetery and with only a light covering of earth. A year later Mussolini's body was stolen and reburied in an unknown spot. We asked Cardinal Schuster whether the Duce had shown any signs of repentance when he saw that his end was approaching. 'None whatever; he was far too arrogant,' was the reply. We said we supposed he had done a certain amount of good for the Church in Italy. 'Certainly,' His Eminence answered; 'but only from carefully calculated political motives, and never from true religious feeling. From his boyhood, as one was, alas, later to experience, he had been without religion and had soon fallen into a loose way of living.' So ended a dictator who, in the course of a decade, had caused the death of millions of his fellow beings.

Early next morning both bishops said Mass at the tomb of St. Charles Borromeo in the crypt of the *Duomo*. We then said farewell to Cardinal Schuster who very kindly gave us provisions for the journey and some Italian money. The early morning sun fell aslant the Cathedral as we took our last look at its gothic towers, the myriad marble finials and figures of saints—a glorious symphony of form and colour. How great that age of faith and ideals must have been when men could give to God such a *Sursum Corda* in religious art. This marvellous work of the human spirit escaped intact the devastation of war.

In peace time the train journey from Milan to Rome is a matter of some 12 hours. It took us twice that time owing to the destruction of bridges and tunnels. At Bologna we again met the French cardinals who had waited there overnight. They invited our bishops to share their *wagon-lit*, and thus it happened that on Thursday night French and German cardinals used the same sleeping compartments. Our Bishop was the guest of the Cardinal of Lille. Although the latter was considerably older than von Galen he insisted on occupying the upper bunk, leaving the lower bed for the Lion of Münster. 'It must be recorded,' said the Bishop, 'as a sign of the times, that at least churchmen know how to try and ease the strain between nations by shaking hands as brothers, thus helping to bring nations together.'[1]

On the forenoon of Friday, after exactly a week of travelling, we reached our destination. A sharp, happy intake of breath— a sudden flooding of the spirit with an inner joy, for there, not far away, rose the domes and towers of the Eternal City . . . so must the pilgrims of old have felt when, after months of weary peregrination, their eyes first fell on *Roma Eterna*, and standing still, they folded their hands in prayer.

[1] Translator's note: The Romans on the station were astonished to see the French and German cardinals leave the train and walk down the platform arm in arm, just as if there had been no war.

CHAPTER 23

IN THE ETERNAL CITY

THERE before us lay the City, her face miraculously unscarred despite the dangerous days of June, 1944. The giant dome of Michelangelo, rising out of a sea of buildings, loomed larger and mightier as we came nearer, and yet in some mysterious way remained distant and isolated in its deep solemnity, mantled by gossamer veils of morning mists through which the warming rays of the rising sun gently penetrated here and there. It is a quite special and private experience for every Catholic whether bishop, priest or layman to see Rome for the first time or to greet it anew after years of absence—this 3000-year-old Rome, the City of the World as it has been called.

And now, only a few months after the cessation of those dire hostilities, came the Holy Father's summons throughout the world to the chief men of the Church's hierarchy to attend a council of the highest senate.

In the midst of discord and dissension they hastened as messengers of charity and conciliation to the Father of Christendom in the Eternal City. Among those Princes gathered from the four corners of the earth (for a short space we must re-live the days that followed our arrival) was the Bishop of Münster or simply 'The Cardinal', as he was known. All Rome was at his feet. Cardinal Frings, preaching the panegyric at his colleague's requiem in Münster a few weeks later, declared, 'He was the undisputed hero of the consistory. . . .' God gave him to our diocese in the most disgraceful period of German history, and now he held the highest honour in the eyes of the whole Christian world.

During their sojourn in Rome bishops usually make a point of residing in one of their national seminaries or colleges. Every Christian nation has possessed at least one such a house for centuries, a sort of island home in the middle of the supra-nationality of the Eternal City; such, for example, is the case with the French, Spanish, the British and the Americans; so

also the Poles and the Dutch; the Portuguese and the Braz-
ilians. We Germans have three such institutions. First comes
the Collegium Germanicum, founded by St. Ignatius of Loyola
in the sixteenth century, and still conducted by Jesuit Fathers.
It houses young students of theology, sent by their local ordin-
aries from Germany, Austria and Hungary to study in Rome
for a period of seven years, after which they are ordained to the
holy priesthood. These *Germaniker* can easily be recognized by
their bright red cassocks. Then there is the *Collegio Santa Maria
dell' Anima,* adjoining which is the German national church;
since the Middle Ages this building has been the hospice for all
German pilgrims to Rome, but for the last hundred years it has
been the residence for German priests who are pursuing special
studies in the papal academies—and above all in Canon Law.
In 1946 four German cardinals stayed there: Innitzer of
Vienna, Faulhaber of München, Graf von Preysing of Berlin
and Graf von Galen of Münster. Cardinal Frings of Cologne
went to the Campo Santo, the third of the German colleges,
which serves the same purpose as the Anima, and is situated
in the immediate neighbourhood of Vatican City.

The first path which bishops tread on reaching Rome is
that leading to the Holy Father. Soon after the arrival of the
German bishops on that Friday morning their names were
announced at the Vatican, and a few hours later we received a
communication: *Private audience on Saturday at 11 a.m.* On that
morning, therefore, the Bishop of Münster, accompanied by his
suite, drove to Vatican City in one of the Papal cars. We went
past venerable churches, through the streaming shopping
crowds, threading our way through booths and market stalls,
a strange and somewhat bizarre sight for Teutonic eyes. One
could buy to one's heart's content had one but money enough.
It was a time of inflation, yet it seemed to us that the Romans
looked more prosperous than the Parisians. The German
cardinals had only marks, which were quite useless abroad; but
the Holy Father and the American prelates were lavish in
coming to their assistance. When the latter paid their respects
in the days following they left a packet of dollars on our Bishop's
table, and shortly after the visit he said to his chaplain: 'The
Cardinal of Chicago was here just now and he has given me a
bulky envelope. Just take a look and see if I'm right!' The banks

in Rome accepted dollars only too gladly, and gave us plenty
of lire in exchange, so that we were able to defray the expenses
incurred by our stay in the German colleges.

Passing over the Tiber by the Ponte Sant' Angelo we
approached the Città del Vaticano, and were again struck by
the splendour and majesty of the great cupola of St. Peter's as
we crossed the huge Piazza with its giant colonnades. Having
arrived in the Cortile di San Damaso, we left the car and,
going through an entrance hall, ascended the wide steps of the
Scala Pia. Our way now led through the spacious *Stanze* of
Raphael, through lofty galleries and past saluting Swiss Guards
who, one sensed, immediately recognized the great Bishop
from the North. They seemed to hold themselves more upright
and bore themselves with special pride. With a smile the Bishop
saluted them paternally, saying in German, '*Grüss Euch Gott,
Ihr Lieben Schweizer Jungs!*' This seemed to please them, for over
several faces there passed a flush of pleasure. At last we
arrived in the Anticamera, which is almost next to the Holy
Father's private study. Involuntarily voices were lowered—
giving place to whispers. The old sculptures, the massive
paintings and enormous tapestries, the busts of popes, the heavy
window curtains, the distant murmur of the metropolis, the
subdued light, the silent tread—everything is tuned to give the
visitor the feeling that here dwells the one who holds in his
hands the helm of the Universal Church. A few more steps
forward and we had the *entrée* to the *Anticamera Segreta*. We were
on the threshold. The two members of Cardinal Fring's suite
were talking to a Privy Chamberlain of the Sword and Cape, a
sign that their Archbishop was having audience of the Holy
Father. At noon precisely, the Cardinal of Cologne emerged
from the library, and our Bishop went in alone. Under his
arm he carried a brief-case containing photographs of churches
destroyed and documents dealing with events in East Germany.
These two great men of the Church had not seen each other
since May 1939. To think what had passed during that period!
The sermons preached by the Bishop in the summer of 1941
at the height of his battle with the forces of darkness had come
into the Pope's hands a few weeks after their delivery, and the
blessing and assurance of prayers which soon followed afforded
the Bishop in Münster deep consolation, and were a strong

support to him in the ensuing years of struggle. Now in this hour of audience the Holy Father was able to thank the great German Bishop personally; and it was indeed for this that he had given him the Sacred Purple in order that his apostolic crusade and his spirit of willing martyrdom might be again remembered and absorbed by the whole world. They spoke too of Germany's present anxieties and problems, and the Holy Father carefully examined the papers laid before him.

When the appointed hour was at an end the door was opened and the Bishop appeared, his features betraying great emotion; he beckoned to his suite, and according to ancient custom, presented them to the Pope. For a few minutes one stood and knelt before the Father of Christendom. He asked us questions in our mother tongue and we replied in the same language. We received from his own hands a Rosary as a memento; then the Holy Father rose, embraced the Cardinal and we slowly withdrew to the *Anticamera*. The tall figure of the Pope makes an unforgettable impression with his slender upright figure, stooping perhaps a little at the shoulders; his complexion is of a tanned olive, eyes large and dark with a lively expression, his voice resonant and full of energy.

The Swiss nun[1] who, with two others, looks after his domestic *ménage* gave us some details of his daily routine. The Pope rises at six and celebrates Holy Mass alone at seven. At nine he is seated at his desk where he works until eleven, when the audiences begin. They last until 1.30 p.m. Luncheon is taken alone, followed by a period of rest until three in the afternoon. Then comes a walk in the Vatican gardens of about an hour's duration. This is the only time in the day when the Pope can be out in the fresh air; even then he always carries a sheaf of papers in his hand rather than remain idle during that period. From twenty minutes past four further work at his desk, after which he takes the evening meal. After dining he says the Rosary with the prelates of his *entourage* and the three nuns. His Office is said from ten to eleven; this done he returns to his study and often works until two in the morning. When he is in good health a short period of sleep is sufficient.

[1] Translator's note: Madre Pascalina, a Franciscan who kept house for the Pope when he was Nuncio in Munich.

A long row of visitors waited in the Anima: priests and nuns as well as lay-people of all ages and standing. They all wanted to have a word with the Bishop and hear about conditions at home in Germany. On Sunday afternoon he preached an important sermon in the Church of the Anima. Although it was recorded by a Swiss company on discs he spoke extempore without preparing notes—there had been no time for this—and his words were plain and very simple, from *il fondo del cuore*. Deeply moved, he thanked the Holy Father for the great love he had shown towards Germany by raising three German bishops to Cardinalitial rank, at a time when all the world, so full of hate, had declared the entire nation guilty. He openly protested against the monstrous horrors then being perpetrated in East Germany, and against the hate-inspired dictum that a whole people must be blamed collectively. He referred to the heroism of many Christians in Germany during that period of satanic tyranny.

It was indeed moving to see the German cardinals kneeling in the beautifully decorated quire to receive Benediction of the Blessed Sacrament. Not only were members of the German colony present, together with hundreds of German Religious, but countless foreigners made up the faithful in the packed nave and side aisles overflowing into the side chapels. Although there were many present who did not understand the German tongue they were content to hear the Bishop's voice, see his huge stature and feel his presence.

The Press could not avoid writing in a sensational way about his tallness: 'He is a giant—fully six feet six inches in height. A colossus, a veritable Saint Michael. . . .' One paper produced a charming and amusing picture. On Saturday morning the Cardinal appeared with a Cistercian Father attached to his titular church of St. Bernard. As both were leaving the main door of the church a Press photographer took up a position in front of them; the shutter clicked and the picture was taken. The picture showed an unusually short Italian monk completely dwarfed by the Gargantuan German Bishop. The Romans were unfeignedly astonished at his appearance, and took him to their hearts with every manifestation of affection whenever they saw him.

Sixty German military chaplains who were prisoners of war

in Italy received permission to come to Rome on the day of the consistory. They stood beneath the Bishop's pulpit and listened avidly to his sermon. When the service was over they were greeted by the Bishop in the sacristy, and for many this was a happy reunion.

Twenty-four hours later our Bishop, accompanied by Cardinal Innitzer of Vienna, drove out to Vicarello, an old monastery north of Rome, in which the German chaplains were quartered. This monastery is situated in wild, romantic hill country where bearded shepherds tend their flocks as they did centuries ago; it was formerly inhabited by German Sisters belonging to the Order *Unserer Lieben Frau*. That evening the two cardinals were ceremonially surrounded by the German priests. Clemens August, who had on his right the only member of the Münster diocese, Padré Lohmann, D.D., gave them an amusing account of the adventurous journey to Rome, and, capturing the hearts of all present, was given a great ovation when he left.

.   .   .   .   .

Consistory week started on Monday, Feb. 18th, and on that day the ceremonies began with the Secret Consistory of the old cardinals. In the *Sala Concistoriale* the Pope, with great pomp and ceremony, announced to the assembled cardinals the names of those he intended to raise to the Cardinalate. The papal couriers of monsignorial rank, attended by a Privy Chamberlain of the Sword and Cape[1] in sixteenth-century Spanish Court dress, waited outside the closed doors. As soon as the Secret Consistory was over these gentlemen were handed the briefs of appointment in great sealed envelopes for transmission to all the new cardinals assembled in Rome. In order to facilitate and expedite their delivery the cardinals of each country hold themselves ready at an agreed place for the reception of the documents. The three German cardinals had gathered at the Monastery of the Salvatorians near St. Peter's Square. They sat on gilded chairs in an assembly hall attended by regular and secular clergy and privileged laymen.

[1] Translator's note: Privy Chamberlains of the Sword and Cape are laymen.

When suddenly the door opened, and three tall Italians appeared, our Bishop at once recognized them as the Pope's nephews. He was much moved for some time after by this signal mark of the Holy Father's kindness in thus sending his nearest relatives on the occasion of their elevation to the Cardinalate. At eleven o'clock there was a sudden hush of expectancy, and the papal couriers were announced. One of the monsignori went first to the Archbishop of Cologne who was, of course, the senior of the three German prelates, spoke a few introductory words and then presented the brief of appointment. It was at once opened and read aloud. The same procedure followed with the Bishops of Berlin and Münster. Cardinal Frings then spoke shortly and to the point in Italian, expressing their thanks to the Pope, after which the three couriers withdrew. Everybody was happy, and hearts were full as the congratulations, the so-called *Visita di calore*, began. Well-wishers pressed in from all sides. Chancing to look up at our Bishop I saw tears in his eyes and his lips quivered. There seemed to be no end to the rows of congratulators who streamed in from all parts of the Eternal City. We noticed the variety of different coloured cassocks belonging to seminarians from all over the world, and there were faces of every complexion and hue: the white of the British and Americans; the olive, brown and yellow of the Spanish, Indian, Chinese and Japanese; the jet black of Africans. It was remarkable to watch the diminutive Asiatics looking up with smiling faces at the tall Cardinal of whose heroic struggle they had heard so much, and the latter, his eyes moist with tears, bending down to put his hand on their shoulders. At such times one experiences in a wonderful way the depth of that love which binds all the nations and races of this world into the kingdom of true peace in the Church of Christ.

When the *Visita di calore* was over an American film company came along and asked permission to make a picture of the German cardinals. As we moved along the terrace in obedience to their instructions, there was a buzz of animated conversation and all the manifestations of unrestrained joy; as we gazed over the Piazza or looked up at the mighty cupola of St. Peter's we could hear the soft clatter of the cine-camera.

Wednesday afternoon. For the first time the newly named

cardinals drove to the Vatican as such. In the Sistine Chapel, which houses the famous painting of Michelangelo's Last Judgement, they came together to receive in the semi-public consistory the solemn conferring of the scarlet biretta.[1] The rays of the setting sun streamed through the high windows, casting a golden veil on that majestic picture, and softly illuminating the painted ceiling with its scenes from the Old Testament, the creation of Adam and the figures of prophets, while below the flashlights of the photographers flared whenever a cardinal arrived with his suite. Each Eminence taking his station according to precedence and protocol donned the cardinalitial *cappa magna*, a kind of cloak with a collar of ermine and a long scarlet train.

Suddenly the British and American Princes of the Church were seen to go up to the Germans: the victors, if we may so put it, came to the vanquished and shook their hands with the greatest cordiality. Cardinal Spellman of New York made a laughing reference to the adventures of the journey to Rome[2] which he had heard about in Paris, and promised to put an American plane at their disposal when the time came to return home. At once a load fell from our minds, for ever since we had arrived in the City this problem had caused us the greatest anxiety.

Six o'clock struck and the procession was formed. At its head went the Patriarch of Armenia, followed by the archbishops and finally five bishops, among whom were Berlin and

[1] Translator's note: After the secret consistory, and normally on the same day the newly created cardinals meet in the Pope's apartments when the scarlet *zucchetto* or skull-cap is handed to them; later the scarlet biretta is placed by the Pope on the head of each. They receive the 'red hat' at the next public consistory after they have taken the customary oath. The author does not mention here the secret ceremony known as *aperitio oris*, the 'opening of the mouth', and at this same secret consistory the *clausura oris*, the 'closing of the mouth', symbolizing their duties to preserve the secrets of their office and to give wise counsel to the Pope. Certain departures from normal custom were made at the consistory described here owing to the unprecedented number of new cardinals at the same time. The Pope also wished that as many as possible should witness the ceremonies.

[2] Translator's note: Before leaving Paris I attended a reception given by the American Ambassador in honour of Cardinal Spellman and Cardinal Tien. I took the opportunity of informing His Eminence of New York about transport difficulties and the fact that the German cardinals were without money, and he generously promised to attend to both matters when he arrived in Rome.

Münster. To the right of each cardinal walked the episcopal secretary and on the left a Privy Chamberlain of the Sword and Cape. The procession passed through the halls and corridors into the Hall of Benedictions, which is situated over the portals of St. Peter's, and can accommodate some 4000 people (St. Peter's is the largest church in the world and can take about 70,000). Slowly the impressive *cortège* moved across the brilliantly lighted Aula where on both sides the faithful sat in packed rows. Against the huge proscenium at the end of the Hall stood the Holy Father's throne on which he had already taken his seat. Many of the spectators held in their hands copies of the papal newspaper, *Osservatore Romano*, containing photographs of the new cardinals with their names. When the tall figure of our Bishop came in sight there was a movement in the rows, a whisper of astonishment and the half-suppressed exclamation, '*Conte di Galen—Vescovo di Münster!*' All heads were turned towards him. A slight, almost embarrassed smile flickered over his face and he whispered to his suite, '*Ist doch peinlich, wenn sie einen hier alle so angucken.*' ('Can't say I relish all this staring.')

Thirty red damask chairs had been arranged in a semi-circle round the papal throne on which the cardinals then sat. There followed the striking ceremony of the bestowal of the biretta. Each cardinal mounted to the throne, knelt down and received the scarlet token of his new dignity. The Pope then delivered an allocution lasting nearly an hour: he spoke of the significance of these appointments; he had called these men to the highest rank of the hierarchy from all nations and countries as a sign that the Church, which is truly Catholic and world-embracing, is given jurisdiction and responsibility not only in Europe but all over the world. (For further details of this speech *vide* Bierbaum, *Cardinal von Galen's Last Journey to Rome*.) At the completion of this ceremony the Holy Father came down from the throne and mounted the *Sedia Gestatoria*, the portable throne that is borne on the shoulders of the red-uniformed *palafrenieri* or footmen. Suspended, so it seemed, above the head of the crowd and clearly visible to one and all, the Holy Father blessed the kneeling thousands. After he had passed them they stood up and loudly acclaimed the Father of Christendom with joyful shouts of '*Evivva il Papa!*' The German

'*Es lebe der Papst!*' was not heard since it is our custom to remain silent on these occasions. These outward expressions and manifestations of loyalty differ according to national temperament.

The Cardinals' procession followed. When our Bishop appeared again and came within touching distance of the bystanders all restraint was cast aside. Breaking through the cordon of the Swiss Guard they pressed round him to kiss his ring. Those who were unsuccessful in this took hold of his robes and pressed them to their lips. How was it that such actions, which caused the Bishop the deepest emotion, could take place? Such expressions of primitive and genuine affection were nothing short of astonishing. They had expected a dignified Prince of the Church, a man of knightly bearing, a stubborn-looking fighter, a man to whom respect and awe was due; and now a totally different picture. True a giant in stature, but so homely, unaffected and natural with the features and expression of a gentle father, and having the eyes of a good shepherd. And so it was that folk in a foreign land went into raptures of enthusiasm and cried out, '*Uomo simpatico!*' It was an enthusiasm and attachment which mounted daily.

.   .   .   .   .

Thursday morning. For the first time in the Church's history the public consistory was held in the central nave of St. Peter's. The papal throne had been erected above the *Confessio*, the tomb of the Apostle, the first Pope, and from here his successor in the twentieth century would award the Red Hat. Two separate stairways, elegantly devised, led up to the *cathedra*. A passageway down the centre of the Basilica was kept open; to the left and the right were rows of seats and the pen-like tribunes. That morning St. Peter's opened its bronze doors to more than 20,000 people gathered in from all nations and from every race: the rich and poor, the simple and the learned. High above this great family of Christian society the huge Petrine dome seemed to float in a lake of light, fed by the beams of early morning sunlight, whose shafts struck down on to the *Confessio Sancti Petri* and blended with the beams of the searchlights. Modern techniques of lighting were united to the splendour, form and colour of the Renaissance in order to preserve those hours of august spectacle.

At 8 a.m. the new cardinals assembled in the Vatican. Having vested in *cappa magna* the procession slowly descended the broad stairs leading to the chapel of the Blessed Sacrament in St. Peter's. Here in the presence of the Eucharistic Saviour they took the oath to defend always the rights of Holy Church. At the same time the Holy Father came down by another way, and entered the chapel of the world-famed Pietà of Michelangelo where the old cardinals were waiting. On the stroke of the great clock the Supreme Pontiff took his seat on the *Sedia Gestatoria* flanked by the *flabelli*, the huge fans of ostrich feathers, and the procession began to move. In front went the Swiss Guards, the Noble and Palatine Guards, the Papal Gendarmes; then followed monsignori, prelates, bishops and cardinals. High from the Loggia of the Aula Magna there rang out the *Marcia Papale*, the Papal March played on the renowned silver trumpets: that strangely moving melody with its measured rhythm exactly fitting the steps and tempo of the processionists. The glory of long past ages sprang to life before us. These are the hours when the Church displays the rich lustre of her tradition and history and girds herself in splendid panoply. There broke forth a mighty storm of applause, great bursts of acclamation greeted the appearance of the Holy Father: it rolled like the murmur of thunder through the immense transepts and aisles of the Basilica and filled those vast spaces with windy sound. Ere long the Pope, wearing the tiara, sat enthroned high above the tomb of St. Peter. In accordance with ancient custom a passage from the document of a beatification process was read aloud and relayed through loud-speakers. Then silence fell as the old cardinals rose from their seats and passed down the central gangway into a side aisle where the cardinals-elect were waiting in prayer before the tabernacle in the Blessed Sacrament chapel. The moment was pregnant with symbolism as the old cardinals fetched their new brothers, received them into their midst, and again forming procession, led them through the tens of thousands of spectators to the Pope. Then they passed into the beams of the spotlights, and the glittering sight was unforgettable as the thirty cardinals-elect from all over the world passed up to the tomb of the Fisherman and his successor.

A whispering rustle of subdued applause was heard, at first

controlled, but becoming louder as each national group in the congregation greeted their cardinal; but when the towering figure of the Cardinal of Münster was seen, the plaudits were redoubled and grew to hurricane force—an *applauso trionfale*, the papers described it—as he slowly mounted the steps of the papal throne, massive and dignified. Complete silence then came over all. The Bishop of Münster was kneeling before the Holy Father. The Red Hat, emblem of the cardinal's exalted and princely rank, was slowly placed on his head, and to him and his brothers the words were spoken each time, 'Receive this hat, emblem of the cardinalitial dignity . . . as a sign that thou wilt defend the rights of Holy Roman Church even to the shedding of thine own blood.'[1] We who watched and knew him intimately said within ourselves, 'Thou who kneelest there hast already shown thyself ready.' The Cardinal rose and the Holy Father leaning forward to embrace him whispered the memorable words, 'God bless you, and God Bless Germany!' Count von Galen turned to face the vast host below. On him were concentrated searchlights and spotlights, cameras and glasses, and the steady gaze of tens of thousands. He was the cynosure of every eye in the Basilica which now re-echoed to a storm of applause, enthusiasm and homage that lasted for minutes on end in which diplomats and cardinals themselves joined. Those from Münster who witnessed this astonishing occurrence felt as in a dream. A senior official in the diplomatic service wrote that day, 'When Bishop von Galen came down from the steps of the Papal throne it seemed to me that at that moment the German name, covered so long in shame and infamy, recovered something of its former lustre in the person of this great bishop.'

The newly created cardinals, surrounded by the old, now took up a position between the *Confessio* and the *Cathedra* hard upon the place where the remains of the Apostle lie buried; there they sank to their knees and stretched their bodies prone

---

[1] Translator's note: The actual words the Pope pronounces are as follows: '*Ad laudem omnipotentis Dei et Sanctae Sedis ornamentum, accipe galerum rubrum, insigne singularis dignitatis cardinalatus, per quod designatur quod usque ad mortem et sanguinis effusionem inclusive pro exaltatione sanctae fidei, pace et quiete populi christiani, augmento et statu sacrosanctae romanae Ecclesiae, te intrepidum exhibere debeas, in nomine Patris, et Filii et Spiritus Sancti.*' As the last few words are said a threefold sign of the cross is made over the cardinal.

upon the ground in the manner prescribed for the Good Friday
liturgy. The *Te Deum* was chanted. The meaning of this impressive act is simple : these men who have risen to the highest
rank of the Church must never forget they are but as dust in the
eyes of God. There is a photograph of our Cardinal lying thus
on the ground, the hood of his *cappa magna* drawn over his head.
Who among those present in St. Peter's could have had any
idea how soon Almighty God would demand from him the
consummation of that symbolic gesture?

On the following afternoon the cardinals were summoned
to the next secret consistory. As the last sign of their rank they
received from the hands of the Pope the sapphire ring.[1]

This took place on Friday, the 22nd of February, at half
past five in the evening. Exactly four weeks later, also on a
Friday and again on the 22nd of a month (March), the Cardinal
died ; it was the sad task of his chaplain to draw from the dead
man's finger the Holy Father's ring.

The whole of Saturday morning was devoted to receiving
visits from foreign cardinals, especially the Spanish and
American. A few days before, the German Princes of the Church
had attended the official reception for the diplomats accredited
to the Holy See and had taken the opportunity of telling them
about events in Germany. Similarly they felt it incumbent on
them to make representations to the prelates outside Germany.
Who else could raise their voices publicly about these terrible
happenings except the German bishops, now that Germany was
without any form of Government of its own? We were all consoled and edified by their complete understanding of the problems involved, and for the moral and material welfare of the
Fatherland. Subsequently in their pastoral letters they did all
that was possible, as protagonists of brotherly love and compassion, to urge the faithful of their dioceses to organize
collections and welfare work for their brethren in Germany.

Our Bishop spent a considerable time with the Cardinal of

[1] Translator's note: At the same time they are assigned a title or
diaconia by which they shall henceforth be known. This is the last of the
consistory ceremonies.

Rio de Janeiro in the Brazilian College Outside-The-Walls. In fluent German he spoke in the warmest terms of the German priests and nuns working in Brazil who came from the Münster diocese.

In the afternoon the newly elected cardinals were invited to an academic *fiesta* in the papal Gregorian University.[1] In the imposing Aula, the Father Rector delivered a speech in impeccable Latin, and this was followed by hymns sung by a choir of students, French, Spanish, American. . . . Others sang solo songs of congratulations to their cardinals. Finally a Chinese theological student sang of his far-off country which evoked great applause. All eyes were turned upon Cardinal Tien, the first Chinese bishop to be raised to the Purple. At the conclusion of the song there was renewed cheering and this student had to sing the only encore allowed, not, shall we say, for any instrinsic merit, but because its hearers felt themselves called spontaneously to express to the sons of Asia the Christian brotherly love for Europe. The friendly and charming Chinese Cardinal expressed his thanks in a shy but impressive manner. When from time to time a cardinal left the University each received an ovation from the students. When our Bishop prepared to leave, he was at once surrounded by a jubilant crowd of philosophers, theologians and canonists from all over the world. They thronged round almost threateningly and the Cardinal was borne, almost 'shoved', along the corridor in an ever-swelling wave. The eloquence and *copia verborum* of the Italians was powerless to quell the storm or control the onset. The chaplain to the right of the Cardinal held his *galero*[2] high above his head to prevent it being crushed, but he was pushed aside. At length the Cardinal succeeded with great difficulty in reaching the car which stood in the forecourt, but the chaplain found his way barred by an impenetrable wall of humanity, and only by constantly shouting '*Sono segretario*' did he eventually fight his way to the car. Someone shouted in broken German: 'Stay with us, Your Eminence! Stay a bit longer. All Rome loves

[1] Translator's note: The Gregorian University is perhaps the most important of the four theological colleges in Rome, the others being the *Collegio di Propaganda Fide*, the *Collegio Angelico* of the Dominicans, and the *Seminario Romano* on the Lateran. The Gregorian is under the direction of the Jesuit Fathers.

[2] Translator's note: The Cardinal's 'town' or 'walking-out' hat.

you!' It was not a question of hysteria, but an expression of genuine love or gratitude on the part of young men for whom the heroic spirit still counted for something, and who were as yet impervious to this blasé age.

On Sunday afternoon the German cardinals were the guests of the Collegium Germanicum. The Cardinal of Budapest, who had also been invited, spoke of the serious international situation in his country. He, too, had had difficulties in connection with his journey from Hungary, and eventually reached Rome in an Allied plane, arriving a day after the consistory had begun. From the Germanicum our Cardinal went straight to the nearby Capuchin church where, under the direction of a German monk, fifty Jewish converts were waiting to hear a few words from the Bishop. It was by a strange ordinance that the Cardinal found himself in a like situation a week later. He had offered the Holy Sacrifice in the Salesian Church in the presence of hundreds of pupils belonging to a charity school; later, when visiting the monastery, the Father Rector begged him to confirm a Jewish boy recently converted. He readily consented, and on that Sunday morning laid his hands on the twelve-year-old boy in the monastery chapel: it was his first Confirmation as a cardinal. Here a singular coincidence must be mentioned. On the morning of March 18th he celebrated his last Mass in the Borromäum at Münster for the eight-year-old daughter of a niece who was making her First Communion. That small child received from his hands her first Holy Communion and the last Host the Bishop was to consecrate on earth; and so to two far separated children he dispensed the holy mysteries, Confirmation and Holy Communion, as if God would say to us all: Lo! a great bishop who, like little children, fulfilled the word of God in his life—in the eyes of men a hero, in God's a child!

CHAPTER 24

FINAL JOURNEYS

TUESDAY, 26th Feb., 7 a.m. The spring blue of an early morning sky curved over the Alban hills as our Vatican car sped over the dry, dusty roads. There had been no rain for months in this district where the inhabitants had been praying daily for this blessing which had been given us so abundantly back home in Germany. The Cardinal's *entourage* sat behind, and on this occasion included the Rev. Dr. Berndorff, then chaplain at the Campo Santo, and organizer of the P.O.W. welfare, but now secretary to the Cardinal Archbishop of Cologne. Our Bishop sat in front, next to the Italian chauffeur: the seat was comfortable and roomy and Clemens August was ever a lover of open windows. During that long drive of 600 km. the keen air streamed into his face. This caused toothache, and some swelling of the lower half of the face, which reached something of a crisis on the following Sunday in Rome. Although his companions urged him to take care, the Cardinal, unfortunately, paid no attention to the trouble. The inflammation disappeared, but later in Münster the doctors declared that, as a result, the *caecum*, kidneys and the heart were probably infected.

Thus it was that on the way to visit his imprisoned brethren in South Italy the Cardinal caught the germs of death and unwittingly gave his life for them. There was not, therefore, the slightest foundation in the persistent rumour which was current for a year afterwards that he had been poisoned by the Secret Service.[1]

Our car went the way of the Via Appia, that ancient military highway through the Apennines into southern Italy. The great panorama of Roman history was unrolled in our

[1] Translator's note: Walking in the funeral procession a month later, my eyes were drawn involuntarily to the words chalked on the ruined walls: *Opfer des englischen Geheimdienst, Clemens August* (Our Cardinal, victim of the Secret Service).

15. The late Cardinal Griffin and Brigadier R. L. Sedgwick* at the funeral of Cardinal von Galen

* The Translator of this book.

16. The funeral procession of Cardinal von Galen through the ruins of Munster, March 28th, 1946

imagination. This road of the Scipios became the Via Triumphalis into the Forum Romanum of the Tiber City. Titus had
passed along it after the fall of Jerusalem; at the end of it we
had seen his triumphal arch with the seven-branchd candle-
stick from the Temple of the Jews on the entablature.

At noon we made a brief halt at the seminary in Benevento,
surprising the professors and students, who knew nothing of our
visit. We northerners, who are always inclined to disparage other
countries, were genuinely astonished at the imaginative and
up-to-date lines on which this college was run.

After lunch we set out again over hills and mountains. A
British captain, driving a small open car, was acting as our
outrider: he had some difficulty in coping with our speed—
typical in these southern parts—and our Italian chauffeur, who
was a positive Jehu, and whose *buon umore* had quite won our
hearts, took a fiendish delight, to judge from his grin, in setting
the pace. The smooth, macadamized road twisted and turned
like a snake through the lovely mountain country, past dreaming olive groves and orange orchards where the first harvest
of the year was being gathered; by the wayside stood tightly
packed baskets—how our German children would have loved
the sight of them!—real, golden-ripe *Apfelsinen* pendant on
real orange trees.

We reached our destination, Taranto, at nine in the evening and drove up to the Archbishop's palace. In the twilight
we could just make out the massive structure, festooned with
garlands and bunting in our honour. Alighting in the inner
courtyard we saw that the steps of the portico were closely
packed with seminarists, young and old, and the serried ranks
continued right up into the reception hall where stood the
Archbishop surrounded by his clergy. As the towering figure of
the Cardinal emerged from the car, somewhat stiffly after the
long ride, the southern temperament was again manifested in
lively fashion, becoming louder and more ebullient as he
embraced the Archbishop to the accompaniment of hand-
clapping and *evvivas*.

The foundations of this venerable building are literally
washed by the waves of the sea; for Taranto is situated on a
bight where the heel of the Italian boot juts out into the
Adriatic or, more properly, the *Mare Ionio*. The soft light of

o

the full moon silvered the balcony of the Cardinal's bedroom as he stepped out on to it, very tired after the long journey; he drank in deeply the refreshing night air, and gazed with far-seeing eyes over the wide sea. He prayed for a few moments quietly, and then said, '*Ja, wie herrlich ist hier Gottes Welt, und doch wie werden unsere armen Gefangenen sich verzehren in Sehnsucht, jeder nach seiner noch viel schöneren Heimat!*' ('Yes, God's world is truly lovely here; yet our poor prisoners are consumed with longing for their own homeland—more beautiful to them than even this!')

Next day, escorted by British officers, we drove out to the enormous flying field of Taranto, part of which formed the P.O.W. camp. Rows of neat tents, intersected by numberless camp-roads, were arrayed behind high fences of barbed wire. As we entered the huge gates of this strange canvas town we could see the first columns marching to an open space. The mens' faces were bronzed by the southern sun, but they looked tired and dejected in their worn-out uniforms. We went up onto a platform and looked down on a poignant spectacle; gazing up at us were some ten thousand of our countrymen, their faces tense, expectant; youngsters of only sixteen, grey-haired men well past fifty, some of them in old railway uniforms. The Cardinal found it hard to find the opening words of greeting. ... But like a father he consoled them; they had been obedient to the call of duty, had fought and suffered for their Fatherland, and now had to undergo the bitter fate of the prisoner. He told them of the Holy Father, who had sent each man a Christmas parcel, irrespective of his religion. 'The German prisoners are dear to me,' the Pope had told him in audience, and he was striving ceaselessly to facilitate their repatriation. The Cardinal then gave them news of Germany which longed so earnestly to welcome back its sons. After describing conditions in the different zones of their country, he concluded by asking who came from the Rhineland and Westphalia, and a forest of arms shot into the air. As we came down the steps of the tribune the Westphalians and Rhinelanders closed in on all sides. The British officers had intentionally moved away before the

Cardinal began speaking so that we could converse *ad libitum*.

After many questions had been put and answered to the best of our ability, many began to whisper with anxious glances backwards, 'Are you allowed to take letters back with you?'

'Strictly speaking, no. We are not supposed to . . .'

At the same time I held up my arms so that the overcoat pockets could be seen and reached. Notes and odd bits of paper, scraps torn from paper bags and the like, on which were scribbled the home address, that of the camp and the words, 'I'm all right,' sufficed. Now and then we glanced round to see whether the British officers had noticed what was going on, but they looked the other way. Inspired by the pure air we followed the dictates of our conscience—indeed one needed a heart of stone to have refused these poor fellows. As we were getting into the car I asked Professor Bierbaum in a low voice, 'Did you get notes too?' 'Yes, I'm full of them,' he replied. 'Give me a pencil quickly or I shall forget some of the names.' We were certainly disobeying the rules and were partly aware of the necessity for such restrictions, but we were able to quieten our consciences by looking upon them as being part of the Cardinal's post and destined for the diplomatic bag, and therefore free from scrutiny.

* * * * * (A few weeks later) : On the Wednesday before Easter I was walking along the Promenade in Münster. Homecoming militiamen were passing by, their few possesssions slung across their shoulders. Suddenly a group of them stopped on the far side, and one of them called out a friendly greeting: 'Don't you recognize us? We are from Taranto. Stop a minute.' I crossed over and was warmly welcomed. At once the tallest of them said: 'I asked you in the camp how things were in Haltern and you replied that nothing much had happened. Do you remember?' It was a bitter drop in the cup of pleasure. . . . 'Yes,' he continued, 'if the Cardinal were still alive we would have gone to him at once, for it was he who freed us and but for him we would not be standing here now.' * * * * *

Each day we went to a different camp. It was always the same, drear picture, but our presence seemed to cheer up our brothers a good bit. Sometimes the Cardinal gave them as many as seven talks in a day. On the first evening we drove back in the dusk to the Archbishop's palace where, in the meantime, representatives of the Italian local administration had turned up to pay their respects to His Eminence. Conspicuous among them were the Prefect of the Taranto province, the chief mayor, the chief of police and the commanding admiral. As was always the case when the Cardinal was to be seen an army of Press reporters were present. The Cardinal found it impossible to cope with them all and delegated his suite to deal with the rest. The British commanding officer in Taranto invited the Cardinal and his suite, the Archbishop and his Vicar-General, to a banquet which a number of British officers attended. They had expressed a strong desire to meet and honour the great German Prince of the Church.

On the following day, we set out to visit camps further north towards Bari, and arrived in the evening at a girls' school conducted by nuns, and there passed the night. A fourteen-year-old girl welcomed the Cardinal in a Latin speech beautifully spoken. Early next morning the P.O.W.s were driven from the neighbouring camps to the largest church in the town where our Bishop celebrated Conventual Mass in the presence of the local archbishop. That morning will indeed live in the memory of all who were present: the strong, masculine singing by a choir of thousands of soldiers, the two elderly Bavarians who served the Mass, and the Bishop in full pontificals. He ended his sermon with the same words he had used in the other camps, 'And now good-bye, my dear friends, until we meet in heaven.'[1]

Almost immediately after the Mass we paid a visit to the church of St. Nicholas where the canons, in choir dress, stood ready to receive us at the west door in order to conduct the Cardinal and the Archbishop of Bari to the crypt and tomb of the great saint.[2] A canon beckoned us to a small door at the foot of the baroque altar which was marvellously wrought in beaten silver. Those accepting the rather adventurous descent had to bend double, and literally crawl through the slender

[1] Translator's note: '*Und nun auf Wiedersehen, meine lieben Freunde, spätestens im Himmel.*'

[2] Translator's note: Nicholas of Myra (or of Bari), Saint, Bishop of Myra in Lycia, d. Dec. 345 or 352. His cult began in Germany under Otto II. Here, of course, the Cardinal's chaplain identifies him with Santa Claus and the German Christmas traditions.

aperture; with the aid of a torch, one could then look through a sort of pipe-line into the depths, at the end of which the saint's bones could be seen lying snow-white in the clear waters of a spring. The relics of St. Nicholas! What a sight for us Germans from Münsterland! The magic of blessed childhood stole over us. We took away with us a few small bottles filled with the miraculous spring waters. Then we stood up— it was just possible—and the doors were shut; the Cardinal and myself were left kneeling in front of the altar. His quiet prayer came to my ears: 'Dear St. Nicholas, please help our children in Germany to recover their Catholic schools and never lose them again.' Oh, this trouble over the Catholic schools which exercises the Catholic conscience all over the world! Only that week our parents at home were voting on this very question, which had pursued the Bishop right up to the actual tomb of the great patron of our children, and had caused him to pray thus, in those simple words, from the depths of his childlike heart as was ever his way.[1] Only a week before in Rome his mind had run on the same lines: when the great celebrations and ceremonies had finished their course at St. Peter's he had driven straight back to the Anima and prayed for the same intention.

The Archbishop of Bari accompanied His Eminence as far as the city boundaries when the time came to leave; from there German officers escorted us to the last of the great P.O.W. camps, namely Foggia. Loudspeakers relayed the Cardinal's words to all parts of the huge square filled with thousands of soldiers. Communist agitators were at work in this camp, but the visit passed off well enough. We dined there by candlelight in a clean, well-furnished hut with the men. We had to reply to innumerable questions about conditions at home, and had some difficulty in minimizing the stories of atrocities current among the captives.

Friday night saw us at Naples where we spent the night with the German Grey Sisters. Through the early morning mist we could just make out the Isle of Capri, and behind us, Vesuvius quietly smoked his pipe. We drove in happy mood

[1] Translator's note: The Education Branch of Military Government completely misunderstood this question and went out of their way to complicate the problem, ignoring the Concordat.

through the great port situated on the most beautiful gulf in Europe; it was less damaged than we had been led to suppose. In Caserta, the Headquarters of the Allies in the Mediterranean, the Cardinal paid a visit to the American Commander-in-Chief, General Lee (successor to the British General Alexander) to thank him for making possible our visits to the German P.O.W. camps. The Cardinal seized the opportunity to express vigorously his views on what he considered the illegal retention of the prisoners, and earnestly entreated the General forthwith to set in motion the machinery for freeing them. All camps in southern and central Italy were disbanded a few weeks later, and most of the inmates were sent home. When we left, the General told us that he had been present in St. Peter's the week before at the public consistory, and heartily endorsed the great public demonstration of honour accorded to our Bishop. These sentiments from a high-ranking American general afforded the Cardinal much satisfaction; but after similar experiences he would always grow serious and would say: '*Jawohl!* The summit of outward praise has indeed been reached, but many good folk in Germany think I can help them in their need: alas, only too soon will they discover how powerless I am in the face of all these fearful events.' He carried these thoughts home with him to Germany—an ever-increasing burden.

At midday on that Saturday—it was the 2nd of March— we came to the town of Monte Cassino, situated at the foot of the mountain of that name, which rises 500 metres above the plain. It was impossible to differentiate between the beginning and end of the town; the car picked its way through an agglomeration of rubble and craters, and here and there the remains of a few walls could be seen. Not even in Germany had we seen such a picture of desolation and destruction. Our car wound its way up to the summit after carefully negotiating the many giant hairpin bends; here the venerable shrine and sanctuary of the Benedictine Order had greeted the landscape for miles around, until that horrible day had dawned, when Allied bombers came and laid in ruins this noble and exalted monument of the Benedictine spirit. In silence we made our way through the wrack to the tomb of the holy founder, miraculously unharmed. A few days before a hundred German prisoners had arrived as volunteers to help in its rebuilding.[1] The first person to greet them was the Bishop of Münster and they were delighted. How much blood has been spilt here! On the slopes of the Mount we remarked many cemeteries where Americans, British and Poles lay buried.

Sunday, March 3rd. The Bishop claimed his titular church. At the time of his appointment the Holy Father assigns to each cardinal a church in Rome from which the new Prince of the Church takes his title, and by which he is henceforth known: this is a symbol of the intimate unity existing between the wearer of the Purple and the Father of Christendom, and the government of the Universal Church.

The impressive ceremony took place in the ancient, round church of San Bernardo, originally one of the corner-halls of the Termae of Diocletian, consecrated in 1600. From his throne he read out an address in Italian followed by a sermon in German. He expressed his joy that it was now his privilege to call the church of St. Bernard his own; he would strive to become like that great monk of the Cistercian Order, who, like St. Benedict centuries before, had wrought so powerfully for the Church of the Occident, and who (here His Eminence spoke with visible emotion), with his pious devotion to the Heart of Jesus and His Mother, was the first to pray, 'O Clement, O Loving, O Sweet Virgin Mary!' Next morning he celebrated Holy Mass in his titular church. The last days in Rome were spent in visiting the seven principal churches, and on Wednesday there was the farewell audience with the Pope which again lasted an hour.

Two years later, in April 1948, our new Bishop, Mgr. Michael Keller, D.D., stood at the microphone of Vatican Radio to speak a few words in memory of his illustrious predecessor, 'Wherever I have been I have heard men speak of the powerful impression his personality made on them, and also of the triumphant reception given him by everybody in St. Peter's.'

.   .   .   .   .   .

[1] Translator's note: Before World War I German monks from the Benedictine Abbey of Beuron near Sigmaringen were responsible for the mosaics in the crypt under the direction of Dom Desiderius Lentz, and the ancient tower of St. Benedict had already been restored and decorated by these artists in the peculiar style of the Beuron school. Whenever the German Emperor visited Italy he always went to Monte Cassino, and contributed generously to the cost of the work his subjects were doing there.

Cardinal Spellman of New York was as good as his word in organizing the homeward journey of their Eminences of Cologne, Berlin and Münster, sending a special plane and a German-American officer from the American Zone. The latter's name was Dengler, and though he himself had been born in the U.S.A., his parents originally hailed from Bingen, and he spoke German with the real Bingen dialect. He clearly thought it a great honour to act as courier to the three cardinals. The flight was made in a four-engined Douglas. We were airborne at 2 p.m. and the pilot gave the cardinals a pleasant surprise by flying low over Rome and Vatican City, and we had a glorious bird's-eye view of the Eternal City. We were able to pick out all the great landmarks: St. Peter's with Bernini's colonnade, the Tiber, the main streets, the old churches, the Colosseum and the innumerable *palazzi*. It gave us tremendous pleasure, and our Cardinal said, 'Yes, now we know what it looks like from heaven!' Heading north we flew along the coast, turning west over Corsica. Below us lay the broad, blue sea, and there was the tiny Island of Monte Cristo, riding the waves like a ship. Between here and Marseilles the Cardinal spent some time in the pilot's cabin. We then made for Paris via Lyons but were compelled to cruise over the French capital for a full hour owing to mist and fog; but we touched down safely at 7 p.m. Waiting cars bore us swiftly to the Grand Hotel where we were received by American chaplains.

On the following morning—it was March 8th—heavy snowfalls were announced and further air-travel was impossible. Instead, we made the journey to Frankfurt by American leave-train. At the station nine British cars stood ready, three for each Cardinal and his *entourage*. The Bishop of Berlin at once flew direct to the capital where his reception had been arranged for the Sunday. Their Eminences of Cologne and Münster returned for the third time to the Sisters of the Marienhospital, where the Bishop of Limburg had hastened to welcome them to his diocese.

On Sunday morning the six British cars, with ample provisions for the journey, left Frankfurt and set out at once for Cologne, which was reached at 2.30 p.m. At three o'clock the people of that city began the festivities for the reception of

their Archbishop. The remaining three cars drove via Duisburg
and Recklinghausen to Haus Merfeld near Dülmen, where
the Cardinal proposed to spend a week with his brother,
Franz. When saying good-bye that evening, he handed his
chaplain 150 marks as a tip for the three British drivers. It was
the only time during the entire itinerary that he had to dip into
his own purse, and he smilingly remarked, 'No one ever
became a cardinal as cheaply as we German bishops have
done!'

In the early hours of a still wintry morning the Cardinal's
car, coming from Dülmen, hastened through the quiet streets
of Münster, past the Franciscan monastery, and out on to the
Telgte road. This was to prove the last visit of his life to his
beloved place of pilgrimage. Gently he wiped the blurred
windows with his hand, and looked at those woods and fields
through which he had so often walked on his pilgrim's way,
rosary in hand, alone with his troubles. Throughout his
episcopacy he had drawn an inner strength by the prayerful
treading of those solitary, woodland paths. Once again the
dear, familiar world of his homeland came before his eyes.
Today was his sixty-eighth birthday, and it was a Saturday—
Our Lady's day; the faithful of his diocese were coming to
welcome him home with all the joy and splendour they could
muster. Telgte was a sea of flags from end to end; from windows and flagstaffs streamed standards and bright bunting;
pride and love shone in the eyes of his people, who stood tightly
packed in the market square, when they saw that towering
figure emerge from the car and receive the salutations of
Landrat and *Bürgermeister*. Into the church people had poured
from all the villages around Telgte until it was filled to overflowing, and there the Cardinal offered the Holy Sacrifice for
them. He personally distributed Holy Communion to those
who came to the altar rails. As he went down from the high-
altar something happened the significance of which struck one
some weeks later. The chaplain assisting him had to let the
Cardinal descend the quire steps alone, as there was a long row
of acolytes and servers kneeling there, and the narrow passage

permitted only one to pass. At that moment the Cardinal stumbled, and no one being there to support him, lost his balance, and fell heavily on to his elbows against the communion rails. As a result, two Hosts fell from the ciborium on to the floor. Whether this severe jolt, combined with the inevitable sudden shock to the whole body, brought about some internal hurt—perhaps causing the perforation of the inflamed appendix—who can say? If this was so, then he had already begun his last way of the cross, at the feet of the *Mater Dolorosa*, whose statue had been carried to that very spot in the quire; and so, as pious minds will think, the Mother of God herself had come to take her son to Heaven.

On leaving the church the jubilant crowd surged round him in ever-increasing numbers, and carried him towards the Provost's house. First among the clergy he greeted the venerable Dean Weckendorf, laying his hand on his shoulder, and handing him the brief appointing him a Privy Chamberlain of the Pope. The good Dean seemed unable to grasp its significance at first, and not until he had sat down at the breakfast-table, on the Cardinal's right, and heard the latter joking about it, did he really understand. After breakfast the Cardinal went up the narrow staircase leading to his room; he appeared to all of us to be in the best of health and in excellent humour. There he wrote the outline of the speech he was to make that afternoon in the Cathedral Square. It was the last thing he ever penned.

At four o'clock the sound of increasing activity in the street could be heard, and then above it in the distance the sharp trot of the Cardinal's equipage. Representatives of the Cathedral Chapter and the Archpriest of Münster then arrived. The team of four white horses from Everswinkel pranced nervously over the Kappellenplatz, and amid cheers and acclamations from the crowd, the Cardinal appeared and stepped into the decorated carriage; he stood up in it and waved to them all once again; it was, moreover, his farewell gesture to Our Lady of Telgte.

The cold, frosty air blew over the countryside. Contrary to his usual habit the Cardinal frequently pulled the rugs tighter round his knees. Was it the chill of his approaching illness? As we drew near the boundaries of Münster the crowds thickened, and a forest of handkerchiefs waved from the road-side. There were more garlands and more triumphal arches with words of welcome hanging from the crosspieces. Many of them were messages of hope for the future. Tears stood in the Bishop's eyes as he looked up at the gaunt ruin of houses in the Warendorfer Strasse, and blessed the people standing there amid the wrack and ravage, which they had tried to hide with flowers and pennons. 'The poor dears will freeze to death this afternoon,' he remarked to his chaplain.

The procession turned into the Salzstrasse. Above the surging exultation of the multitude a clear and gladsome paean rang out from the few bells which had survived the fire-storms of war. At this moment a sudden, impressive hush marked this homecoming. For the first time in the centuries-old history of the Münster diocese a cardinal was taking possession of the see. His features were transfigured by a devout gravity that harmonized with the solemn silence as he stood on the podium at the foot of the Lambertiturm to receive the freedom of the city from the chief burgomaster. In the shadow of the old town and market church, whose pulpit had witnessed his great sermons, the son of the Red Soil was crowned with the laurel. Before him passed an immense procession drawn from every corner of the diocese despite the difficulties of transport; before him filed its bannered youth, its endless rows of clergy regular and secular. The scarlet fire of the Cardinal's hat coruscated in the spent rays of the afternoon sun beneath the brocaded baldachin. As of old the highest dignitaries of the Cathedral Chapter stood assembled in St. Michael's Square, where formerly fine gates had given access to the Precincts, there to hail their chief shepherd. And so within the *Dom* the home-comer knelt at journey's end—knelt betwixt the time-honoured walls of the *Paradisus*, where a canopy had been erected to housel the Eucharistic Saviour during those after-noon hours.

Fifty thousand people congregated on and round the great mountain of rubble at the west door. For the wearer of the Purple a throne had been set up in the lee of the burnt-out towers. The faithful of the city and the entire diocese here spoke their love and loyalty to their beloved Bishop through the mouths of the Lord Lieutenant, the Lord Mayor, and the speakers for the Catholic committees, and youth organizations. Then the Cardinal stood up in his full height. The rays of the fast-setting sun illumined his robes, the purple of joy and suffering.

An intense stillness fell on the tens of thousands as his lips opened to speak those words destined to be a valediction to his diocese. The mighty concourse looked up at him eagerly, as he stood there in the débris, and inspired by the immensity of the hour began to form the sentences which echoed over the Cathedral through the loud-speakers. As he spoke all marked the effulgence of his countenance.

He referred to the goodness of the Holy Father in calling him to the highest tribunal of Holy Church, thus expressing to all the world his paternal gratitude to all the Catholics of Germany, and to the diocese of Münster. There followed sentiments of simple humility about his fight made possible, he said, only by their unshakeable Faith; there were words of love for his Fatherland, and praise for the heroic deeds of our soldiers. A shudder gripped all hearts as he said, in a voice choked with tears, that only the steadfast spirit of his indomitable diocese had prevented his receiving the crown of martyrdom. As the procession moved through the struggling crowds, priests and laymen declared that never had the Bishop spoken with such earnest and moving conviction. At the entrance to his room in the Borromäum stood little children dressed as cherubs: as they conducted him on the last stages of his *via triumphalis*, their little bells tinkled softly and flowers fell beneath his feet. Was it already the distant echo of the funeral knell? *In paradisum deducant te angeli*—'May angels lead thee into Paradise!'

Darkness had enfolded the Bishop's city. Youthful feet clattered through the ruins of the *Dom*; fireworks and rockets shot up into the night high above the lofty splendour of the four-square towers, and the cracked walls trembled at their lambent touch. Washed in a shimmering lake of light the ruined cathedral stood transformed, and the solemn metamorphosis proclaimed its sure uprising once again from the glory now engulfed.

Fire-drenched, the Cardinal stood in his cathedral close; the Chapter around him. His eyes went up to the highest

pinnacle of the Lambertiturm riding over the night sky, and
from whose lonely top-gallant a flambeau flamed in the wind:
its light grew smaller and fainter, and then spent itself. A grisly
iciness clutched at his soul. As he returned to the Borromäum
he shivered and grew silent.

CHAPTER 25

REQUIEM AETERNAM

ON THE Sunday morning, Clemens August celebrated his first
and last Pontifical High Mass. For the last time he climbed the
steps of a pulpit. Mitred and crozier in hand, our good shepherd's last official words were an exhortation to papal loyalty,
especially in the person of the present Holy Father. The powerful strains of Bruckner's *Te Deum* sung by the Gregorius choir
soared through the high arches of the Church of the Holy Cross.
Seemingly worn out, the Cardinal sank to his knees on the steps
of the high altar, his head supported in his hands. When the
Mass was over the procession led him through the lane of
jubilant gonfaloniers to the carriage drawn by the four white
horses. We were near the apotheosis; the last episcopal blessing
was to be given, and he returned to the Borromäum. It was
striking twelve when he took a little food—the first for fourteen
hours. The hall was packed with visitors who swarmed through
his room; he had a friendly handshake, and a good-humoured
word for everyone, including senior representatives of Military
Government. At 1.15 p.m., when the last guest had gone, a
sudden faintness drove the Cardinal to his armchair; his face
became a strange colour, and his hands trembled. But later,
despite the misgivings of the Vicar-General, he assisted at an
academic celebration and then retired to his study. Hearing
Archpriest Berghaus express some anxiety about His Eminence's
condition, I went up at once to enquire. Smiling painfully, he
complained of a stomach-ache and took a little fruit juice.
Downstairs, the remaining clergy were all of the opinion that
the trouble was no doubt due to the great strain imposed upon
the Bishop during the last weeks, and could be put down to
nervous exhaustion, and perhaps a strained heart.

Next morning he offered the Holy Sacrifice for the last time
and gave Holy Communion to the child of one of his relatives as
we have mentioned elsewhere. After the Mass, and with all
that was left of his strength, he said a *Pater Noster* for the intention of the Catholic Schools; he then devoted a short time

to his relatives although he had not yet taken any sustenance, and set about climbing the stairs to his room. He moved as if dead tired. He thought it would be sufficient if he rested in the chair at his desk or at most lay down on the sofa. But he could not be prevailed upon to go to bed. Only a fortnight before in Rome, he had jestingly declared in the presence of the other German cardinals that he had not spent a day in bed since 1890, and that in 1938, when the trouble with his knee had deteriorated, neither the nurse nor the doctor who were then called in could alter his habit in this respect.

He would allow no doctor to be called before the Tuesday morning. Unfortunately, as many will say today, the Cardinal's brother also respected this wish; consequently, it was not until early on Tuesday morning that, at the urgent instigation of Director Weinand, Doctors Langenkamp and Schlief had the opportunity of making a diagnosis. The Auxiliary Bishop informed the Cardinal that their findings were serious and that an operation should be performed that day. The Cardinal took the news calmly and agreed; he expressed the wish to receive the Last Sacraments that afternoon in the presence of the entire Cathedral Chapter. With like calm he then proceeded to transact diocesan business with his chaplain, and with a characteristic smile, said he supposed they would be keeping him at the hospital for some days.

The ambulance arrived at four. It was a shocking picture: the Bishop sat on the edge of his bed, a long, black cloak thrown over his broad shoulders—his hair dishevelled; the haggard face, the sick, tired expression—the giant strength broken. He said, pointing to the window: 'That red-bound book over there—you know it well—we brought it back from Rome. You can read in it after, how a Cardinal is buried.' This cut us to the heart, and we turned away to hide our emotion. The stretcher-bearers were standing ready in the next room, and he wanted to go there without support, which, however, we would not allow. Workmen, who were busy in the house, helped to lift up the stretcher so that the Cardinal could lie down on it the more easily, but there were moments of terrible pain for him in the effort. Covered in rugs and secured by straps he was carried below and put into the car. The doors were closed. On the way he gave me these instructions: 'First and foremost you must bury me in one of the towers of the cathedral or in The Paradise. The chapel of St. Ludger won't do because of the damage. This cardinal's ring is to go to my brother Franz, and at his death it is to pass into the family property at Haus Assen.' These were his only words on the way to the Franciscan hospital whither the Chapter and other clergy had repaired in the meantime. The Capuchin Father, Dr. Bernardin Göbel, who was convalescing at the hospital, heard the Cardinal's last confession. Just before the Auxiliary Bishop entered the sick room with the Blessed Sacrament the Bishop spoke to those standing round his bed: 'Today is the anniversary of my baptism, and also the Feast of St. Joseph, the patron of the dying. . . .' Then his voice failed.

We who were there will never forget the inspiration of that hour. With what simple piety, calmness and recollection did he join in the prayers! When all had left the room he called back Director Bothe, his old classmate, and begged: 'If I am to die tonight you must come to me. I don't want to be alone then.' Towards evening Dr. Schlief, the specialist attached to the Franciscan hospital, assisted by other leading surgeons, performed the operation. Military Government put an aeroplane at the disposal of a Bonn specialist who hastened to the theatre. The operation revealed perforation of the *caecum* and intestinal paralysis.

How helpless is man in the face of that inexorable passage of events which God alone controls! People with anxious faces stood outside scanning the bulletins affixed to the hospital doors. With noiseless tread, the hospital personnel passed through the corridors, with many a fearful glance at the door behind which lay the man beloved by millions. The imploring cry went up from all hearts, 'Lord, do not let him die!' The news of his desperate condition ran through the diocese and all German lands like a nightmare horror. Daily the bulletins grew worse. Fully conscious, calmly and quietly, the Cardinal moved to the end of his course. Often in earlier years he had prayed that God would grant him, when on his deathbed, the grace of seeing death face to face, in full possession of his faculties. Truly nature was strong in him, and he wanted to hold on to life, but his trust and resignation in God's holy will always came first. In this spirit of submissiveness, he

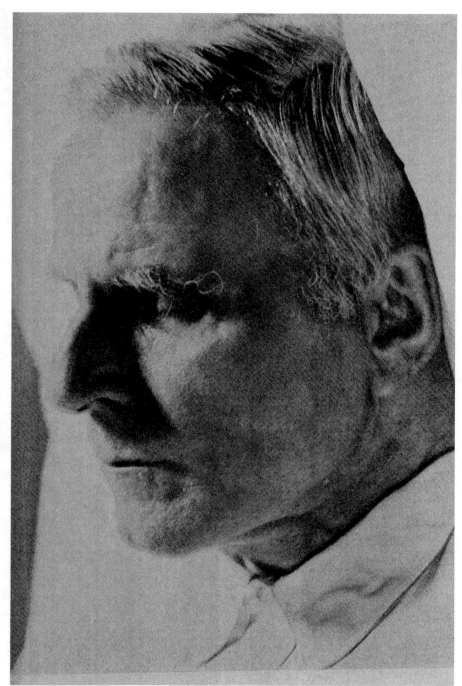

17. Requiem aeternam

18. Cardinal von Galen's successor

thanked all those who strove day and night to save his life, patiently submitting to the many painful processes he had to undergo, including injections of penicillin sent to him by the British authorities.[1]

On Friday morning I drove to Telgte with three members of the Cardinal's family to say Mass at the shrine of the *Mater Dolorosa*. It was an anniversary Mass for one of Count Franz's sons, a nephew of the Cardinal, who had been killed in battle a year previously. His name, too, was Clemens. Was this anniversary to be the day of the Cardinal's death also? I asked myself.

At noon Professor Sunder-Plassmann arrived at the Caritashaus where the Cardinal's closest relatives were staying to take them in his car to the hospital. Deeply moved, he explained that unless a miracle happened the end was expected that afternoon; he told us that after watching the Bishop during those last days of illness he would honour him as a saint for the rest of his life. The Cathedral Canons, together with a few other relations, and those priests who had been close friends, had already arrived. We assembled in the waiting-room; from time to time the Sisters came in and told us how the Cardinal had been praying for the diocese, the Fatherland, and for the children; in the morning, during his delirium, he had asked repeatedly for his carriage: he wanted to drive in it to the cathedral to give a last blessing from the ruins, to his town and diocese—*urbi et orbe*; then, he said, they could bring him back to the hospital and he would die content. His last words on earth were: 'As God wills! May God reward you! May He protect the dear Fatherland. . . . I beg you to go on working for it. O sweet Saviour . . . !'

At half past four a Sister appeared to announce the fast-approaching end. We went to the death-chamber. Unbleached candles for the dying were burning. We knelt down, and the

---

[1] Translator's note: I took penicillin to Münster as soon as I heard of the Cardinal's illness, but unfortunately could not see him. The gesture was misunderstood by some elements and may have given rise to the rumours already referred to by the author.

Auxiliary Bishop began the last prayers. The dying man breathed slowly and with difficulty, in great gusts. The huge form lay there stiff and helpless on its back; unconscious now, with eyes wide open that stared into the far distance, his arms outstretched to their full extent. Hot tears were in our eyes. At about five the breathing became weaker—then suddenly the great Cardinal breathed his last. That heart so beloved by God and man was stilled. Blood and water flowed from the mouth and nostrils. The profound silence of death held us motionless in grip inflexible. Then looking down on him we saw that a wondrous peace had spread over his features. Everybody in Germany is familiar with that picture of tranquillity in death, captured for ever by the camera a few hours later. It is the most beautiful likeness we possess of the Cardinal, portraying, as does no other, the innermost depths of his great and noble soul. It is the image of one glorified—of true consummation.

In death doth honour from thy forehead glow
Princely, as shines forth on a mountain-height
A rock, that earliest rays triumphant smite
From Sun new-risen. Pure as driven snow,
Thy locks wave white above thy martyred brow.
Thine eyelids are closed softly and thy sight
Turns inward, where thou dost behold God's light.
Of naught death robs thee and doth all bestow.
Thy lips now silently God's glory praise,
Thy fearless eyes naught save His Kingdom see.
Asleep thy mind is laid in charity,
That alway calmed thy thought. Lo, all man's pride
Is before God as dross. By travel tried,
Thou restest in the haven of God's Grace.

WILHELM VERNEKOHL
(*Translated by J. Slingsby Roberts*).

Over the Bishop's city the tolling of bells gave bitter tongue. People stood about the streets in silent groups; many gave way to tears and went into the nearest church to pray. Some hurried to the hospital. Next morning, in the quietude of the churches, sobs could be heard as priests announced the sad news to the faithful, who felt they had lost their own father. The lying-in-state lasted four days, during which an unending procession

passed by the catafalque which was placed in the Erphochapel
of the Church of St. Maurice.

.   .   .   .   .

On March 28th he was borne to his grave like a king. Three
Princes of the Church, including Cardinal Griffin of West-
minster, and many other bishops escorted him on that last
journey. The same priests, who only a few days before had
walked in triumph before their Bishop, now sang the *Miserere*
for their departed master. The same voices, raised on that
occasion in the joyful strains of the *Te Deum* to welcome him
home, now chanted the mourning cadences of *Dona ei Requiem*
for him who had gone Home. The same proud standards of
our diocesan youth, so recently unfurled in the storms of
enthusiasm, now hung prone in their heavy crêpe. The same
crowds, that had shouted in sheer love and joy to their Cardinal,
now stood silent and stunned in the ruined streets, and bowed
low as the huge coffin, drawn by four brown horses, passed by.
How quickly here on earth can joy be changed into sorrow, and
how bitterly this truth came home to them as they followed
the *cortège*.

A few days before a door had been made in the Galen
chapel; it had been walled-up since the seventeenth century
when the last Prince-Bishop, Christoph Bernard von Galen, was
interred there. Now they carried the dead Cardinal to this ancestral resting-place. When the coffin had been lowered into the
ground, and the first clods of earth were falling, there rose from
the vast crowd all round a mighty volume of sound—triumphant over the mourning, and as their expression of the un-
conquerable hope of Christians over the powers of death, the
Easter Hymn '*Wahrer Gott wir glauben Dir*' resounded through
the ruins of the *Dom*. Hymn of the Resurrection, anthem of the
victorious battle of the redeemed! May his strength inspire our
souls as we stand with folded hands in the still and gutted
chantry chapel before his simple tombstone! When, as once
it did, the cathedral stood in untouched splendour around us
here, the figure of St. Ludger could be seen in one of the
chantry windows. A demon army trod the nether air: coiled in
throng confused, they hurl themselves with hellish rage upon

the man who had dared to wage battle against them; erect and dauntless St. Ludger held up the cross in front of the infernal spirits, who fled before its power.

There the Cardinal now lies buried, where the Ludger-Window once reflected in glorious colours the Saint's apostolate for the prayerful man to see and comprehend; but the nether world, depicted in the beautiful *grisaille* glass, has become our world, and it is not man who will hurl the dragon of the Apocalypse into the bottomless pit—but God. God gave to the great Bishop of Münster, Clemens August, Cardinal von Galen, a part of that angelic strength with which to stem, bulwark-wise, the satanic powers of our own century.

REQUIESCAT IN PACE SANCTA!

SOURCES

THE foregoing book describes for the most part personal experiences of the writer, which he, as Bishop's Chaplain from 1938 to 1946, had the opportunity to record in diaries he kept regularly. For a certain number of small anecdotes it is needless to enumerate authorities as the names of those who reported them are mentioned in connection with the incidents themselves. Apart from these sources, I have drawn on the following: the records of the von Galen family, those of the parish of St. Lambert at Münster, jottings taken down from time to time by Count Franz von Galen, those made by Father Holstein, who, as a curate, had known the Cardinal in Berlin and afterwards as a parish priest at Münster, those of Dr. Eising, my predecessor as his chaplain, those of the Marist Father Boesch at Sendenhorst and those of the former Cathedral-Vicar, Dr. Kamp, who in 1945 accompanied the Bishop as interpreter. Finally, the past numbers of the official diocesan gazette and all the documents and papers left by the Cardinal stood at my disposal. The present volume presents a biographical completion and continuation of the writings already published by the author, i.e. *Bishop von Galen Speaks, An Apostolic Contest and its Echo* (Herder, 1946), *The Bishop of Münster, the Reverberations of a Struggle for God's Right and the Rights of Man* (Aschendorff, 1946), Documents concerning the Bishop of Münster (Aschendorff, 1948). The two books published by the firm of Aschendorff are in all quotations designated as Vol. I and Vol. II. I wish to express my sincere gratitude to all those who have contributed to the formation of this book. I owe particular thanks to Mgr. Quiel, Mgr. Coppenrath, Vicar-General Ricking and Herr Helmert for their services in revising the proofs.

APPENDIX

BEING EXTRACTS FROM CARDINAL VON GALEN'S
WARTIME SERMONS

Translated by R. L. Sedgwick

The First Sermon, preached in the Lambertikirche on the 13th of July after a heavy R.A.F. raid on Münster in July, 1941.

The sermon refers to these raids by the 'external enemy', as the Bishop called them, to give point to his protestation and denunciation of the Gestapo, which he designates the 'internal' enemies of the Fatherland. The subject of the sermon is the confiscation and sequestration of Church property in the diocese.

My dear Catholics of St. Lambert's,

I have felt it necessary to come here in person to deliver my pastoral letter on the events of last week from the pulpit of Münster's parish church, and to express my heartfelt sympathy particularly to my old parishioners. Here you have suffered heavy casualties and damage as elsewhere in the city. It was my intention to say something about the meaning of the visitations, to say that God visits us to take us to Himself. But these thoughts I must lay aside, for today I feel compelled to speak out publicly on another matter—of an appalling event which has befallen us at the end of this week of horror.

Münster has not yet recovered from the terrible devastation which the external and military enemy has inflicted on us. On top of all this, yesterday, at the end of this dreadful week, on July 12th, the Gestapo seized both of the Jesuit houses in the city, Sentmaring House in the Weserlerstrasse and Ignatius House in the Köenigstrasse. Only yesterday they evicted the owners, and forced the Reverend Fathers to leave immediately not only their houses, not only our city, but also Westphalia and the Rhine Province. The same cruel fate has overtaken the good Sisters in Steinfurtstrasse. Their convent, too, has been confiscated and they must leave the city by six o'clock this evening. The houses of the two Orders, all that is in them, and

231

all their possessions have been commandeered for the Gauleitung of Northern Westphalia.

Thus we see that the rape of the religious houses, which has been raging for a considerable time in Southern Germany, in Austria, in the recently acquired territories of Western Poland, Luxembourg, Lorraine and in other parts of the Reich, has now been extended to Westphalia. We must be prepared for the repetition of such dreadful news in the next few days, when one monastery after another will be sequestered by the Gestapo, and their inmates, our brethren, the children of our families, loyal Germans, will be thrown into the streets like dissolute slaves and hunted from the country as so much riffraff. And all this takes place at a time when everyone is apprehensive of more air-raids which may well kill us all, and which may turn any one of us into a homeless refugee. At this very moment, innocent and estimable men are being chased from their humble homes. German citizens—our fellow townsmen—become fugitives. Why? I am informed that the reasons are political. No other reasons have been given. Not a single Religious has been accused of any offence or summoned before a court or indeed sentenced. If any one of them is guilty, let him by all means be indicted. But why should the innocent suffer?

The Bishop then goes on to pay tribute to the work of the Jesuit Fathers and the Sisters of the Immaculate Conception. He then returns to the charge against the Gestapo.

My dear children in Christ! If the Gestapo ignores those events which have made hundreds of our compatriots homeless, if it continues to throw our blameless fellow citizens into the streets and to banish them from their home province at a time like this, then I no longer hesitate to protest publicly and with every justification and to utter this grave warning. During the last few weeks even two members of my Cathedral Chapter were suddenly dragged from their dwellings by the Gestapo and exiled to distant places which they have been compelled to accept as their domicile. And for what reason? Because *I*, their Bishop, have displeased the Government. When, in the course of the last two years, four vacancies in the Cathedral Chapter were filled, the Government announced in three cases that it disapproved of the appointments. Under the terms of the Prussian Concordat of 1929, interference from the Government is explicitly forbidden. I therefore confirmed two of the appointments. Let them hale *me* before the courts if they think I have contravened the law. I am certain that no independent German court of justice could condemn me for my action in filling the canonries.

Is the reason why the Gestapo has been instituted to replace the ordinary courts, the fact that the Gestapo's actions in the Reich are not, unfortunately, themselves subject to juridical revision? No German citizen has any defence against the power of the Gestapo. I repeat that he is utterly defenceless. Not one of us is certain, though he be the most loyal, the most conscientious citizen, though he knows himself innocent, I say that not one of us is certain that he will not any day be dragged from his house and carried off to the cells of some concentration camp.

I know full well that this may happen to me, perhaps now or on some future day. And it is because I shall then no longer be able to speak out publicly that I do so today. I openly warn them not to pursue these actions which I am firmly convinced will call down God's punishment and bring our people to misery and ruin.

My brethren in Christ! the incarceration of many innocent men who are without defence and without a legal verdict, the restrictions on the liberty of the two Canons, the sequestration of religious houses, the expulsion of blameless monks and nuns, of our brothers and sisters, compel me today publicly to remind you of the eternal and unassailable truth: *Justitia est fundamentum regnorum.*

The right to live and to be free, the right to inviolability is an essential part of every moral social order. No one denies the State the authority to restrict the rights of its citizens by way of punishment, but this applies only to those who break the law, whose guilt must be proven by impartial juridical procedure. Any State which over-rides this divinely imposed limit, and allows or causes the punishment of blameless men, undermines its own authority and the respect for its dignity in the conscience of its citizens.

Here the Bishop gives further names of his proscribed clergy and then refers to the imprisonment of the Protestant Pastor Niemöller who was arrested by the Nazis in 1937 and imprisoned until the end of the war.

My brethren, the name of an Evangelical pastor, who in the last war risked his life for Germany as a submarine commander, and has for years now been deprived of his liberty, is known to all of you. We have the very greatest respect for his courage and the fortitude with which this estimable German confesses to his Christian belief. So you will see from this last example, that the demand which I make openly today is not confined to denomination or for Catholics only but something which *affects all Christians; it is a request for something fundamentally human, religious, and national.*

The foundation of the State is justice. We grieve to see today this foundation being shaken and we deplore that the natural and Christian virtue of justice, which is indispensable to the ordered condition of every human community, is not being dispensed and maintained unequivocally for all. We beg, we ask—nay, we *demand* justice not only in defence for the rights of Holy Church, not only for the rights of the individual, but also because we love our people and are deeply anxious about our Fatherland.

Only if those in authority show a proper respect for the royal majesty of justice and use the rod of punishment in the service of justice alone, can they with any hope of lasting success, honestly oppose the illegal use of force by those who happen to be stronger; only then can they rightly oppose the degrading of the weak to disgraceful serfdom. Those in power can only rely on the true adherence and the unfettered service of decent men if their punitive measures are seen in the light of impartial scrutiny to be untainted by despotism and in harmony with the stainless scales of justice. Therefore the exercise of judgment and punishment without defence or trial tends to a feeling that there *is* no justice and to *an attitude of anxious pusillanimity and cringing cowardice, which will end by disrupting the national character and community.*

When the Gestapo inflicts its punishments, jurisdiction on the part of the administration goes by the board. Since none of us knows how to control impartially measures taken by the Gestapo, its curtailment of personal liberty, its deportations, its imprisonments of German citizens in concentration camps, there now exists a widespread feeling of a want of justice and indeed of cowardly impotence which sorely injures our country.

My office as Bishop demands me to uphold the moral order and I have sworn an oath before God and the representative of the Government, to prevent, as far as in me lies, all harm which may imperil the German State, and it therefore urges me to make this public warning about the actions of the Gestapo.

No doubt, my dear brethren, there are those who will upbraid me, alleging that I am weakening the home front in using such straight speaking in war-time. To any such reproach I answer: It is not I who am the cause of any weakening of our home front . . . but rather those men who ill-treat our fellow countrymen, our brothers and sisters, by stealing their property and sending them into exile; it is *they* who weaken and undermine the security of the Reich and the trust in our Government. In the name of the righteous German people, and in the interests of the solidarity of the home front, I therefore raise my voice. As a Catholic Bishop, as the representative of the Christian faith, as a German and a law-abiding citizen, I cry out: We demand Justice! If this plea is unheard and unheeded, if the rule of true justice is not brought back, our German nation will, notwithstanding the bravery of our soldiers and their splendid victories, collapse from internal corruption and uncleanness.

The sermon ends with an impassioned call to prayer.

.   .   .   .   .

The Second Sermon, preached on Sunday, July 20th, 1941, in the Überwasserkirche, Münster. The Bishop returns to his charge against the Gestapo.

In the first part of this sermon the Bishop gives in detail the names of further Church property to be taken over by the Gestapo since his sermon a week before, and he again speaks of the 'attacks of *our enemies within this country*'. After speaking of the plight of the exiled inmates of these institutions he continues:

On Monday, July 14th, I called on the Provincial Vice-President and demanded that the liberty and property of innocent Germans might be protected. He explained that the Gestapo is an independent organization and that he could do nothing. However, he promised to forward my complaints and petitions to the Gauleiter, Dr. Meyer. There was no result. On the same day I wired to the Führer's Chancellery in Berlin to this effect:

'After enemy attempts since July 6th to destroy Münster by aerial bombardment, the Gestapo began on July 12th to seize the monasteries and institutions of religious orders in the city and environs of Münster and to expropriate them and their furniture. The inmates, guiltless men and women, members of respectable German families whose relatives are now fighting in the armed forces for the Fatherland, are being deprived of their homes and property, turned into the streets and banished from their home province. I implore the Führer and Reich Chancellor, in the name of justice and in the interests of the solidarity of the home front, to protect the freedom and property of German citizens against the arbitrary measures of the Gestapo and against their sequestration on behalf of the Gauleitung.'

I despatched similar telegrams to Reich Marshal Göring, to the Minister of Home Affairs, and finally to the High Command of the Army as well.

It was my hope that if no consideration of justice, then at least a realization of the bad effect on the home front would in war-time have some influence with the powers that be in halting such deeds against our kinsfolk. I did not imagine they would refuse chivalrous protection to innocent German women. My protests availed nothing: the actions continued. What I had long anticipated and indeed prophesied has now come about. *We are now contemplating the ruins of inner national unity, which during these last few days has been foully overthrown.*

I pointed out with considerable emphasis to the recipients of the telegrams that these outrages can only spring from a deep-rooted hatred of the Christian religion and the Catholic Church and that suchlike chicanery but serves to sabotage national unity. How can we feel one with men who hound our religious brothers and sisters from the country like outlaws without cause, defence or trial? We can't! I have nothing in common, neither in thought nor sentiment, with these men and all others responsible for these actions. I do not hate them but I wish from the bottom of my heart that they may acknowledge their sins and repent. We must therefore pray for all those who persecute and denigrate us in obedience to Our Blessed Lord's mandate. But as long as they continue to act as they are now doing I withhold any kind of fellowship. . . .

It is true we Christians must not start revolutions. We must continue to do our duty conscientiously in obedience to the Divine Will and out of love for our people and country. Our soldiers will continue to fight and die for their Fatherland but not for those men who, by their hateful deeds against our beloved Religious, break our hearts and bring down shame on the German name before God and man. We shall continue our fight against the external enemy, but we cannot fight with weapons against the enemy *within our own gates*, who strikes and tortures us. The only way we can hit back is by strong, prolonged and stubborn endurance. Steel yourselves and hold fast! We can perceive clearly enough what lies behind the new *credenda* which they have imposed upon us for some years now, how they have forbidden religious teaching from our schools, suppressed our societies and are now intending to ban the Catholic kindergartens. Their motive springs from a deep-rooted hatred of Christianity which they intend to deracinate. I repeat, steel yourselves and hold fast! At this moment we are not the hammer, but the anvil. Others, chiefly intruders and apostates, hammer at us; they are striving violently to wrench us, our nation and our youth from our belief in God. We are the anvil, I say, and not the hammer, but what happens in the forge? Go and ask the blacksmith and see what he says. Whatever is beaten out on the anvil receives its shape from the anvil as well as the hammer. The anvil cannot and need not strike back. It need only be hard and firm. If it is tough enough it invariably outlives the hammer. No matter how vehemently the hammer falls, the anvil remains standing in quiet strength, and for a long time will play its part in helping to shape what is being moulded. And so it is with the wrongly imprisoned, the blameless who have been driven out, and the exiled God will strengthen them so that they lose not the shape and bearing of Christian fortitude when the hammer of persecution strikes them sore blows and inflicts upon them unmerited wounds. It is our monks and nuns, our brethren, who are being tried in the fire now. The day before yesterday I paid a visit to some of those so proscribed in their temporary refuge and to converse with them. The brave attitude of these good people both edified and inspired me, roughly and ruthlessly driven as they have been from the conventual roof, and deprived of the Eucharistic Presence in the Tabernacle. Upright in bearing, knowing that they are innocent of any crime, they tread the way of exiles trusting in Him who feeds the birds of the air and clothes the lilies of the field. They rejoice with that joy which Our Blessed Lord commends to His disciples: 'Blessed are those who suffer persecution in the cause of right, the kingdom of heaven is theirs. Blessed are you, when men revile you, and persecute you, and speak all manner of evil against you falsely, because of Me. Be glad and light-hearted, for a rich reward awaits you in heaven!'[1] These men and women are nothing less than paragons of the Divine Forge. Our youth is now being pressed between hammer and anvil—a youth still growing up but not yet adult, still malleable. We cannot save them from the

[1] Translator's note: Knox version.

hammer blows of scepticism, of hatred of Christianity, of false doctrines and morals. What sort of instruction is forced upon them at their clubs and youth organizations which, we are informed, they have joined voluntarily and with the parental permission? What sort of books do they read? Christian parents! Do but examine these books, especially the history texts used in the secondary schools. You will be appalled at the disregard for historical truth, at the attempt to inculcate simple children with distrust for Christianity and the Church and indeed with hatred of the teaching of Christ. In the privileged State schools, that is the Hitler schools, the new training colleges for future teachers, all Christian influence—in fact every kind of religious activity— is disallowed on principle. And what of our children last spring who were evacuated to distant parts to escape the air raids? What are they being taught about their holy religion? Can they even practise it? Christian parents! You must look to these things, otherwise you are neglecting your religious duties and you will not be able to satisfy the exigencies of your own con- science and of Him Who entrusted you with children that you might set them on the path to Heaven.

We are the anvil, not the hammer. . . . Make your home, make your love and loyalty as parents, make your exemplary Christian life the stalwart, hard, fast and unyielding anvil that will support the pressure of the hostile blows and tempers the strength still frail into a weapon of God's will, at no time departing from His service.

Nearly every one of you is being forged at this time . . . we are the anvil for all the blows that beat down upon us. We must persevere in loyal service to our nation but we must always be prepared to show courage and sacrifice when it comes to obeying God before man. God communicates with us through con- science that is moulded by faith and you must always courageous- ly obey that inner voice. Remember the example of the Prussian Minister of Justice in bygone days. Frederick the Great ordered him to annul a lawful verdict of the courts to gratify the King's whim, but the minister returned this splendid answer: 'My head is at your Majesty's disposal, but not my conscience. I am ready to die for the King and will obey him even unto death, my life is his but my conscience belongs to God.' Are suchlike chivalrous men extinct? Do Prussian servants of this same metal no longer exist? Are burghers and peasants, craftsmen and labourers no longer possessed of the same outlook and nobility of thought? That I cannot and will not believe. And so

I say again: 'Harden yourselves and yield not an inch. Stand firm like the anvil. Obedience to God and conscience may well cost us life, liberty and home; but let us die rather than commit sin. May God's grace, without which we can do nothing, grant us and sustain in us this adamant resolution.

My dear Catholics of Münster! After the ambulatory of the cathedral had been pierced by a bomb during the night of July 7th, another which struck the outer wall on the following night destroyed the fountain of St. Ludger, the memorial to the late Bishop Johann Bernhard's return from exile in 1844. The effigies of the two bishops Suitger and Erpho on both sides of the memorial are badly damaged; but the stone figure of the first bishop of Münster was left untouched. He raises his right hand in benediction, pointing heavenwards, as though, by means of this almost miraculous preservation of the statue, he wished to urge us, come what may, to hold steadfast to the Catholic Faith, revealed by God and committed to us by our forefathers. Amidst all this annihilation of human works, amidst the storm and stress I exhort you in the words spoken to the persecuted Christians by the first Supreme Pontiff: 'Bow down, then, before the strong hand of God; He will raise you up, when His time comes to deliver you. Throw back on Him the burden of all your anxiety; He is concerned for you. Be sober, and watch well; the devil, who is your enemy, goes about roaring like a lion, to find his prey, but you, grounded in the faith, must face him boldly; you know well enough that the brotherhood you belong to pays, all the world over, the same tribute of suffering. And God, the giver of all grace, who has called us to enjoy, after a little suffering, His eternal glory in Christ Jesus, will Himself give you mastery, and steadiness, and strength. To Him be glory and power through endless ages, Amen.'[1]

Let us pray for our relatives and for our religious Orders, for the innocent who are suffering, for all in trouble, for our soldiers, for Münster and its inhabitants, for our nation and Fatherland and for its leader. Amen. (Here the vast congregation shouted, 'And for our beloved Bishop!')

.   .   .   .   .   .

The Third Sermon, preached in the Church of St. Lambert's on August 3rd, 1941, in which the Bishop attacks the Nazi practice of euthanasia and condemns the 'mercy killings' taking place in his own diocese.

[1] Translator's note: Knox version.

My Beloved Brethren,

In today's Gospel we read of an unusual event: Our Saviour weeps. Yes, the Son of God sheds tears. Whoever weeps must be either in physical or mental anguish. At that time Jesus was not yet in bodily pain and yet here were tears. What depth of torment He must have felt in His heart and Soul, if He, the bravest of men, was reduced to tears. Why is He weeping? He is lamenting over Jerusalem, the holy city He loved so tenderly, the capital of His race. He is weeping over her inhabitants, over His own compatriots because they cannot foresee the judgment that is to overtake them, the punishment which His divine prescience and justice have pronounced. 'Ah, if thou too couldst understand, above all in this day that is granted thee, the ways that can bring thee peace!' Why did the people of Jerusalem not know it? Jesus had given them the reason a short time before. 'Jerusalem, Jerusalem . . . how often have I been ready to gather thy children together, as a hen gathers her chickens under her wings; and thou didst refuse it! I your God and your King wished it, but you would have none of Me. . . .' This is the reason for the tears of Jesus, for the tears of God. . . . Tears for the misrule, the injustice and man's wilful refusal of Him and the resulting evils, which, in His divine omniscience, He foresees and which in His justice He must decree. . . . It is a fearful thing when man sets his will against the will of God, and it is because of this that Our Lord is lamenting over Jerusalem.

My faithful brethren! In the pastoral letter drawn up by the German Hierarchy on the 26th of June at Fulda and appointed to be read in all the churches of Germany on July 6th, it is expressly stated: 'According to Catholic doctrine, there are doubtless commandments which are not binding when obedience to them requires too great a sacrifice, but there are sacred obligations of conscience from which no one can release us and which we must fulfil even at the price of death itself. At no time, and under no circumstances whatsoever, may a man, except in war and in lawful defence, take the life of an innocent person.'

When this pastoral was read on July 6th I took the opportunity of adding this exposition:

For the past several months it has been reported that, on instructions from Berlin, patients who have been suffering for a long time from apparently incurable diseases have been forcibly removed from homes and clinics. Their relatives are later informed that the patient has died, that the body has been cremated and that the ashes may be claimed. There is little doubt that these numerous cases of unexpected death in the case of the insane are not natural, but often deliberately caused, and result from the belief that *it is lawful to take away life which is unworthy of being lived.*

This ghastly doctrine tries to justify the murder of blameless men and would seek to give legal sanction to the forcible killing of invalids, cripples, the incurable and the incapacitated. I have discovered that the practice here in Westphalia is to compile lists of such patients who are to be removed elsewhere as 'unproductive citizens', and after a period of time put to death. This very week, the first group of these patients has been sent from the clinic of Marienthal, near Münster.

Paragraph 21 of the Code of Penal Law is still valid. It states that anyone who deliberately kills a man by a premeditated act will be executed as a murderer. It is in order to protect the murderers of these poor invalids—members of our own families —against this legal punishment, that the patients who are to be killed are transferred from their domicile to some distant institution. Some sort of disease is then given as the cause of death, but as cremation immediately follows it is impossible for either their families or the regular police to ascertain whether death was from natural causes.

I am assured that at the Ministry of the Interior and at the Ministry of Health, no attempt is made to hide the fact that a great number of the insane have already been deliberately killed and that many more will follow.

Article 139 of the Penal Code expressly lays down that anyone who knows from a reliable source of any plot against the life of a man and who does not inform the proper authorities or the intended victim, will be punished. . . .

When I was informed of the intention to remove patients from Marienthal for the purpose of putting them to death I addressed the following registered letter on July 29th to the Public Prosecutor, the Tribunal of Münster, as well as to the Head of the Münster Police:

'I have been informed this week that a considerable number of patients from the provincial clinic of Marienthal are to be transferred as citizens alleged to be "unproductive" to the institution of Richenberg, there to be executed immediately; and that according to general opinion, this has already been carried out in the case of other patients who have been removed in like manner. Since this sort of procedure is not only contrary to moral law, both divine and natural, but is also punishable by

Q

death, according to Article 211 of the Penal Code, it is my
bounden obligation in accordance with Article 139 of the same
Code to inform the authorities thereof. Therefore I demand at
once protection for my fellow countrymen who are threatened
in this way, and from those who purpose to transfer and kill them,
and I further demand to be informed of your decision.'

I have received no news up till now of any steps taken by
these authorities. On July 26th I had already written and
dispatched a strongly worded protest to the Provincial Administration of Westphalia which is responsible for the clinics to
which these patients have been entrusted for care and treatment.
My efforts were of no avail. The first batch of innocent folk have
left Marienthal under sentence of death, and I am informed
that *no less than eight hundred cases* from the institution of Waestein
have now gone. And so we must await the news that these
wretched defenceless patients will sooner or later lose their lives.
Why? Not because they have committed crimes worthy of death,
not because they have attacked guardians or nurses as to cause
the latter to defend themselves with violence which would be
both legitimate and even in certain cases necessary, like killing
an armed enemy soldier in a righteous war.

No, these are not the reasons why these unfortunate patients
are to be put to death. It is simply because that according to
some doctor, or because of the decision of some committee, they
have no longer a right to live because they are 'unproductive
citizens'. The opinion is that since they can no longer make
money, they are obsolete machines, comparable with some old
cow that can no longer give milk or some horse that has gone
lame. What is the lot of unproductive machines and cattle? They
are destroyed. I have no intention of stretching this comparison
further. The case here is not one of machines or cattle which
exist to serve men and furnish them with plenty. They may be
legitimately done away with when they can no longer fulfil
their function. Here we are dealing with human beings, with our
neighbours, brothers and sisters, the poor and invalids . . . unproductive—perhaps! But have they, therefore, lost the right to
live? Have you or I the right to exist only because we are
'productive'? If the principle is established that unproductive
human beings may be killed, then God help all those invalids
who, in order to produce wealth, have given their all and
sacrificed their strength of body. If all unproductive people
may thus be violently eliminated, then woe betide our brave
soldiers who return home, wounded, maimed or sick.

Once admit the right to kill unproductive persons . . . then none of us can be sure of his life. We shall be at the mercy of any committee that can put a man on the list of unproductives. There will be no police protection, no court to avenge the murder and inflict punishment upon the murderer. Who can have confidence in any doctor? He has but to certify his patients as unproductive and he receives the command to kill. If this dreadful doctrine is permitted and practised it is impossible to conjure up the degradation to which it will lead. Suspicion and distrust will be sown within the family itself. A curse on men and on the German people if we break the holy commandment 'Thou shalt not kill' which was given us by God on Mount Sinai with thunder and lightning, and which God our Maker imprinted on the human conscience from the beginning of time! Woe to us German people if we not only licence this heinous offence but allow it to be committed with impunity!

I will now give you a concrete example of what is taking place here. A fifty-five-year-old peasant from a country parish near Münster—I could give you his name—has been cared for in the clinic of Marienthal for some years suffering from some mental derangement. He was not hopelessly mad, in fact he could receive visitors and was always pleased to see his family. About a fortnight ago he had a visit from his wife and a soldier son who was home on leave from the front. The latter was devoted to his sick father. Their parting was sad, for they might not see each other again as the lad might fall in battle. As it happens this son will never set eyes on his father again because he is on the list of the 'unproductives'. A member of the family who was sent to see the father at Marienthal was refused admission and was informed that the patient had been taken away on the orders of the Council of Ministers of National Defence. His whereabouts was unknown. The family would receive official notification in due course. What will this notice contain? Will it be like all the others, namely that the man is dead and that the ashes of his body will be sent on the receipt of so much money to defray expenses? And so the son who is now risking his life at the front for his German compatriots will never again see his father. These are the true facts and the names of all those concerned are available.

'Thou shalt not kill.' God engraved this commandment on the souls of men long before any penal code laid down punishment for murder, long before any court prosecuted and avenged homicide. Cain, who killed his brother Abel, was a murderer

long before courts or states came into existence, and plagued
by his conscience he confessed, 'Guilt like mine is too great to
find forgiveness . . . and I shall wander over the earth, a fugitive;
anyone I meet will slay me.'

Because of His love for us God has engraved these commandments in our hearts and has made them manifest to us. They
express the need of our nature created by God. They are the
unchangeable and fundamental truths of our social life grounded
on reason, well pleasing to God, healthful and sacred. God, Our
Father, wishes by these precepts to gather us, His children, about
Him as a hen shelters her brood under her wings. If we are
obedient to His commands, then we are protected and preserved
against the destruction with which we are menaced, just as the
chicks beneath the wings of the mother. 'Jerusalem, Jerusalem
. . . how often have I been ready to gather thy children together,
as a hen gathers her chickens under her wings; and thou didst
refuse it!'

Does history again repeat itself here in Germany, in our land
of Westphalia, in our city of Münster? Where in Germany and
where, here, is obedience to the precepts of God? The eighth
commandment requires 'Thou shalt not bear false witness against
thy neighbour'. How often do we see this commandment
publicly and shamelessly broken? In the seventh commandment we read, 'Thou shalt not steal'. But who can say that
property is safe when our brethren, monks and nuns, are
forcibly and violently despoiled of their convents, and who
now protects property if it is illegally sequestered and not given
back?

The sixth commandment tells us, 'Thou shalt not commit
adultery'. Consider the instructions and assurances laid down on
the question of free love and child-bearing outside the marital
law in the notorious open letter of Rudolf Hess, who has since
vanished, which appeared in the Press. In this respect look at
the immorality and indecency everywhere in Münster today.
Our young people have little respect for the propriety of dress
today. Thus is modesty, the custodian of purity, destroyed, and
the way for adultery lies open.

How do we observe the fourth commandment which enjoins
obedience and respect to parents and superiors? Parental
authority is at a low ebb and is constantly being enfeebled by the
demands made upon youth against the wishes of the parents.
How can real respect and conscientious obedience to the authority of the State be maintained, to say nothing of the Divine

commandments, if one is fighting against the one and only true God and His Faith?

The first three commandments have long counted for nothing in the public life of Germany and here also in Münster. . . . The Sabbath is desecrated; Holy Days of Obligation are secularized and no longer observed in the service of God. His name is made fun of, dishonoured and all too frequently blasphemed. As for the first commandment, 'Thou shalt not have strange gods before me'; instead of the One, True, Eternal God, men have created at the dictates of their whim, their own gods to adore—Nature, the State, the Nation or the Race. In the words of St. Paul, for many their god is their belly, their ease, to which all is sacrificed down to conscience and honour for the gratification of the carnal senses, for wealth and ambition. Then we are not surprised that they should claim divine privileges and seek to make themselves overlords of life and death.

'And as He drew near, and caught sight of the city, He wept over it, and said: "Ah, if thou too couldst understand, above all in this day that is granted thee, the ways that can bring thee peace! As it is, they are hidden from thy sight. The days will come upon thee when thy enemies will fence thee round about, and encircle thee, and press thee hard on every side, and bring down in ruin both thee and thy children that are in thee, not leaving one stone of thee upon another; and all because thou didst not recognize the time of My visiting thee."'[1]

Jesus saw only the walls and towers of the city of Jerusalem with His human eye, but with His divine prescience He saw far beyond and into the inmost heart of the city and its inhabitants. He saw its wicked obstinacy, terrible, sinful and cruel. Man, a transitory creature, was opposing his mean will to the Will of God. That is the reason why Jesus wept for this fearful sin and its inevitable punishment. God is not mocked.

Christians of Münster! Did the Son of God in His omniscience see only Jerusalem and its people? Did He weep only on their behalf? Is God the protector and Father of the Jews only? Is Israel alone in rejecting His divine truth? Are they the only people to throw off the laws of God and plunge headlong to ruin? Did not Jesus, Who sees everything, behold also our German people, our land of Westphalia and the Lower Rhine, and our city of Münster? Has He not also wept for us? For a thousand years He has instructed us and our forbears in the Faith. He has led us by His law. He has nourished us with His

[1] Translator's note: Knox version.

grace and has gathered us to Him as the hen does her brood beneath its wings. Has the all-knowing Son of God seen that in *our* own time He would have to pronounce on us that same dread sentence? 'Not leaving one stone of thee upon another; and all because thou didst not recognize the time of My visiting thee.' That would indeed be a terrible sentence.

My dearly Beloved, I trust that it is not too late. It is time that we realized today what alone can bring us peace, what alone can save us and avert the divine wrath. We must openly, and without reserve, admit our Catholicism. We must show by our actions that we will live our lives by obeying God's commandments. Our motto must be: Death rather than sin. By pious prayer and penance we can bring down upon us all, our city and our beloved German land, His grace and forgiveness.

But those who persist in inciting the anger of God, who revile our Faith, who hate His commandments, who associate with those who alienate our young men from their religion, who rob and drive out our monks and nuns, who condemn to death our innocent brothers and sisters, our fellow human beings, we shun absolutely so as to remain undefiled by their blasphemous way of life, which would lay us open to that just punishment which God must and will inflict upon all those who, like the thankless Jerusalem, oppose their wishes to those of God.

O my God, grant to us all now on this very day, before it is too late, a true realization of the things that are for peace. O Sacred Heart of Jesus, oppressed even unto tears by the blindness and sins of men, help us by Thy grace to seek always what is pleasing to Thee and reject what is displeasing, so that we may dwell in Thy Love and find rest in our souls. Amen.

And now let us pray for those who are sick, for those who lie under the sentence of death, for our Religious in exile, for our soldiers, our country and our leader.

INDEX

DATE DUE

NO 2 3 71			
GAYLORD			PRINTED IN U.S.A.

CPSIA information can be obtained
at www.ICGtesting.com
Printed in the USA
BVHW051043270223
659294BV00010B/345